PEARL of PANDARIA

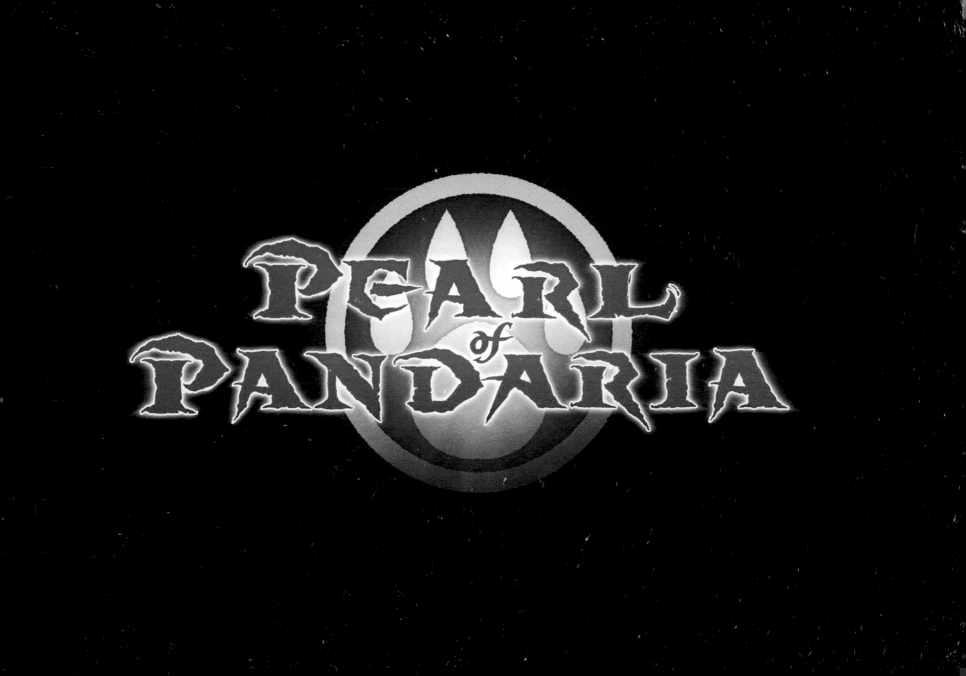

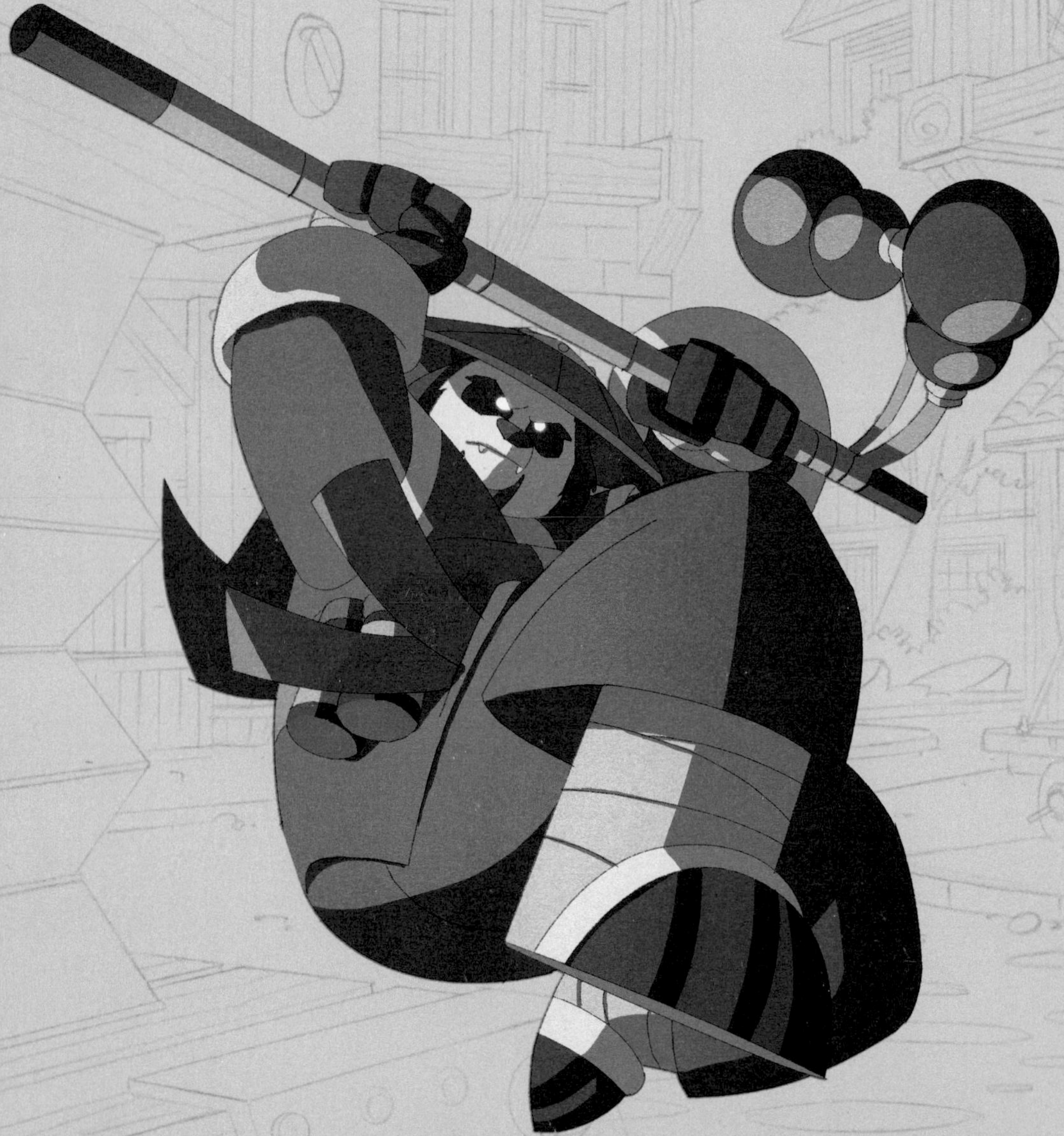

WRITTEN BY:
MICKY NEILSON

ART AND COVER BY:
SEAN "CHEEKS" GALLOWAY

LETTERING BY:
SAIDA TEMOFONTE

Additional 'Behind the Scenes' Layouts by:
Sean "Cheeks" Galloway

Blizzard Special Thanks:
Chris Metzen, Sam Didier, Cameron Dayton,
Doug A. Gregory and Glenn Rane.

Sean "Cheeks" Galloway Special Thanks:
Table Taffy Studio's Derek Laufman, DJ Welch,
Dario Brizuela, Caleb Sawyer, Hwang Nguyen and Ryan Odagawa.

ertainment:

Kanalz & Sarah Gaydos	Editors
n Brosterman	Design Director – Books
Berry	Publication Design
arras	VP – Editor-in-Chief

Nelson	President
Dio and Jim Lee	Co-Publishers
Johns	Chief Creative Officer
Rood	Executive VP – Sales, Marketing and Business Development
enkins	Senior VP – Business and Legal Affairs
ardiner	Senior VP – Finance
oison	VP – Publishing Operations
Chiarello	VP – Art Direction and Design
unningham	VP – Marketing
unningham	VP – Talent Relations and Services
Gill	Senior VP – Manufacturing and Operations
Kanalz	Senior VP – Digital
ogan	VP – Business and Legal Affairs, Publishing
lahan	VP – Business Affairs, Talent
apolitano	VP – Manufacturing Administration
ohja	VP – Book Sales
ney Simmons	Senior VP – Publicity
ayne	Senior VP – Sales

) OF WARCRAFT: Pearl of Pandaria, published by DC Comics, 1700 Broadway, New
Y 10019.

nics, a Warner Bros. Entertainment Company.

78-1-4012-2699-2

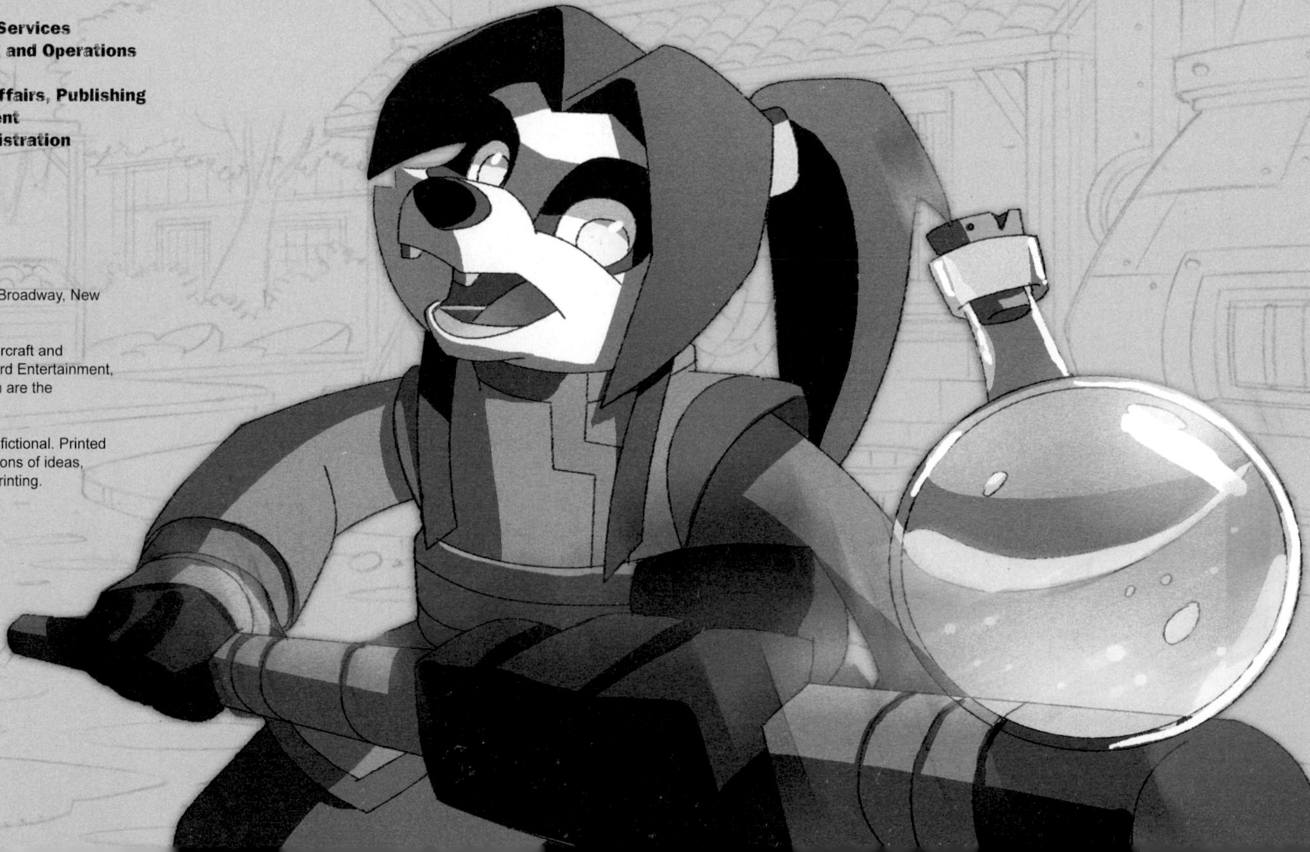

CHAPTER ONE

The Song of Liu Lang

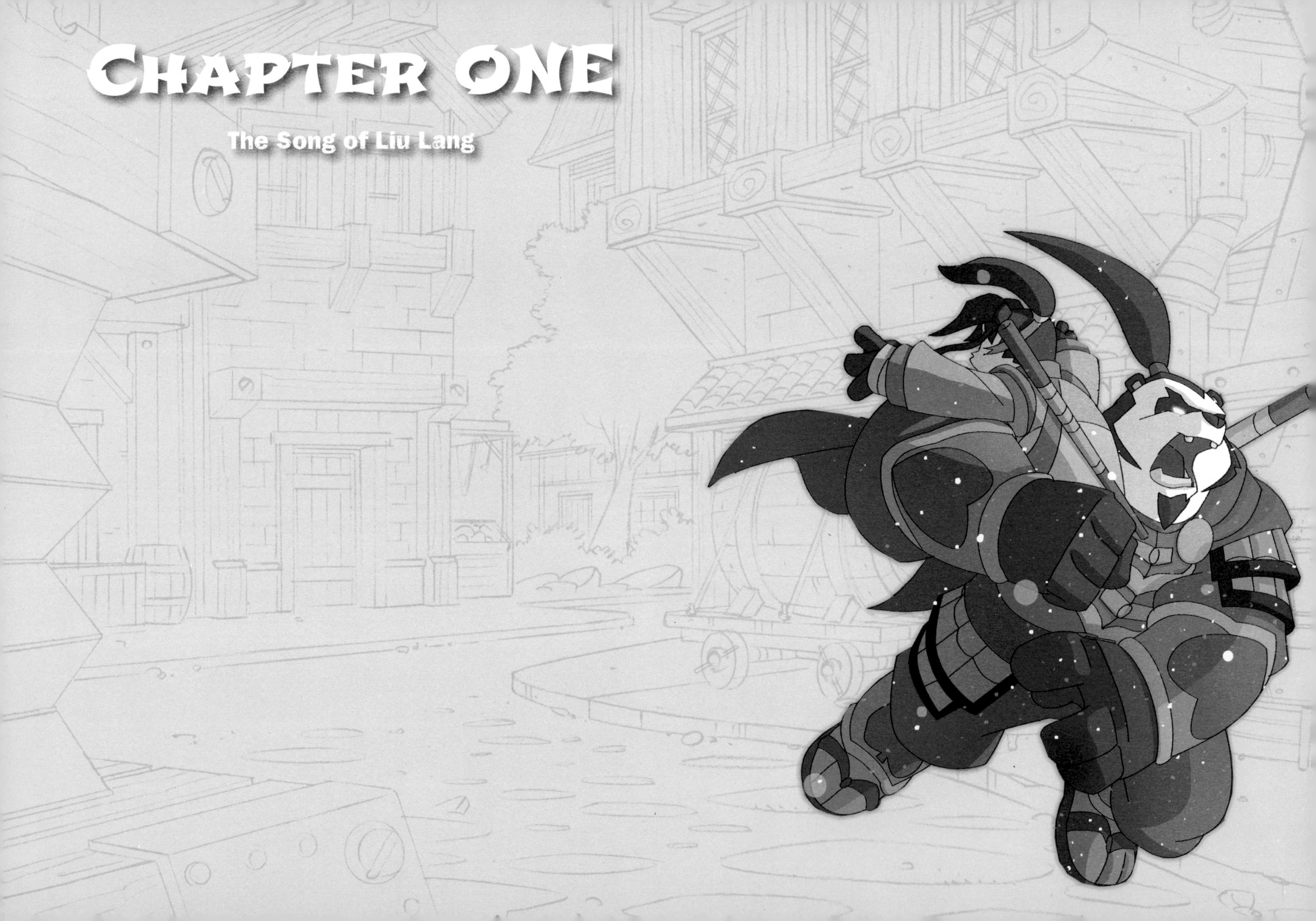

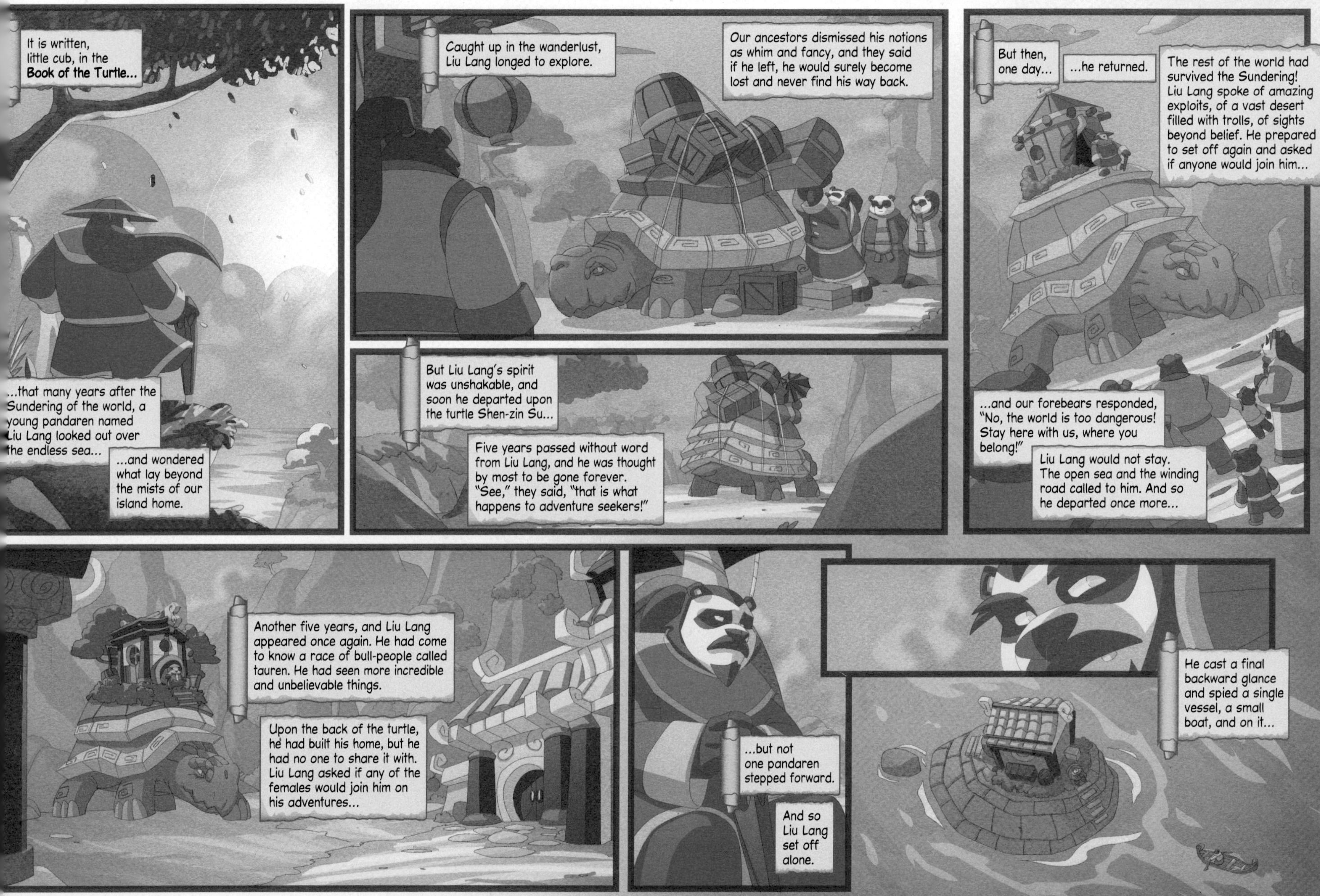
It is written, little cub, in the **Book of the Turtle...**
...that many years after the Sundering of the world, a young pandaren named Liu Lang looked out over the endless sea...
...and wondered what lay beyond the mists of our island home.
Caught up in the wanderlust, Liu Lang longed to explore.
Our ancestors dismissed his notions as whim and fancy, and they said if he left, he would surely become lost and never find his way back.
But Liu Lang's spirit was unshakable, and soon he departed upon the turtle Shen-zin Su...
Five years passed without word from Liu Lang, and he was thought by most to be gone forever. "See," they said, "that is what happens to adventure seekers!"
But then, one day...
...he returned.
The rest of the world had survived the Sundering! Liu Lang spoke of amazing exploits, of a vast desert filled with trolls, of sights beyond belief. He prepared to set off again and asked if anyone would join him...
...and our forebears responded, "No, the world is too dangerous! Stay here with us, where you belong!"
Liu Lang would not stay. The open sea and the winding road called to him. And so he departed once more...
Another five years, and Liu Lang appeared once again. He had come to know a race of bull-people called tauren. He had seen more incredible and unbelievable things.
Upon the back of the turtle, he had built his home, but he had no one to share it with. Liu Lang asked if any of the females would join him on his adventures...
...but not one pandaren stepped forward.
And so Liu Lang set off alone.
He cast a final backward glance and spied a single vessel, a small boat, and on it...

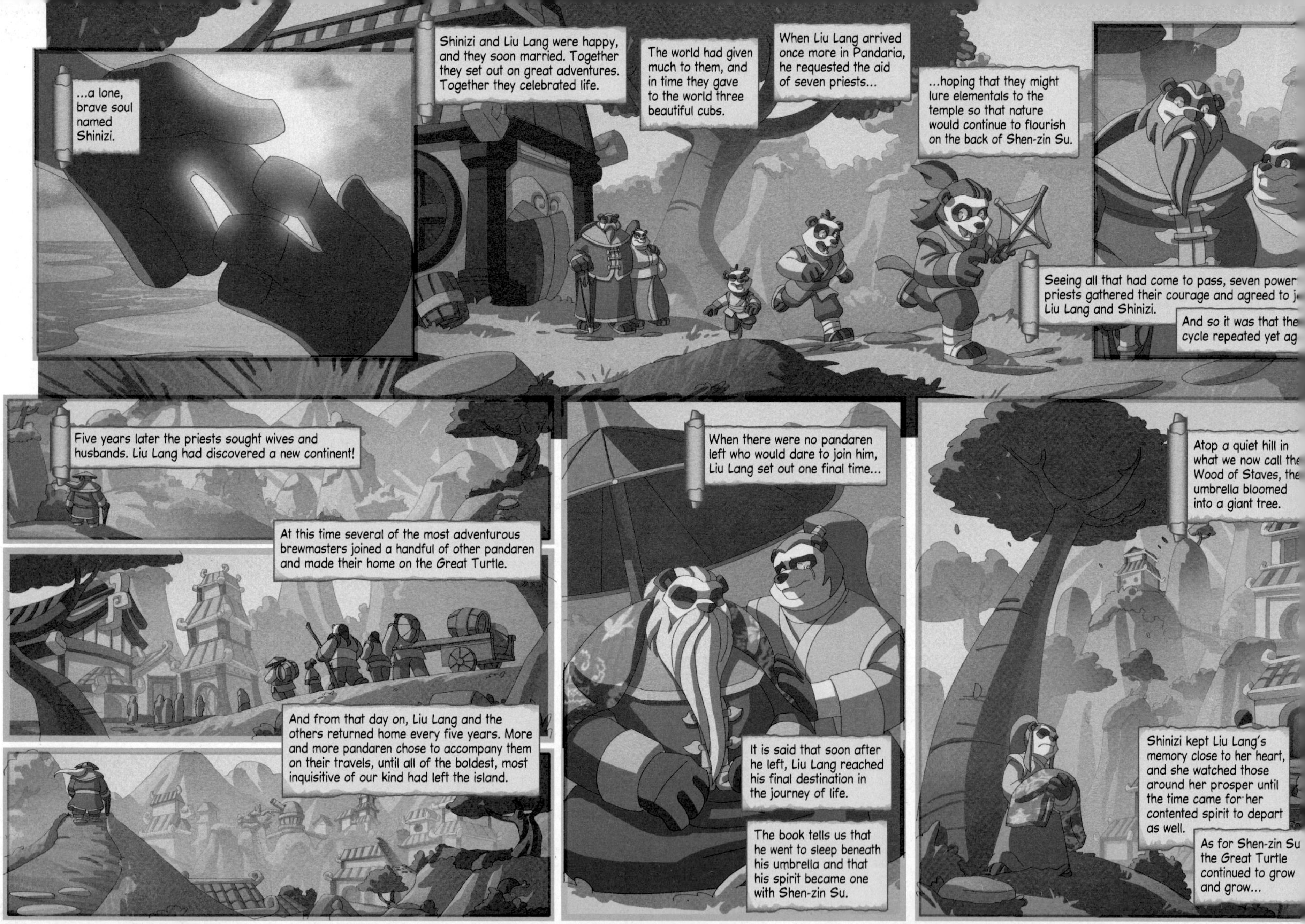
...a lone, brave soul named Shinizi.
Shinizi and Liu Lang were happy, and they soon married. Together they set out on great adventures. Together they celebrated life.
The world had given much to them, and in time they gave to the world three beautiful cubs.
When Liu Lang arrived once more in Pandaria, he requested the aid of seven priests...
...hoping that they might lure elementals to the temple so that nature would continue to flourish on the back of Shen-zin Su.
Seeing all that had come to pass, seven power priests gathered their courage and agreed to j Liu Lang and Shinizi.
And so it was that the cycle repeated yet ag
Five years later the priests sought wives and husbands. Liu Lang had discovered a new continent!
At this time several of the most adventurous brewmasters joined a handful of other pandaren and made their home on the Great Turtle.
And from that day on, Liu Lang and the others returned home every five years. More and more pandaren chose to accompany them on their travels, until all of the boldest, most inquisitive of our kind had left the island.
When there were no pandaren left who would dare to join him, Liu Lang set out one final time...
It is said that soon after he left, Liu Lang reached his final destination in the journey of life.
The book tells us that he went to sleep beneath his umbrella and that his spirit became one with Shen-zin Su.
Atop a quiet hill in what we now call the Wood of Staves, the umbrella bloomed into a giant tree.
Shinizi kept Liu Lang's memory close to her heart, and she watched those around her prosper until the time came for her contented spirit to depart as well.
As for Shen-zin Su the Great Turtle continued to grow and grow...

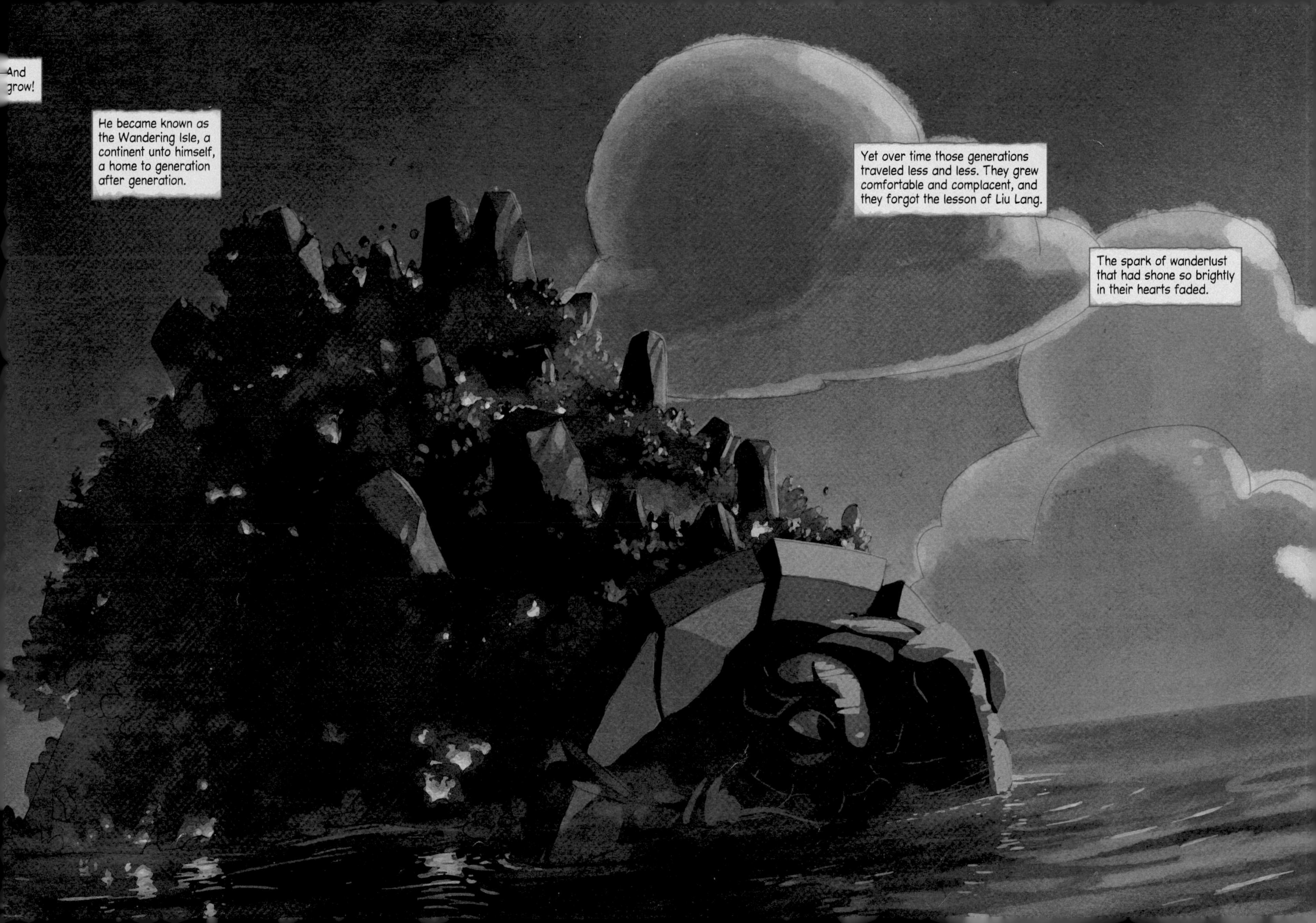

—And grow!
He became known as the Wandering Isle, a continent unto himself, a home to generation after generation.
Yet over time those generations traveled less and less. They grew comfortable and complacent, and they forgot the lesson of Liu Lang.
The spark of wanderlust that had shone so brightly in their hearts faded.

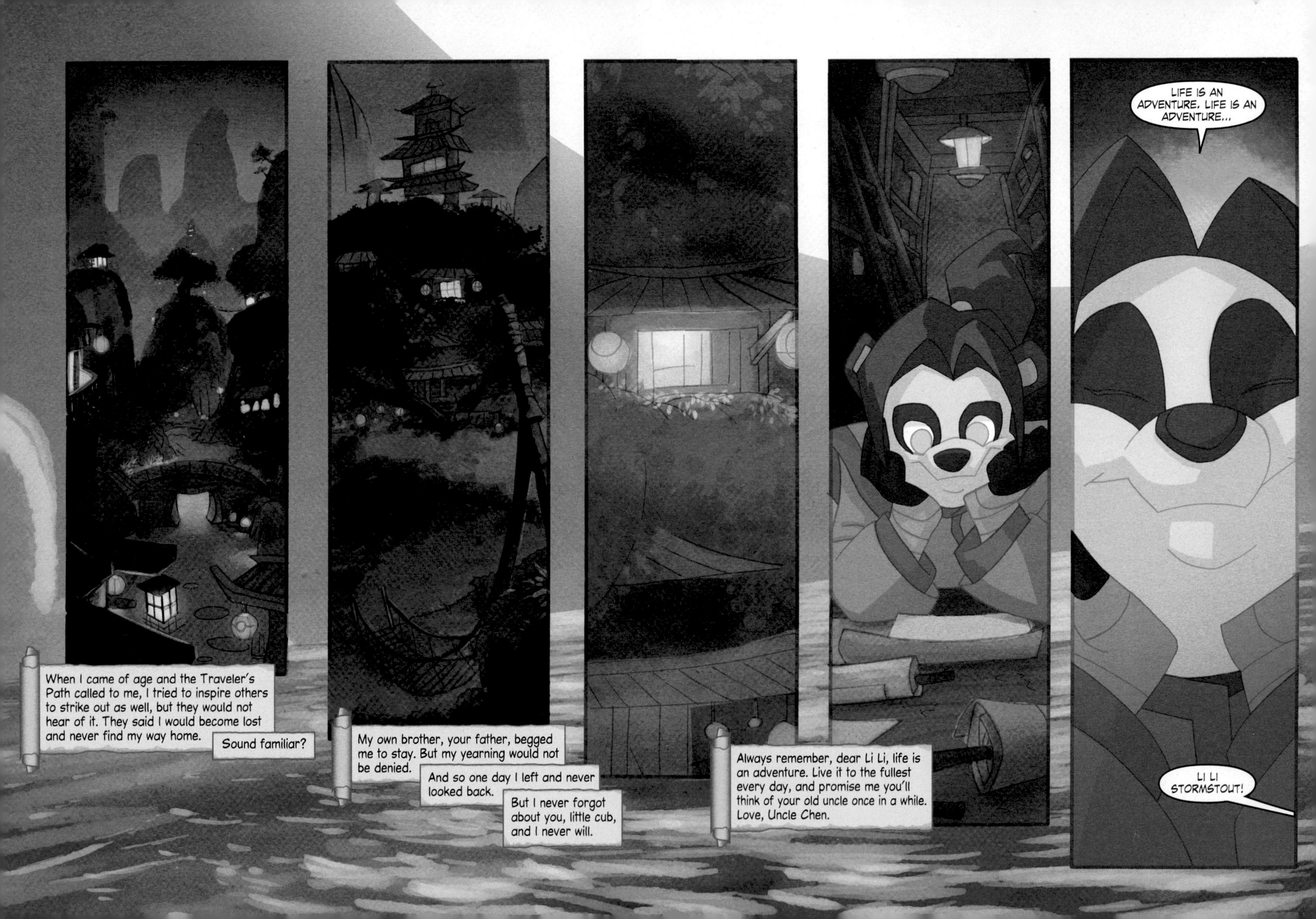
When I came of age and the Traveler's Path called to me, I tried to inspire others to strike out as well, but they would not hear of it. They said I would become lost and never find my way home.
Sound familiar?
My own brother, your father, begged me to stay. But my yearning would not be denied.
And so one day I left and never looked back.
But I never forgot about you, little cub, and I never will.
Always remember, dear Li Li, life is an adventure. Live it to the fullest every day, and promise me you'll think of your old uncle once in a while. Love, Uncle Chen.
LIFE IS AN ADVENTURE. LIFE IS AN ADVENTURE...
LI LI STORMSTOUT!

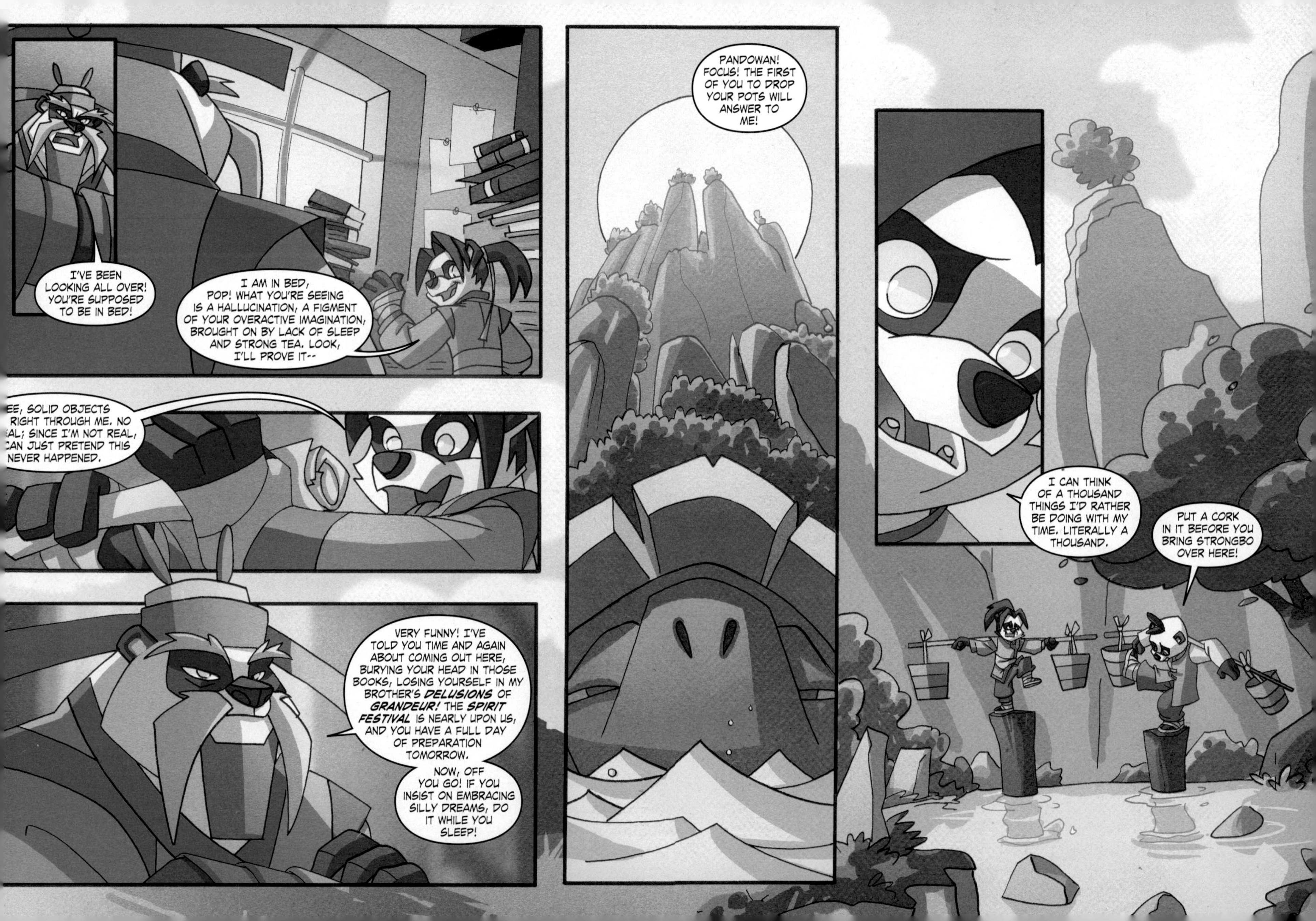
I'VE BEEN LOOKING ALL OVER! YOU'RE SUPPOSED TO BE IN BED!
I AM IN BED, POP! WHAT YOU'RE SEEING IS A HALLUCINATION, A FIGMENT OF YOUR OVERACTIVE IMAGINATION, BROUGHT ON BY LACK OF SLEEP AND STRONG TEA. LOOK, I'LL PROVE IT--
EE, SOLID OBJECTS RIGHT THROUGH ME. NO AL; SINCE I'M NOT REAL, CAN JUST PRETEND THIS NEVER HAPPENED.
VERY FUNNY! I'VE TOLD YOU TIME AND AGAIN ABOUT COMING OUT HERE, BURYING YOUR HEAD IN THOSE BOOKS, LOSING YOURSELF IN MY BROTHER'S *DELUSIONS OF GRANDEUR!* THE *SPIRIT FESTIVAL* IS NEARLY UPON US, AND YOU HAVE A FULL DAY OF PREPARATION TOMORROW.
NOW, OFF YOU GO! IF YOU INSIST ON EMBRACING SILLY DREAMS, DO IT WHILE YOU SLEEP!
PANDOWAN! FOCUS! THE FIRST OF YOU TO DROP YOUR POTS WILL ANSWER TO ME!
I CAN THINK OF A THOUSAND THINGS I'D RATHER BE DOING WITH MY TIME. LITERALLY A THOUSAND.
PUT A CORK IN IT BEFORE YOU BRING STRONGBO OVER HERE!

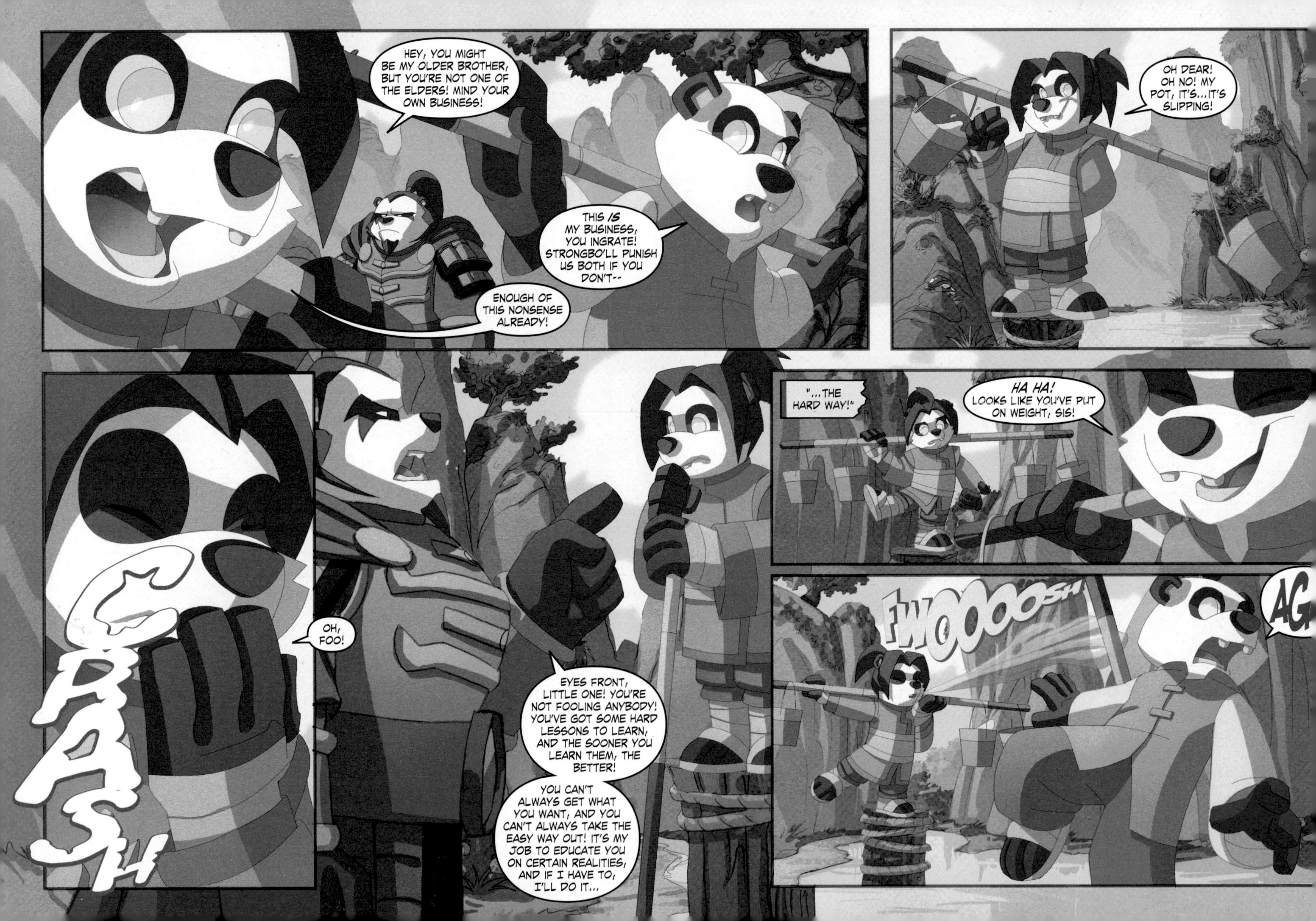
HEY, YOU MIGHT BE MY OLDER BROTHER, BUT YOU'RE NOT ONE OF THE ELDERS! MIND YOUR OWN BUSINESS!
THIS *IS* MY BUSINESS, YOU INGRATE! STRONGBO'LL PUNISH US BOTH IF YOU DON'T--
ENOUGH OF THIS NONSENSE ALREADY!
OH DEAR! OH NO! MY POT, IT'S...IT'S SLIPPING!
CRASH
OH, FOO!
EYES FRONT, LITTLE ONE! YOU'RE NOT FOOLING ANYBODY! YOU'VE GOT SOME HARD LESSONS TO LEARN, AND THE SOONER YOU LEARN THEM, THE BETTER!
YOU CAN'T ALWAYS GET WHAT YOU WANT, AND YOU CAN'T ALWAYS TAKE THE EASY WAY OUT! IT'S MY JOB TO EDUCATE YOU ON CERTAIN REALITIES, AND IF I HAVE TO, I'LL DO IT...
"...THE HARD WAY!"
HA HA! LOOKS LIKE YOU'VE PUT ON WEIGHT, SIS!
FWOOOOOSH
AG

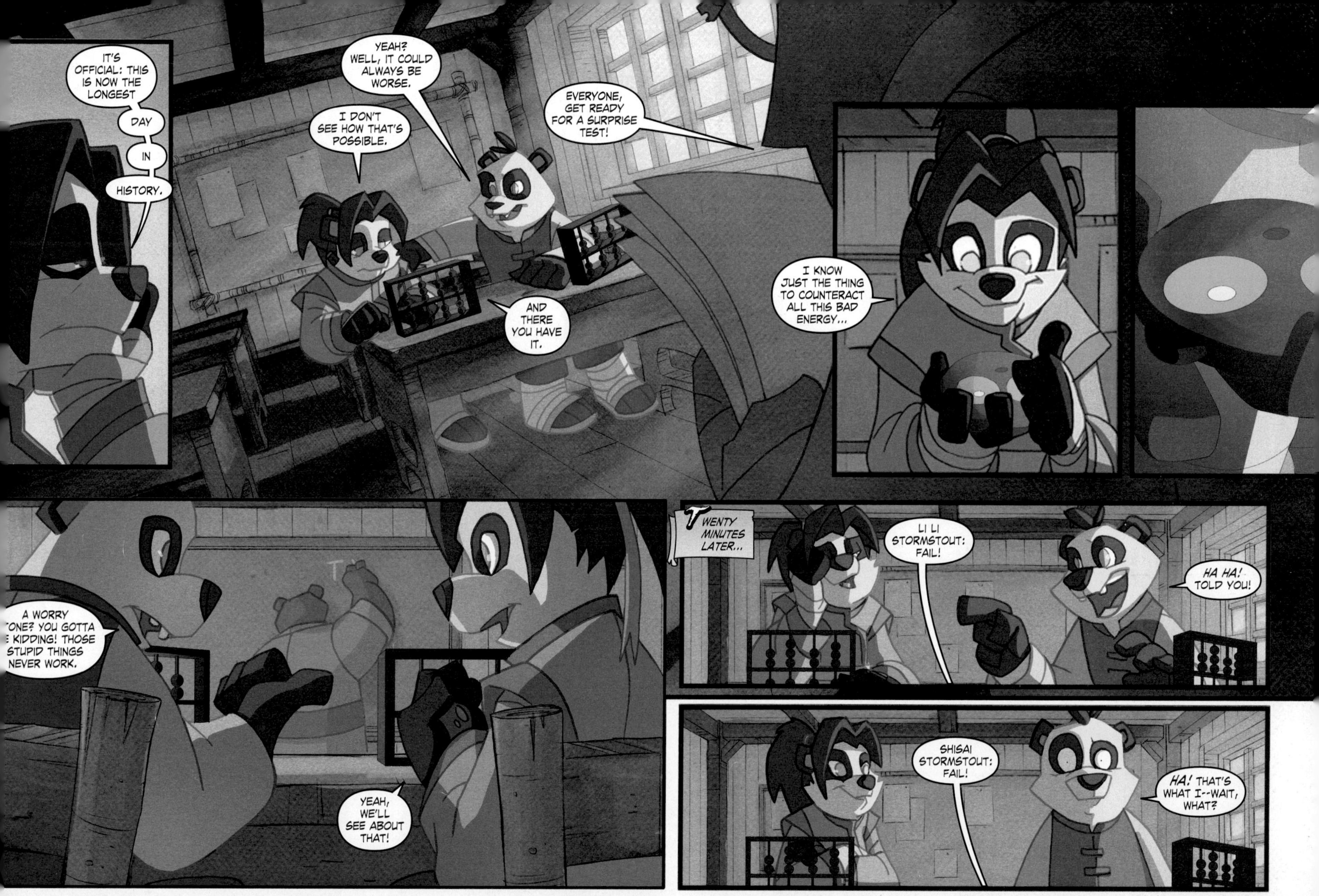
IT'S OFFICIAL: THIS IS NOW THE LONGEST DAY IN HISTORY.
I DON'T SEE HOW THAT'S POSSIBLE.
YEAH? WELL, IT COULD ALWAYS BE WORSE.
EVERYONE, GET READY FOR A SURPRISE TEST!
AND THERE YOU HAVE IT.
I KNOW JUST THE THING TO COUNTERACT ALL THIS BAD ENERGY...
A WORRY STONE? YOU GOTTA BE KIDDING! THOSE STUPID THINGS NEVER WORK.
YEAH, WE'LL SEE ABOUT THAT!
TWENTY MINUTES LATER...
LI LI STORMSTOUT: FAIL!
HA HA! TOLD YOU!
SHISAI STORMSTOUT: FAIL!
HA! THAT'S WHAT I--WAIT, WHAT?

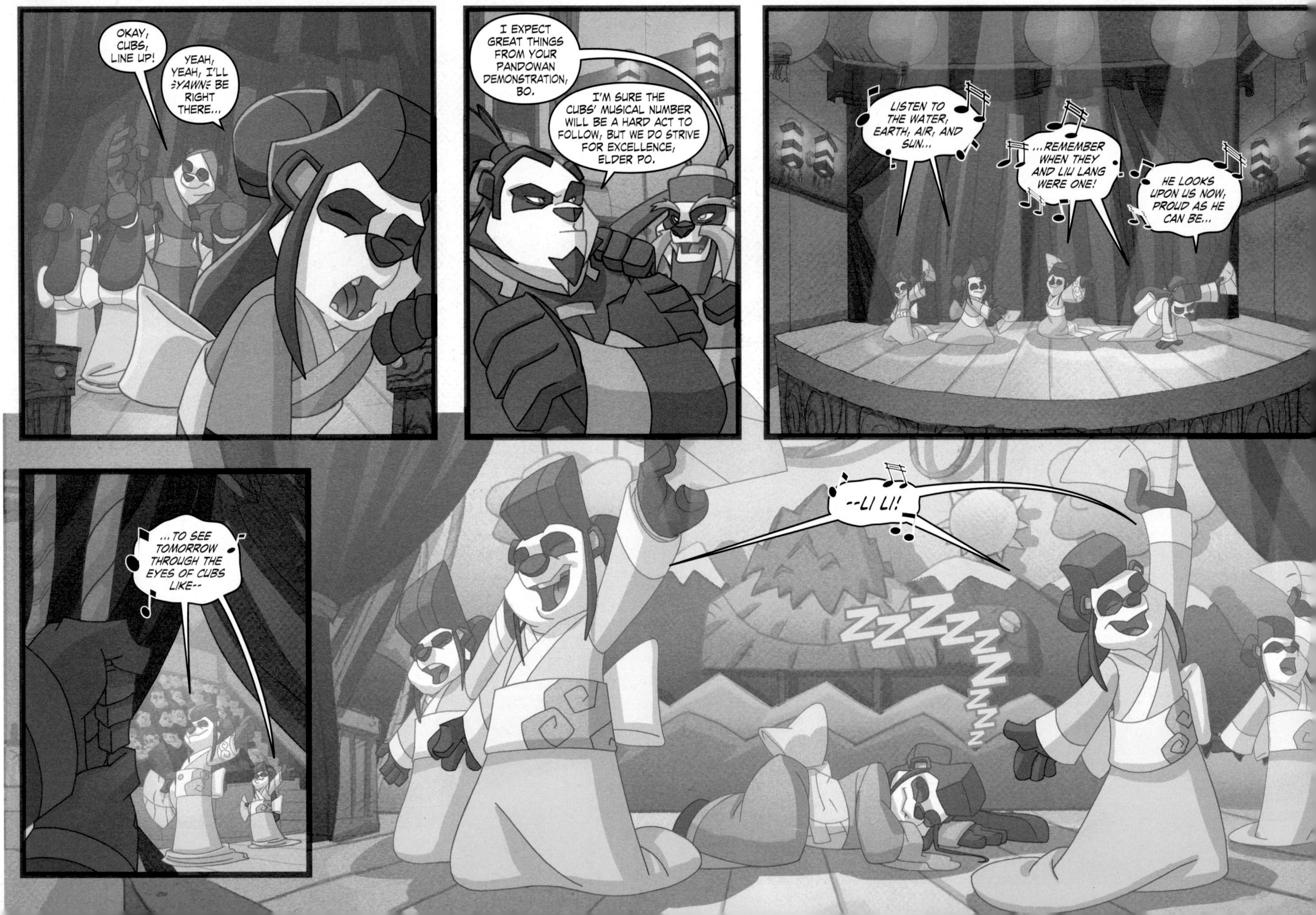
OKAY, CUBS, LINE UP!
YEAH, YEAH, I'LL ≶YAWN≷ BE RIGHT THERE...
I EXPECT GREAT THINGS FROM YOUR PANDOWAN DEMONSTRATION, BO.
I'M SURE THE CUBS' MUSICAL NUMBER WILL BE A HARD ACT TO FOLLOW, BUT WE DO STRIVE FOR EXCELLENCE, ELDER PO.
LISTEN TO THE WATER, EARTH, AIR, AND SUN...
...REMEMBER WHEN THEY AND LIU LANG WERE ONE!
HE LOOKS UPON US NOW, PROUD AS HE CAN BE...
...TO SEE TOMORROW THROUGH THE EYES OF CUBS LIKE--
--LI LI!
ZZZZZZZZZZ

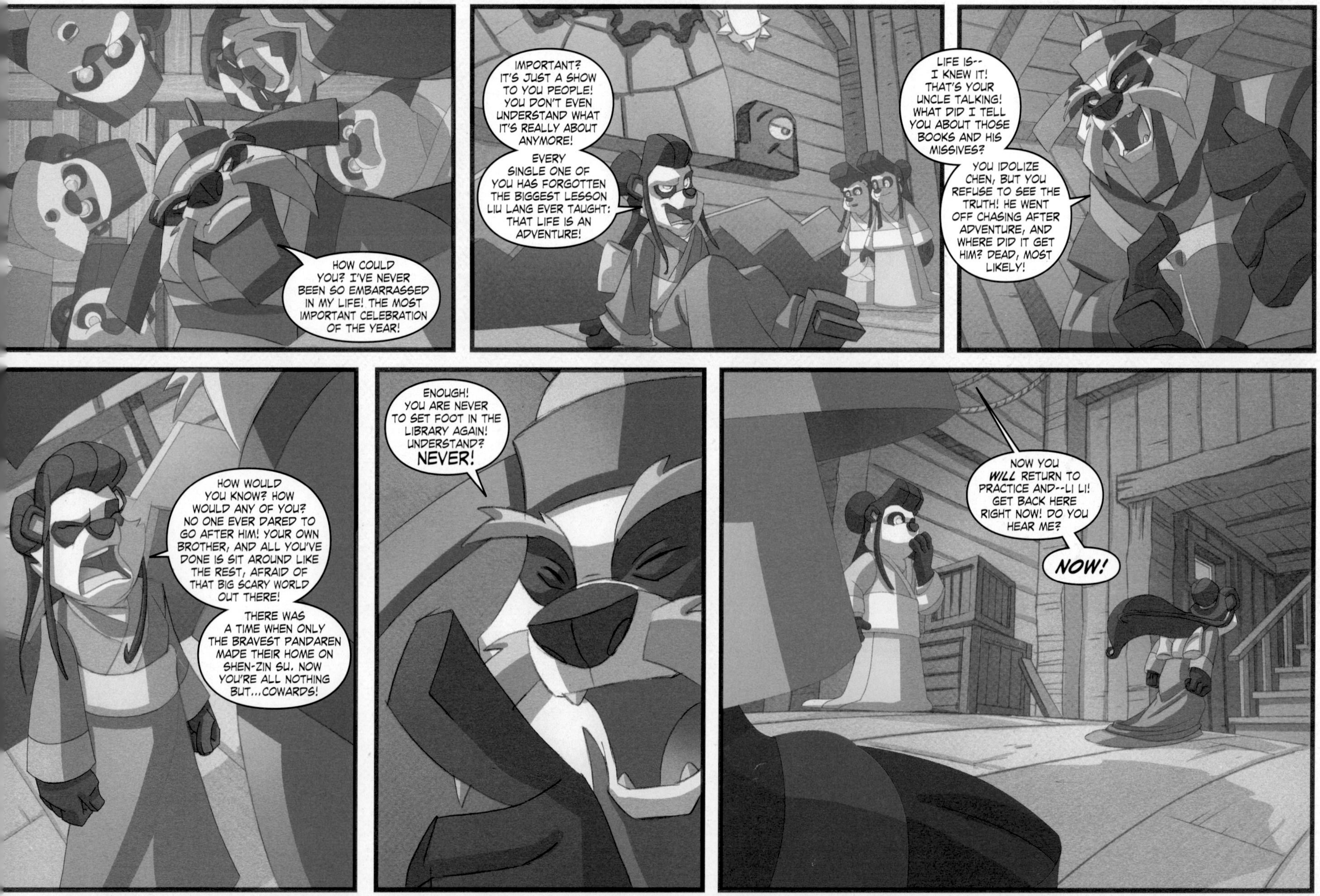
HOW COULD YOU? I'VE NEVER BEEN SO EMBARRASSED IN MY LIFE! THE MOST IMPORTANT CELEBRATION OF THE YEAR!
IMPORTANT? IT'S JUST A SHOW TO YOU PEOPLE! YOU DON'T EVEN UNDERSTAND WHAT IT'S REALLY ABOUT ANYMORE!
EVERY SINGLE ONE OF YOU HAS FORGOTTEN THE BIGGEST LESSON LIU LANG EVER TAUGHT: THAT LIFE IS AN ADVENTURE!
LIFE IS-- I KNEW IT! THAT'S YOUR UNCLE TALKING! WHAT DID I TELL YOU ABOUT THOSE BOOKS AND HIS MISSIVES?
YOU IDOLIZE CHEN, BUT YOU REFUSE TO SEE THE TRUTH! HE WENT OFF CHASING AFTER ADVENTURE, AND WHERE DID IT GET HIM? DEAD, MOST LIKELY!
HOW WOULD YOU KNOW? HOW WOULD ANY OF YOU? NO ONE EVER DARED TO GO AFTER HIM! YOUR OWN BROTHER, AND ALL YOU'VE DONE IS SIT AROUND LIKE THE REST, AFRAID OF THAT BIG SCARY WORLD OUT THERE!
THERE WAS A TIME WHEN ONLY THE BRAVEST PANDAREN MADE THEIR HOME ON SHEN-ZIN SU. NOW YOU'RE ALL NOTHING BUT...COWARDS!
ENOUGH! YOU ARE NEVER TO SET FOOT IN THE LIBRARY AGAIN! UNDERSTAND? NEVER!
NOW YOU WILL RETURN TO PRACTICE AND--LI LI! GET BACK HERE RIGHT NOW! DO YOU HEAR ME?
NOW!

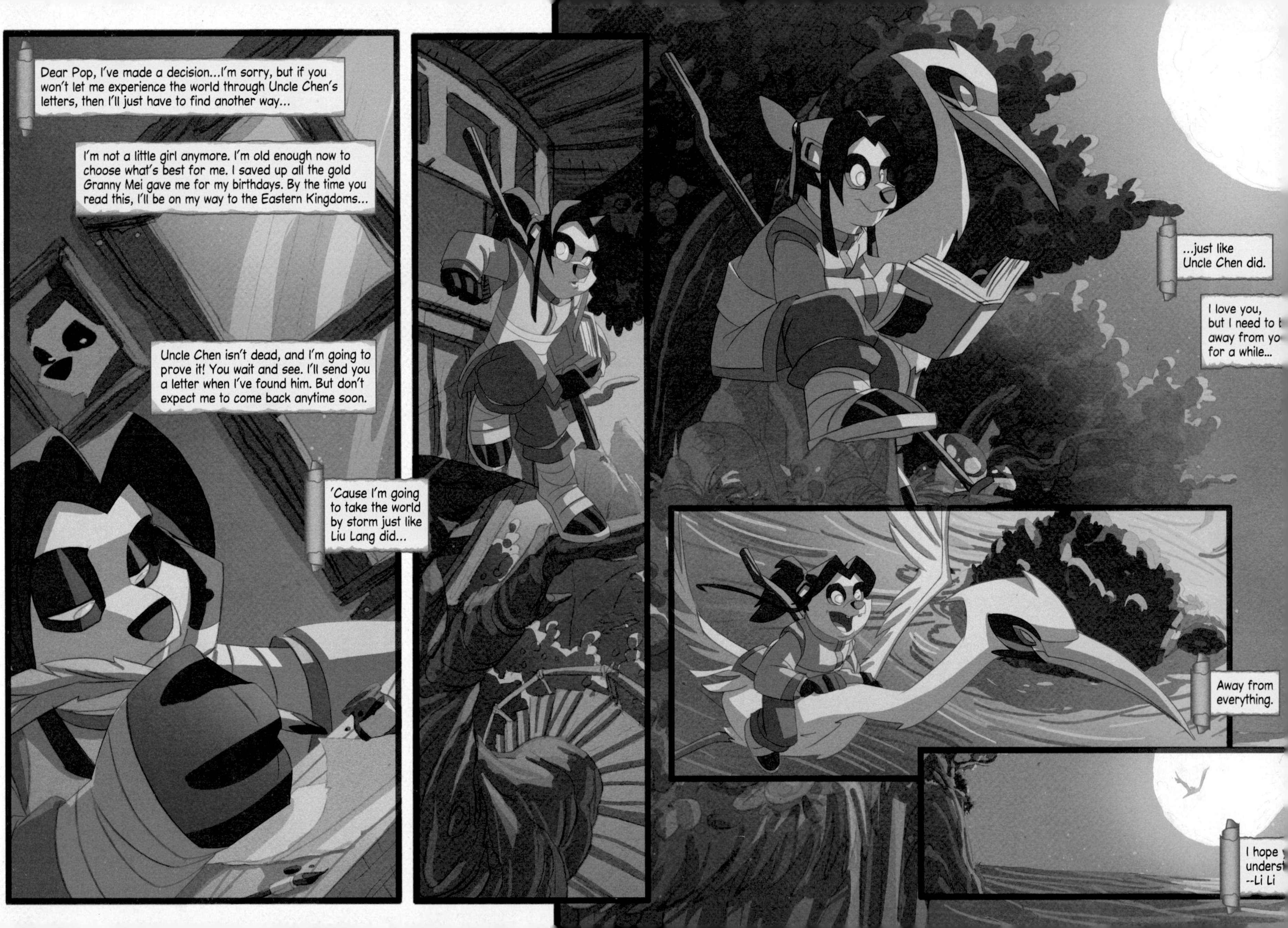

Dear Pop, I've made a decision...I'm sorry, but if you won't let me experience the world through Uncle Chen's letters, then I'll just have to find another way...
I'm not a little girl anymore. I'm old enough now to choose what's best for me. I saved up all the gold Granny Mei gave me for my birthdays. By the time you read this, I'll be on my way to the Eastern Kingdoms...
Uncle Chen isn't dead, and I'm going to prove it! You wait and see. I'll send you a letter when I've found him. But don't expect me to come back anytime soon.
'Cause I'm going to take the world by storm just like Liu Lang did...
...just like Uncle Chen did.
I love you, but I need to away from for a while...
Away from everything.
I hope --Li Li

CHAPTER TWO

Wanderlust

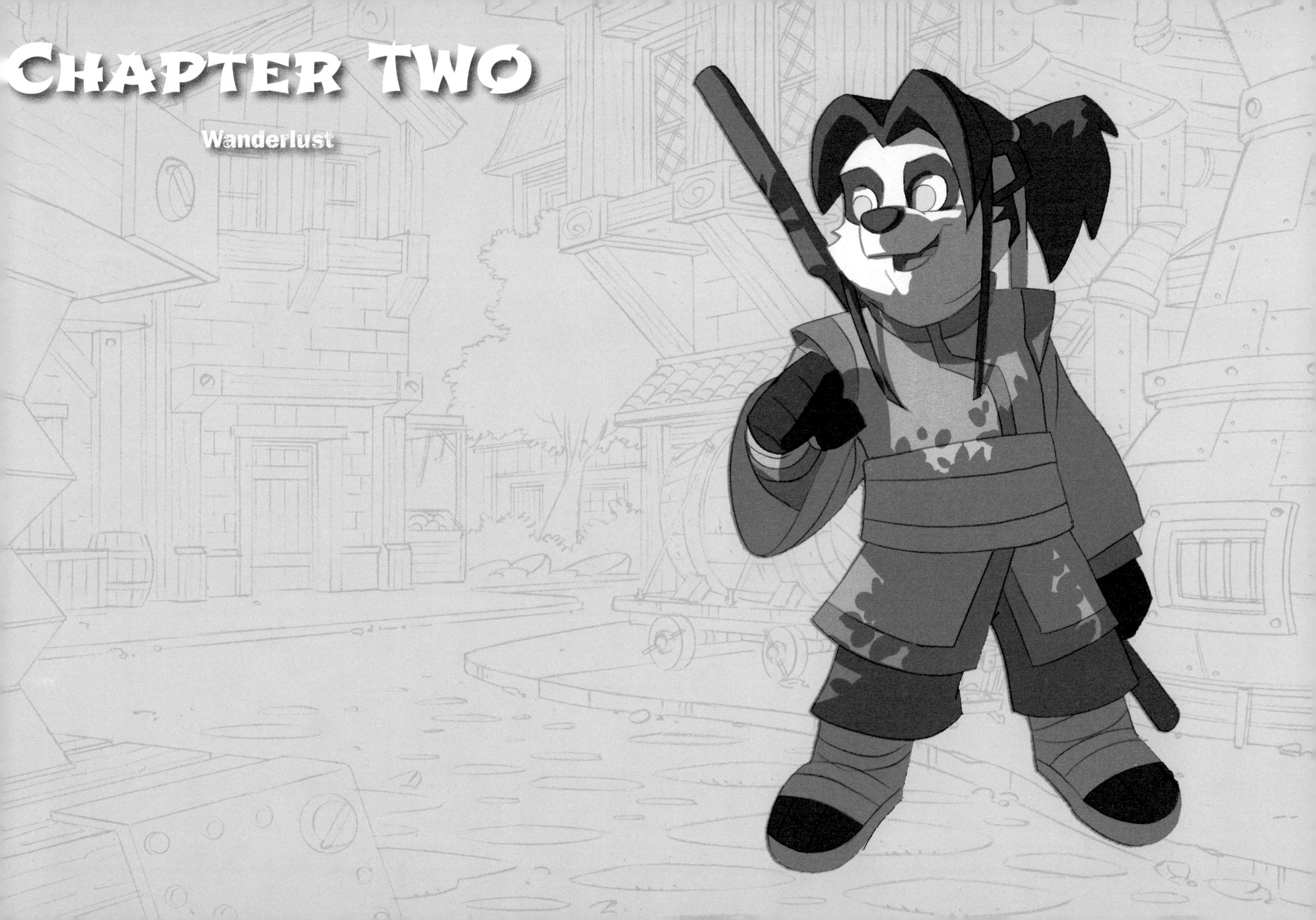

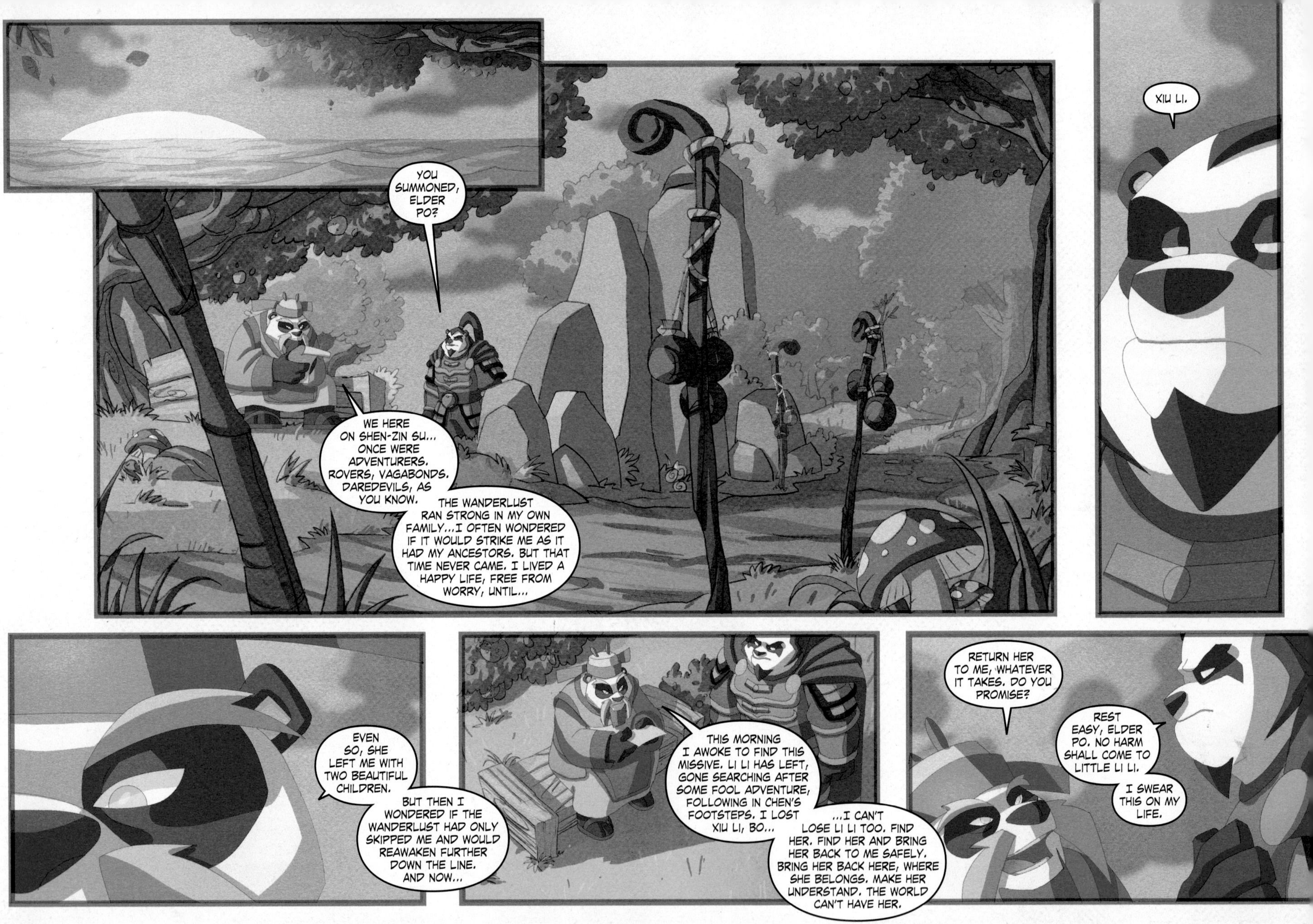

YOU SUMMONED, ELDER PO?
WE HERE ON SHEN-ZIN SU... ONCE WERE ADVENTURERS. ROVERS, VAGABONDS. DAREDEVILS, AS YOU KNOW.
THE WANDERLUST RAN STRONG IN MY OWN FAMILY...I OFTEN WONDERED IF IT WOULD STRIKE ME AS IT HAD MY ANCESTORS. BUT THAT TIME NEVER CAME. I LIVED A HAPPY LIFE, FREE FROM WORRY, UNTIL...
XIU LI.
EVEN SO, SHE LEFT ME WITH TWO BEAUTIFUL CHILDREN.
BUT THEN I WONDERED IF THE WANDERLUST HAD ONLY SKIPPED ME AND WOULD REAWAKEN FURTHER DOWN THE LINE. AND NOW...
THIS MORNING I AWOKE TO FIND THIS MISSIVE. LI LI HAS LEFT, GONE SEARCHING AFTER SOME FOOL ADVENTURE, FOLLOWING IN CHEN'S FOOTSTEPS. I LOST XIU LI, BO...
...I CAN'T LOSE LI LI TOO. FIND HER. FIND HER AND BRING HER BACK TO ME SAFELY. BRING HER BACK HERE, WHERE SHE BELONGS. MAKE HER UNDERSTAND. THE WORLD CAN'T HAVE HER.
RETURN HER TO ME, WHATEVER IT TAKES. DO YOU PROMISE?
REST EASY, ELDER PO. NO HARM SHALL COME TO LITTLE LI LI.
I SWEAR THIS ON MY LIFE.

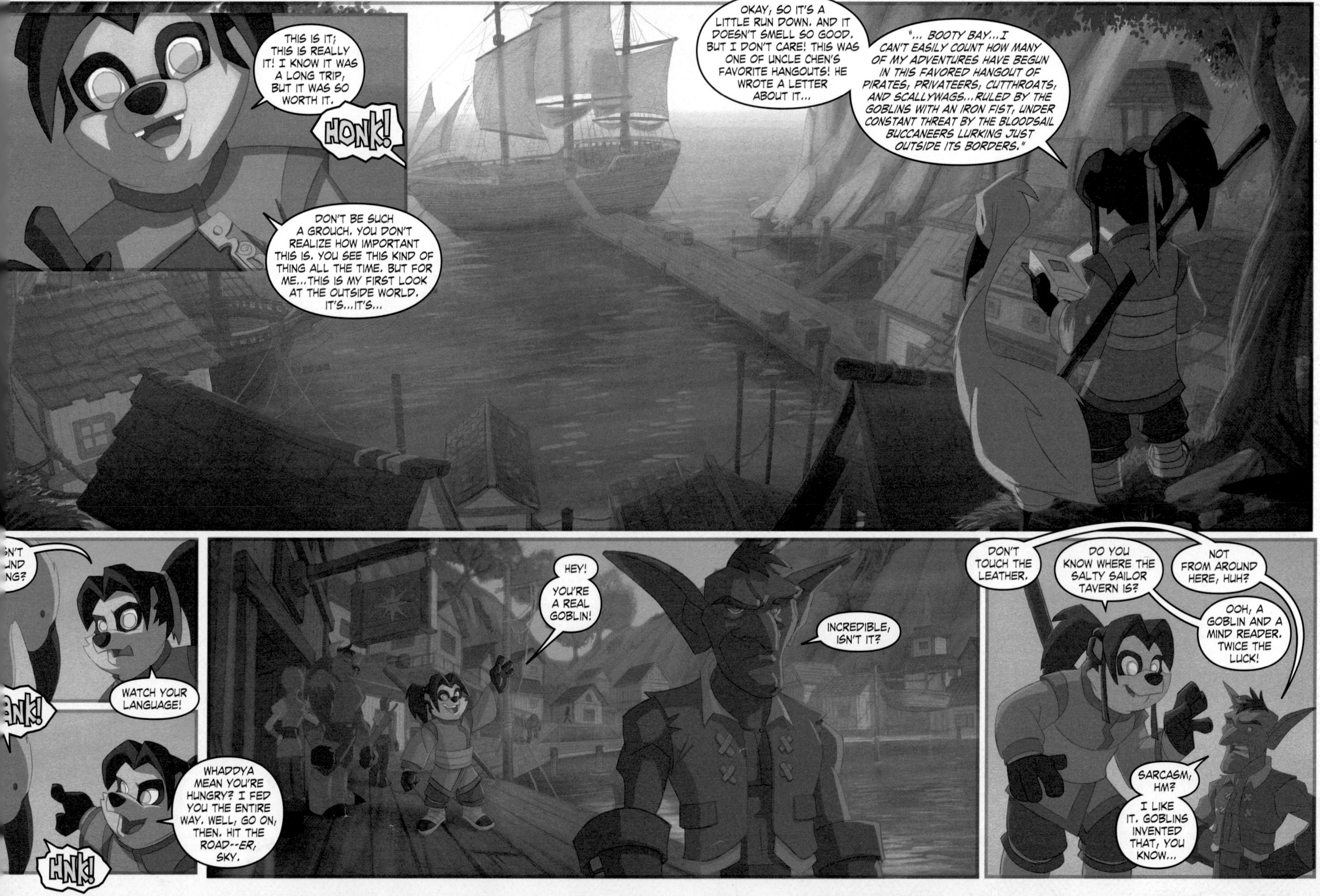

THIS IS IT; THIS IS REALLY IT! I KNOW IT WAS A LONG TRIP, BUT IT WAS SO WORTH IT.
HONK!
DON'T BE SUCH A GROUCH. YOU DON'T REALIZE HOW IMPORTANT THIS IS. YOU SEE THIS KIND OF THING ALL THE TIME. BUT FOR ME...THIS IS MY FIRST LOOK AT THE OUTSIDE WORLD. IT'S...IT'S...
OKAY, SO IT'S A LITTLE RUN DOWN. AND IT DOESN'T SMELL SO GOOD. BUT I DON'T CARE! THIS WAS ONE OF UNCLE CHEN'S FAVORITE HANGOUTS! HE WROTE A LETTER ABOUT IT...
"... BOOTY BAY...I CAN'T EASILY COUNT HOW MANY OF MY ADVENTURES HAVE BEGUN IN THIS FAVORED HANGOUT OF PIRATES, PRIVATEERS, CUTTHROATS, AND SCALLYWAGS...RULED BY THE GOBLINS WITH AN IRON FIST, UNDER CONSTANT THREAT BY THE BLOODSAIL BUCCANEERS LURKING JUST OUTSIDE ITS BORDERS."
WATCH YOUR LANGUAGE!
WHADDYA MEAN YOU'RE HUNGRY? I FED YOU THE ENTIRE WAY. WELL, GO ON, THEN. HIT THE ROAD--*ER,* SKY.
HNK!
HEY!
YOU'RE A REAL GOBLIN!
INCREDIBLE, ISN'T IT?
DON'T TOUCH THE LEATHER.
DO YOU KNOW WHERE THE SALTY SAILOR TAVERN IS?
NOT FROM AROUND HERE, HUH?
OOH, A GOBLIN AND A MIND READER. TWICE THE LUCK!
SARCASM, HM?
I LIKE IT. GOBLINS INVENTED THAT, YOU KNOW...

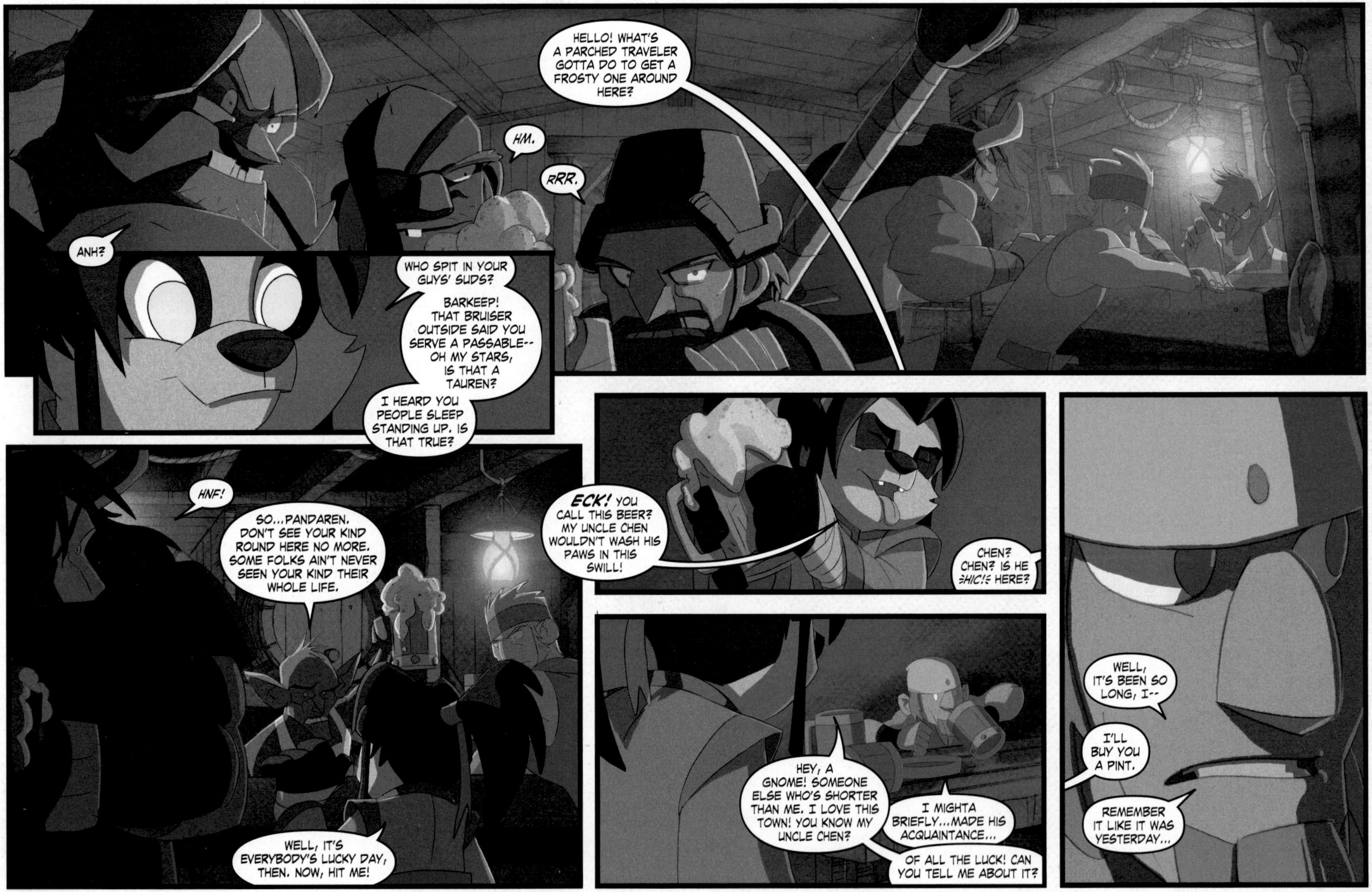
HELLO! WHAT'S A PARCHED TRAVELER GOTTA DO TO GET A FROSTY ONE AROUND HERE?
HM.
RRR.
ANH?
WHO SPIT IN YOUR GUYS' SUDS?
BARKEEP! THAT BRUISER OUTSIDE SAID YOU SERVE A PASSABLE-- OH MY STARS, IS THAT A TAUREN?
I HEARD YOU PEOPLE SLEEP STANDING UP. IS THAT TRUE?
HNF!
SO...PANDAREN. DON'T SEE YOUR KIND ROUND HERE NO MORE. SOME FOLKS AIN'T NEVER SEEN YOUR KIND THEIR WHOLE LIFE.
WELL, IT'S EVERYBODY'S LUCKY DAY, THEN. NOW, HIT ME!
ECK! YOU CALL THIS BEER? MY UNCLE CHEN WOULDN'T WASH HIS PAWS IN THIS SWILL!
CHEN? CHEN? IS HE *HIC!* HERE?
HEY, A GNOME! SOMEONE ELSE WHO'S SHORTER THAN ME. I LOVE THIS TOWN! YOU KNOW MY UNCLE CHEN?
I MIGHTA BRIEFLY...MADE HIS ACQUAINTANCE...
OF ALL THE LUCK! CAN YOU TELL ME ABOUT IT?
WELL, IT'S BEEN SO LONG, I--
I'LL BUY YOU A PINT.
REMEMBER IT LIKE IT WAS YESTERDAY...

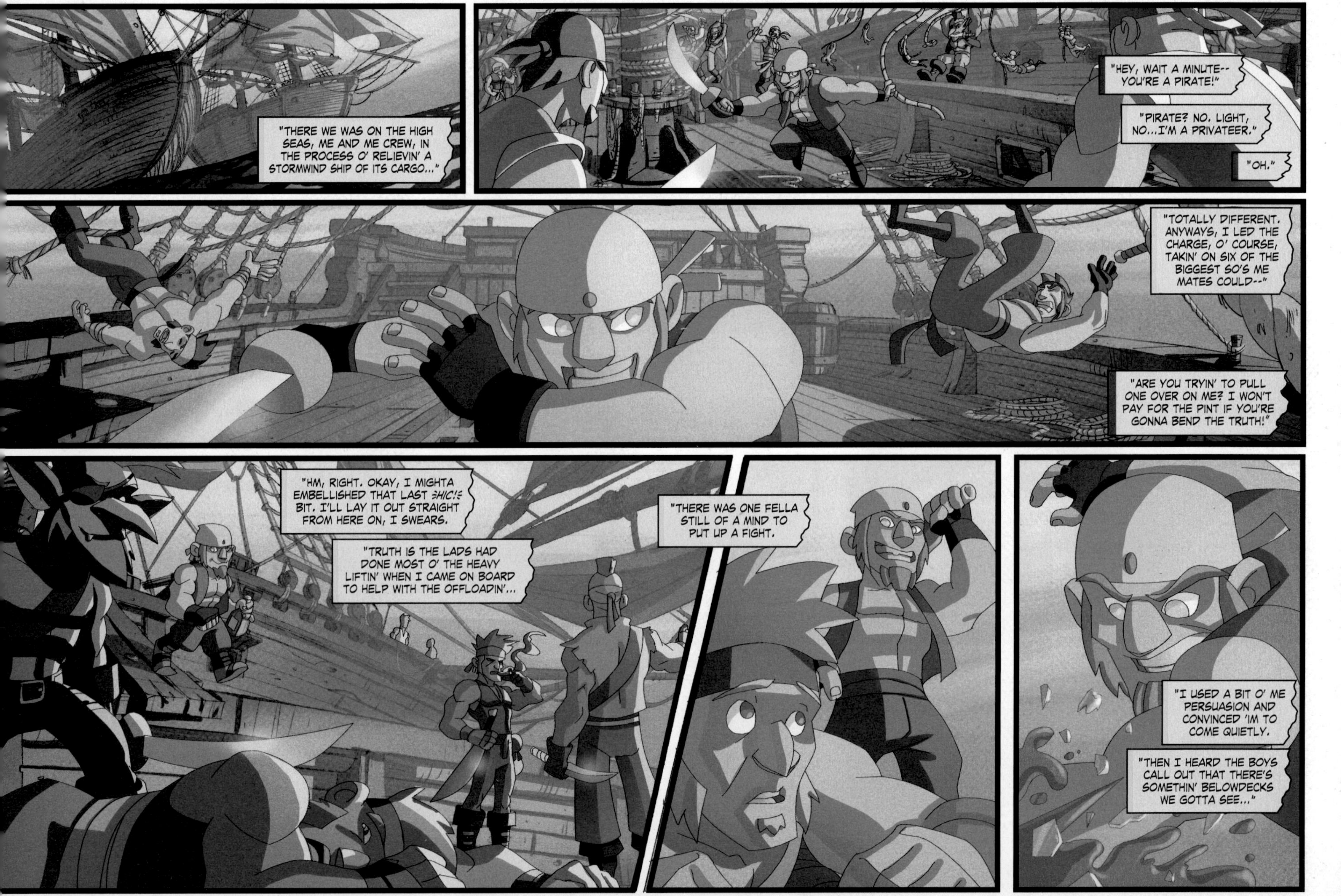
"THERE WE WAS ON THE HIGH SEAS, ME AND ME CREW, IN THE PROCESS O' RELIEVIN' A STORMWIND SHIP OF ITS CARGO..."
"HEY, WAIT A MINUTE-- YOU'RE A PIRATE!"
"PIRATE? NO. LIGHT, NO...I'M A PRIVATEER."
"OH."
"TOTALLY DIFFERENT. ANYWAYS, I LED THE CHARGE, O' COURSE, TAKIN' ON SIX OF THE BIGGEST SO'S ME MATES COULD--"
"ARE YOU TRYIN' TO PULL ONE OVER ON ME? I WON'T PAY FOR THE PINT IF YOU'RE GONNA BEND THE TRUTH!"
"HM, RIGHT. OKAY, I MIGHTA EMBELLISHED THAT LAST *HIC!* BIT. I'LL LAY IT OUT STRAIGHT FROM HERE ON, I SWEARS.
"TRUTH IS THE LADS HAD DONE MOST O' THE HEAVY LIFTIN' WHEN I CAME ON BOARD TO HELP WITH THE OFFLOADIN'...
"THERE WAS ONE FELLA STILL OF A MIND TO PUT UP A FIGHT.
"I USED A BIT O' ME PERSUASION AND CONVINCED 'IM TO COME QUIETLY.
"THEN I HEARD THE BOYS CALL OUT THAT THERE'S SOMETHIN' BELOWDECKS WE GOTTA SEE..."

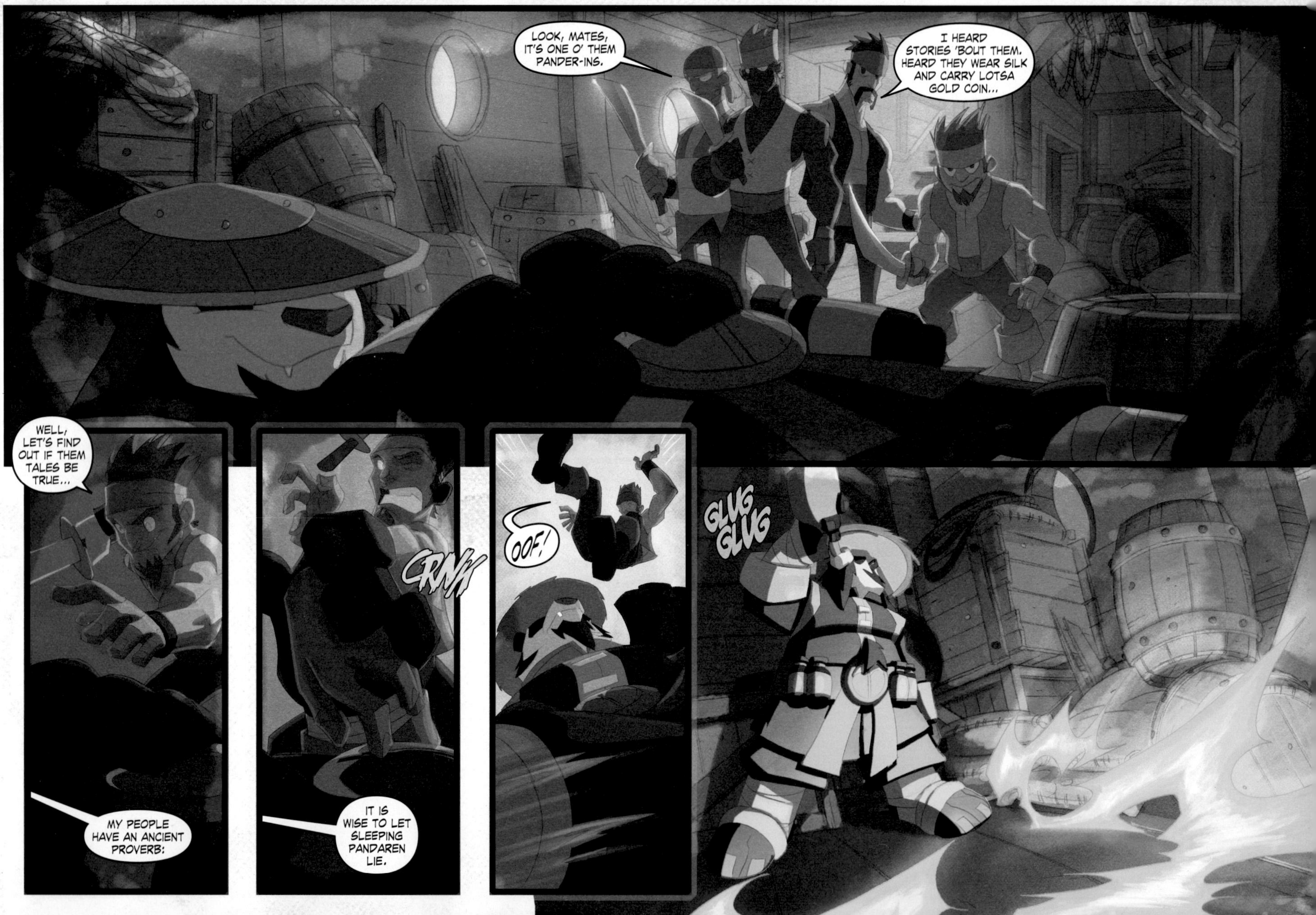
LOOK, MATES, IT'S ONE O' THEM PANDER-INS.
I HEARD STORIES 'BOUT THEM. HEARD THEY WEAR SILK AND CARRY LOTSA GOLD COIN...
WELL, LET'S FIND OUT IF THEM TALES BE TRUE...
MY PEOPLE HAVE AN ANCIENT PROVERB:
CRNK
IT IS WISE TO LET SLEEPING PANDAREN LIE.
OOF!
GLUG GLUG

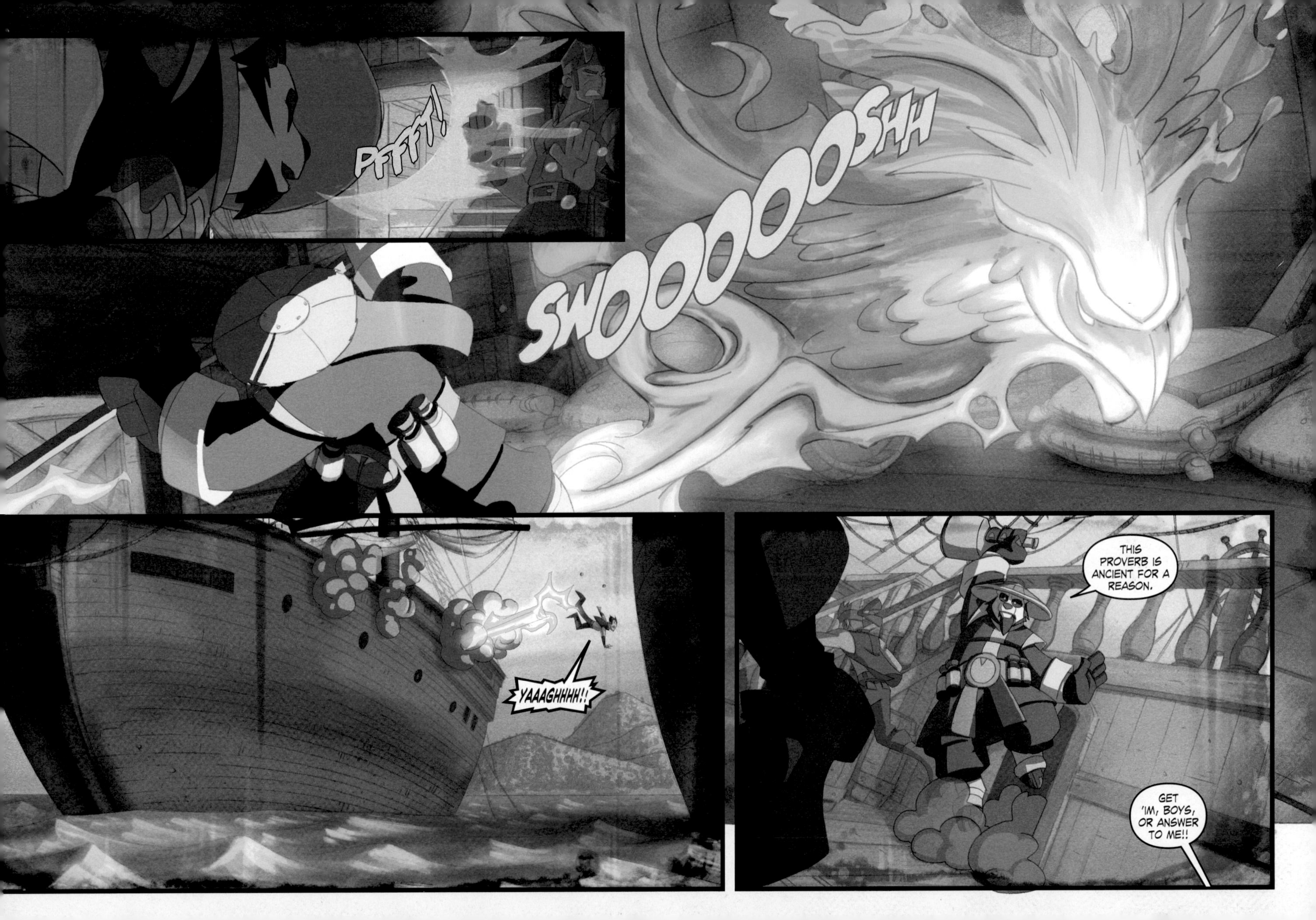
PFFFT!
SWOOOOOOOSHH
YAAAGHHHH!!
THIS PROVERB IS ANCIENT FOR A REASON.
GET 'IM, BOYS, OR ANSWER TO ME!!

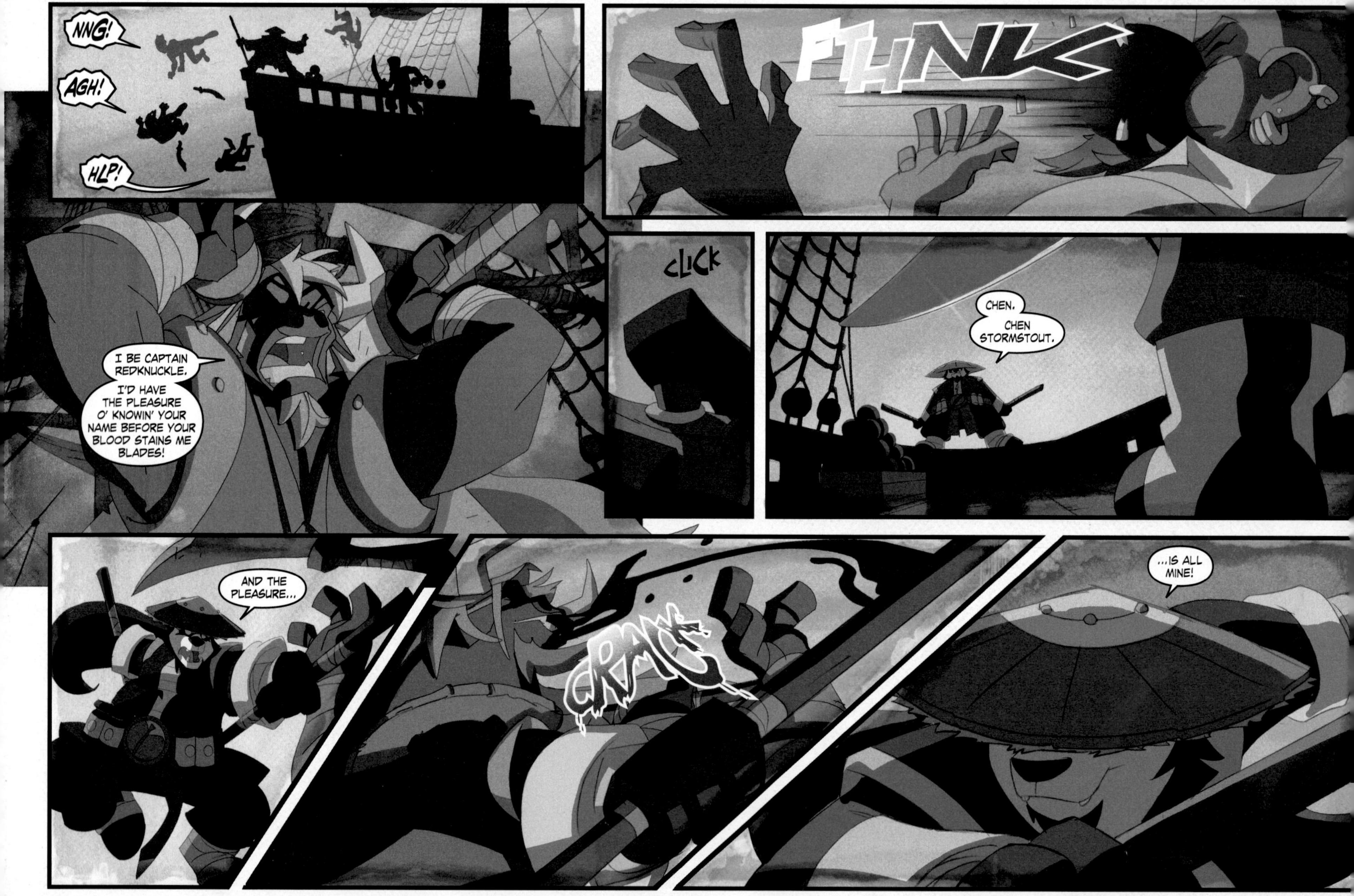
NNG!
AGH!
HLP!
FTHNK
I BE CAPTAIN REDKNUCKLE.
I'D HAVE THE PLEASURE O' KNOWIN' YOUR NAME BEFORE YOUR BLOOD STAINS ME BLADES!
CLICK
CHEN.
CHEN STORMSTOUT.
AND THE PLEASURE...
CRACK
...IS ALL MINE!

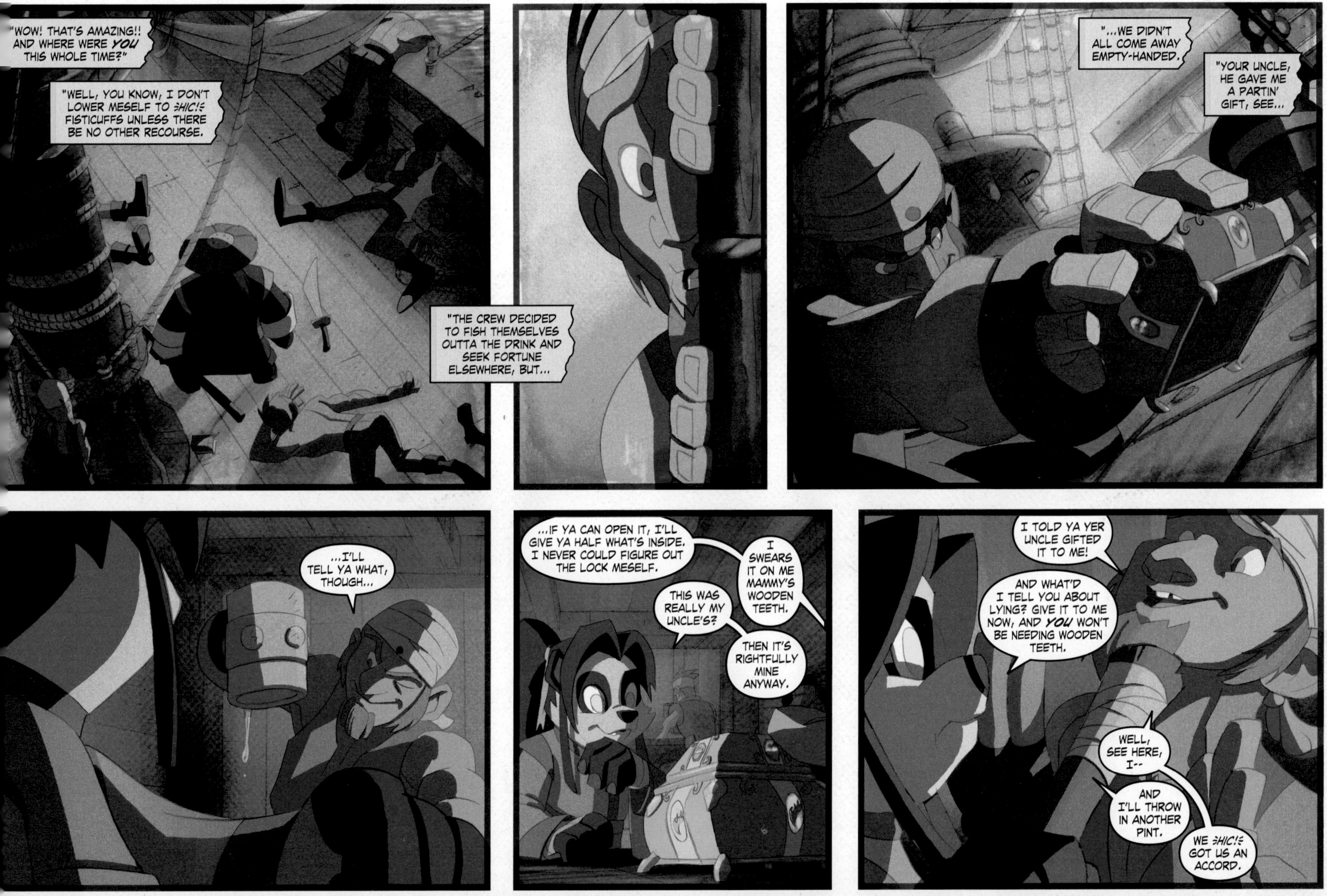
"WOW! THAT'S AMAZING!! AND WHERE WERE *YOU* THIS WHOLE TIME?"
"WELL, YOU KNOW, I DON'T LOWER MESELF TO HIC! FISTICUFFS UNLESS THERE BE NO OTHER RECOURSE.
"THE CREW DECIDED TO FISH THEMSELVES OUTTA THE DRINK AND SEEK FORTUNE ELSEWHERE, BUT...
"...WE DIDN'T ALL COME AWAY EMPTY-HANDED.
"YOUR UNCLE, HE GAVE ME A PARTIN' GIFT, SEE...
...I'LL TELL YA WHAT, THOUGH...
...IF YA CAN OPEN IT, I'LL GIVE YA HALF WHAT'S INSIDE. I NEVER COULD FIGURE OUT THE LOCK MESELF.
I SWEARS IT ON ME MAMMY'S WOODEN TEETH.
THIS WAS REALLY MY UNCLE'S?
THEN IT'S RIGHTFULLY MINE ANYWAY.
I TOLD YA YER UNCLE GIFTED IT TO ME!
AND WHAT'D I TELL YOU ABOUT LYING? GIVE IT TO ME NOW, AND *YOU* WON'T BE NEEDING WOODEN TEETH.
WELL, SEE HERE, I--
AND I'LL THROW IN ANOTHER PINT.
WE HIC! GOT US AN ACCORD.

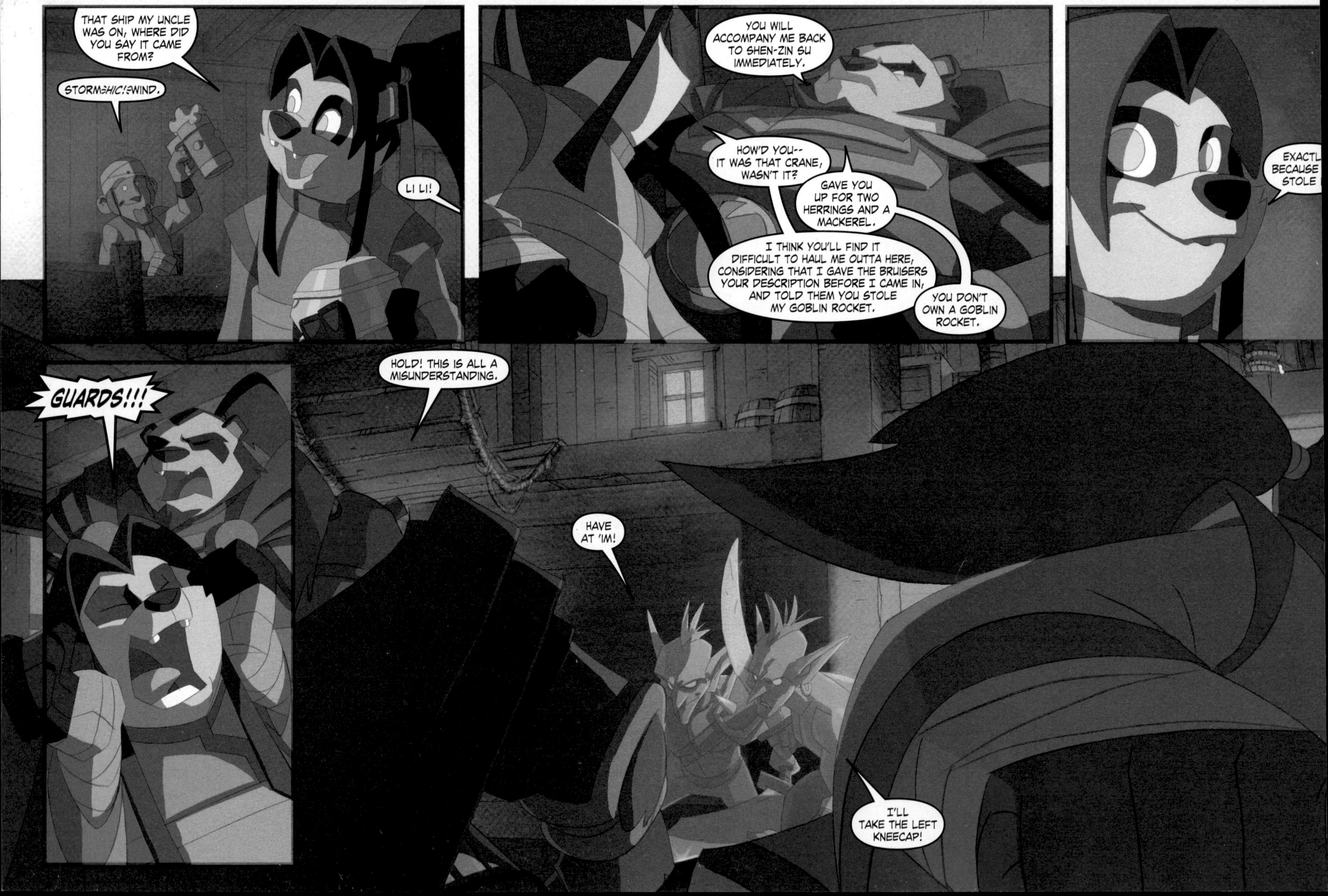

THAT SHIP MY UNCLE WAS ON, WHERE DID YOU SAY IT CAME FROM?
STORM-HIC!-WIND.
LI LI!
YOU WILL ACCOMPANY ME BACK TO SHEN-ZIN SU IMMEDIATELY.
HOW'D YOU-- IT WAS THAT CRANE, WASN'T IT?
GAVE YOU UP FOR TWO HERRINGS AND A MACKEREL.
I THINK YOU'LL FIND IT DIFFICULT TO HAUL ME OUTTA HERE, CONSIDERING THAT I GAVE THE BRUISERS YOUR DESCRIPTION BEFORE I CAME IN, AND TOLD THEM YOU STOLE MY GOBLIN ROCKET.
YOU DON'T OWN A GOBLIN ROCKET.
EXACTL BECAUSE STOLE
GUARDS!!!
HOLD! THIS IS ALL A MISUNDERSTANDING.
HAVE AT 'IM!
I'LL TAKE THE LEFT KNEECAP!

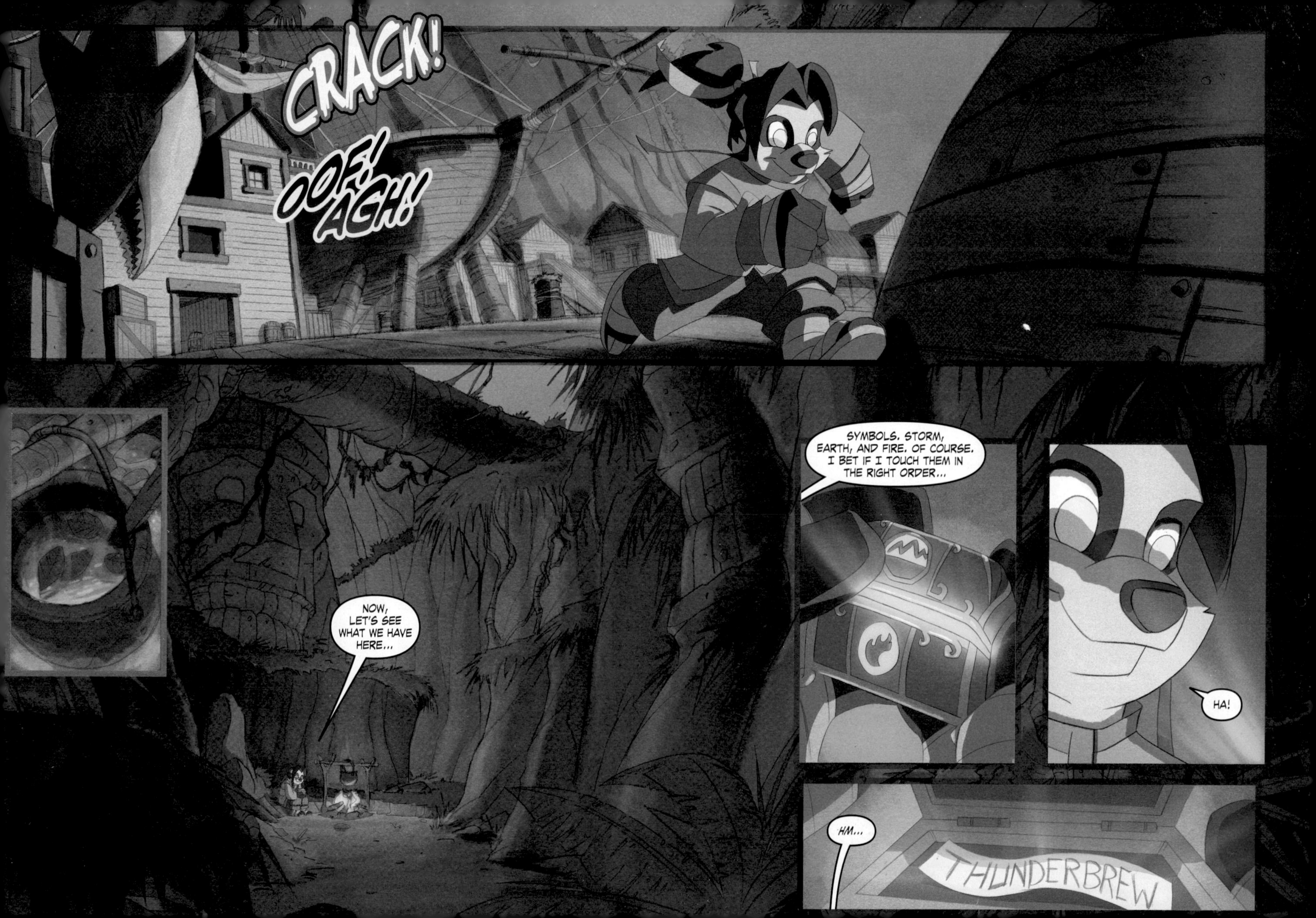
CRACK!
OOF! AGH!
NOW, LET'S SEE WHAT WE HAVE HERE...
SYMBOLS. STORM, EARTH, AND FIRE. OF COURSE. I BET IF I TOUCH THEM IN THE RIGHT ORDER...
HA!
HM...
THUNDERBREW

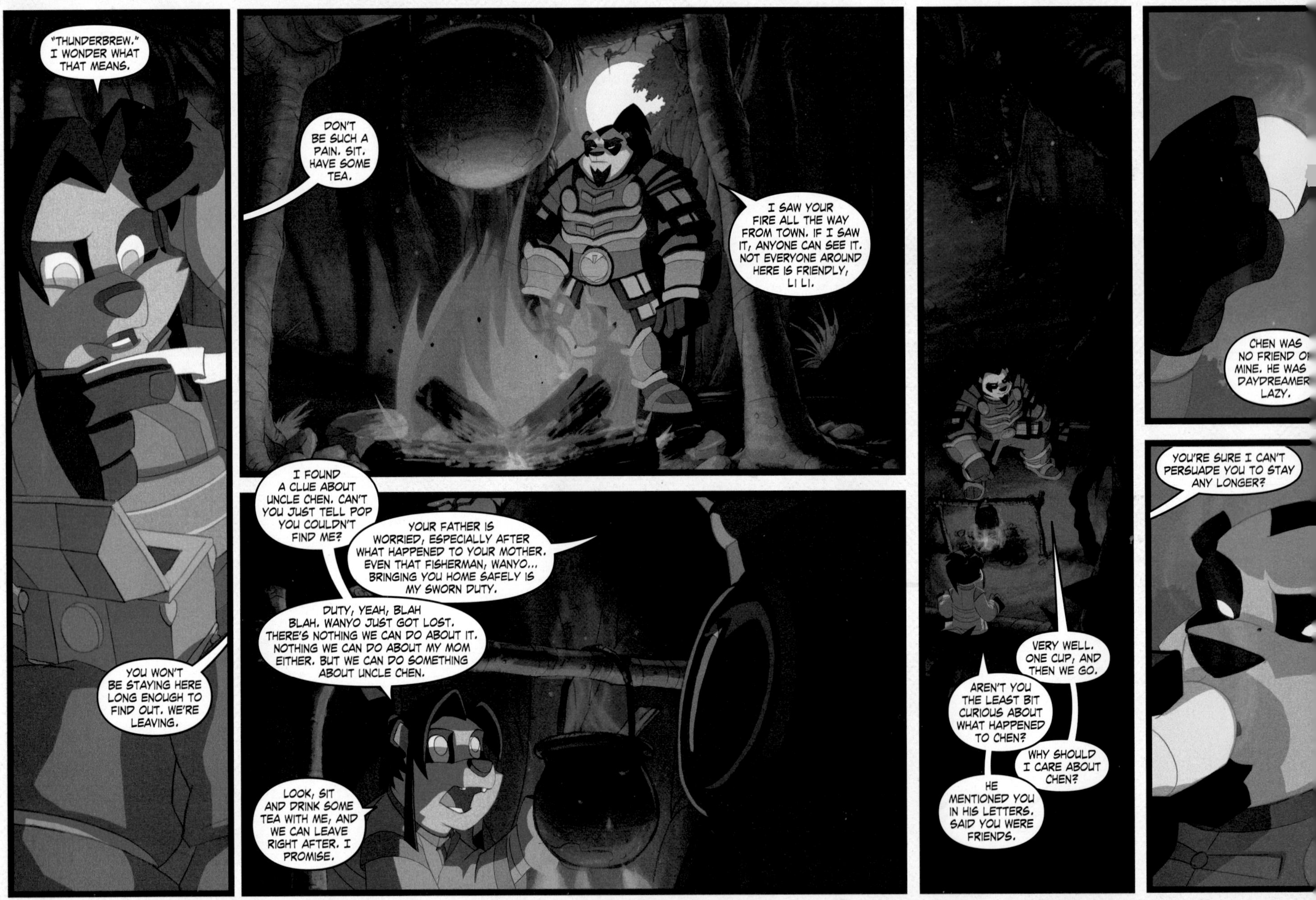

"THUNDERBREW." I WONDER WHAT THAT MEANS.
I SAW YOUR FIRE ALL THE WAY FROM TOWN. IF I SAW IT, ANYONE CAN SEE IT. NOT EVERYONE AROUND HERE IS FRIENDLY, LI LI.
YOU WON'T BE STAYING HERE LONG ENOUGH TO FIND OUT. WE'RE LEAVING.
DON'T BE SUCH A PAIN. SIT. HAVE SOME TEA.
I FOUND A CLUE ABOUT UNCLE CHEN. CAN'T YOU JUST TELL POP YOU COULDN'T FIND ME?
YOUR FATHER IS WORRIED, ESPECIALLY AFTER WHAT HAPPENED TO YOUR MOTHER. EVEN THAT FISHERMAN, WANYO... BRINGING YOU HOME SAFELY IS MY SWORN DUTY.
DUTY, YEAH, BLAH BLAH. WANYO JUST GOT LOST. THERE'S NOTHING WE CAN DO ABOUT IT. NOTHING WE CAN DO ABOUT MY MOM EITHER. BUT WE CAN DO SOMETHING ABOUT UNCLE CHEN.
LOOK, SIT AND DRINK SOME TEA WITH ME, AND WE CAN LEAVE RIGHT AFTER. I PROMISE.
AREN'T YOU THE LEAST BIT CURIOUS ABOUT WHAT HAPPENED TO CHEN?
WHY SHOULD I CARE ABOUT CHEN?
HE MENTIONED YOU IN HIS LETTERS. SAID YOU WERE FRIENDS.
VERY WELL. ONE CUP, AND THEN WE GO.
CHEN WAS NO FRIEND O
MINE. HE WAS DAYDREAMER
LAZY.
YOU'RE SURE I CAN'T PERSUADE YOU TO STAY ANY LONGER?

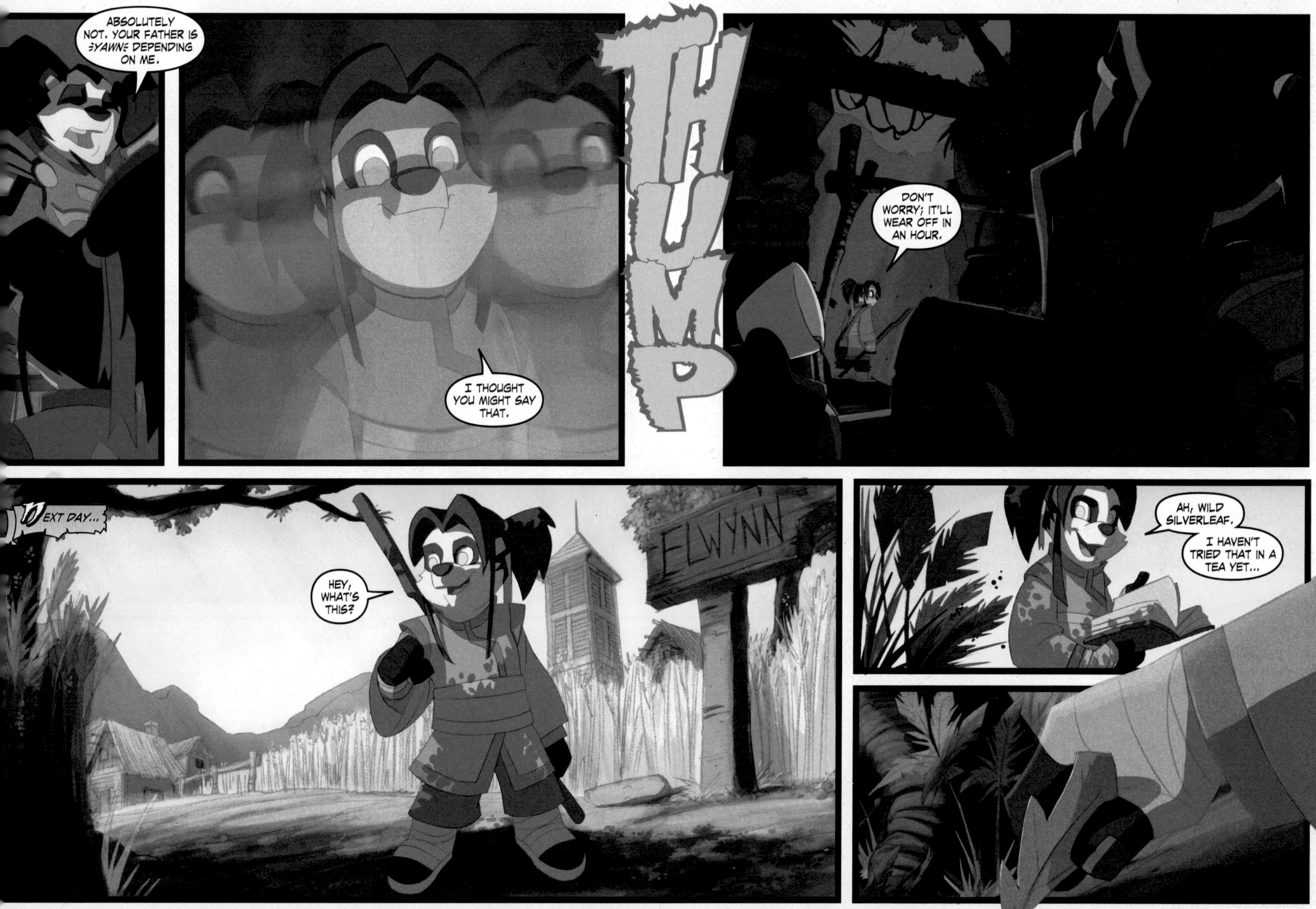
ABSOLUTELY NOT. YOUR FATHER IS =YAWN= DEPENDING ON ME.
I THOUGHT YOU MIGHT SAY THAT.
THUMP
DON'T WORRY; IT'LL WEAR OFF IN AN HOUR.
NEXT DAY...
HEY, WHAT'S THIS?
ELWYNN
AH, WILD SILVERLEAF.
I HAVEN'T TRIED THAT IN A TEA YET...

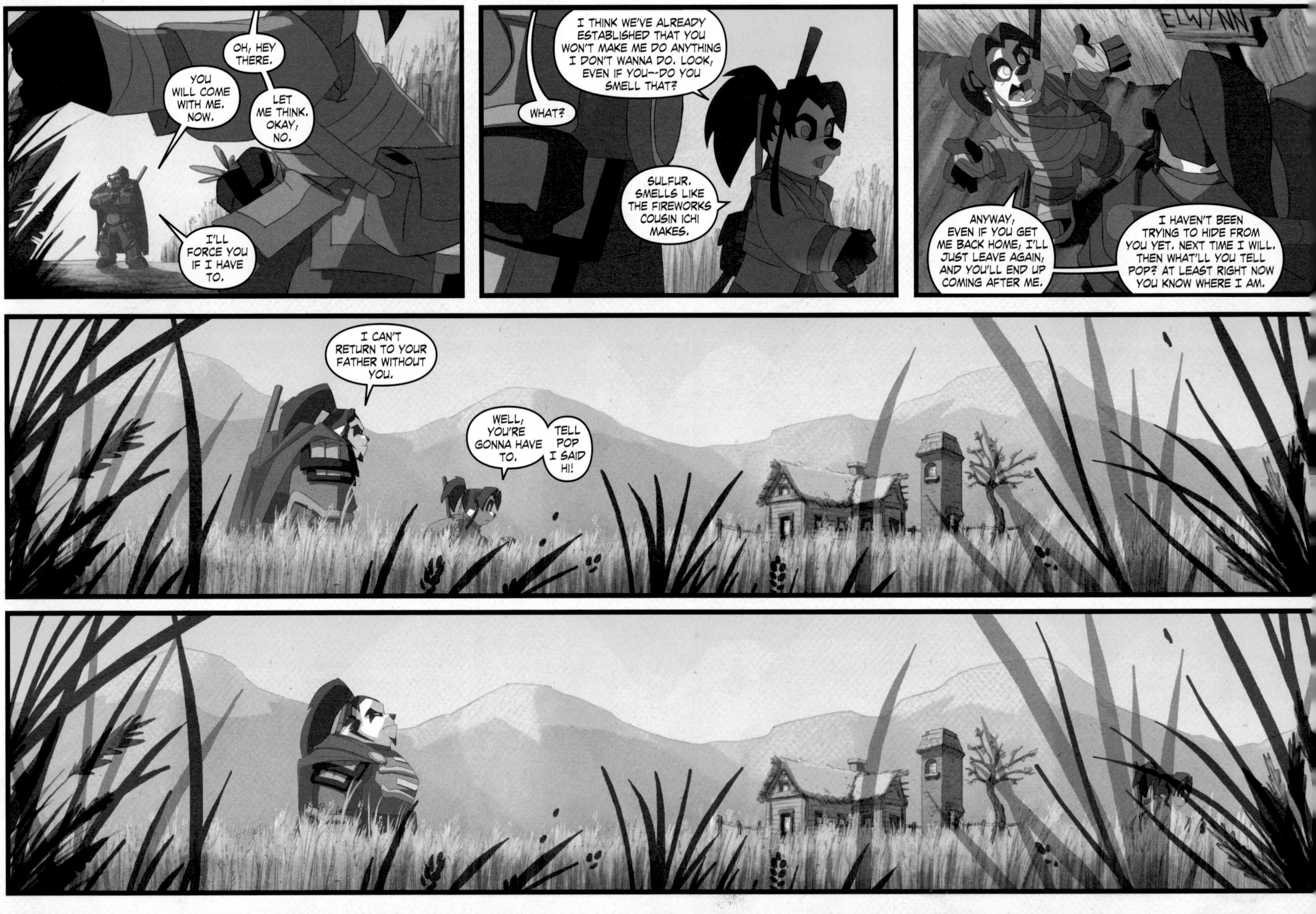
OH, HEY THERE.
YOU WILL COME WITH ME. NOW.
LET ME THINK. OKAY, NO.
I'LL FORCE YOU IF I HAVE TO.
I THINK WE'VE ALREADY ESTABLISHED THAT YOU WON'T MAKE ME DO ANYTHING I DON'T WANNA DO. LOOK, EVEN IF YOU--DO YOU SMELL THAT?
WHAT?
SULFUR. SMELLS LIKE THE FIREWORKS COUSIN ICHI MAKES.
ELWYNN
ANYWAY, EVEN IF YOU GET ME BACK HOME, I'LL JUST LEAVE AGAIN, AND YOU'LL END UP COMING AFTER ME.
I HAVEN'T BEEN TRYING TO HIDE FROM YOU YET. NEXT TIME I WILL. THEN WHAT'LL YOU TELL POP? AT LEAST RIGHT NOW YOU KNOW WHERE I AM.
I CAN'T RETURN TO YOUR FATHER WITHOUT YOU.
WELL, YOU'RE GONNA HAVE TO.
TELL POP I SAID HI!

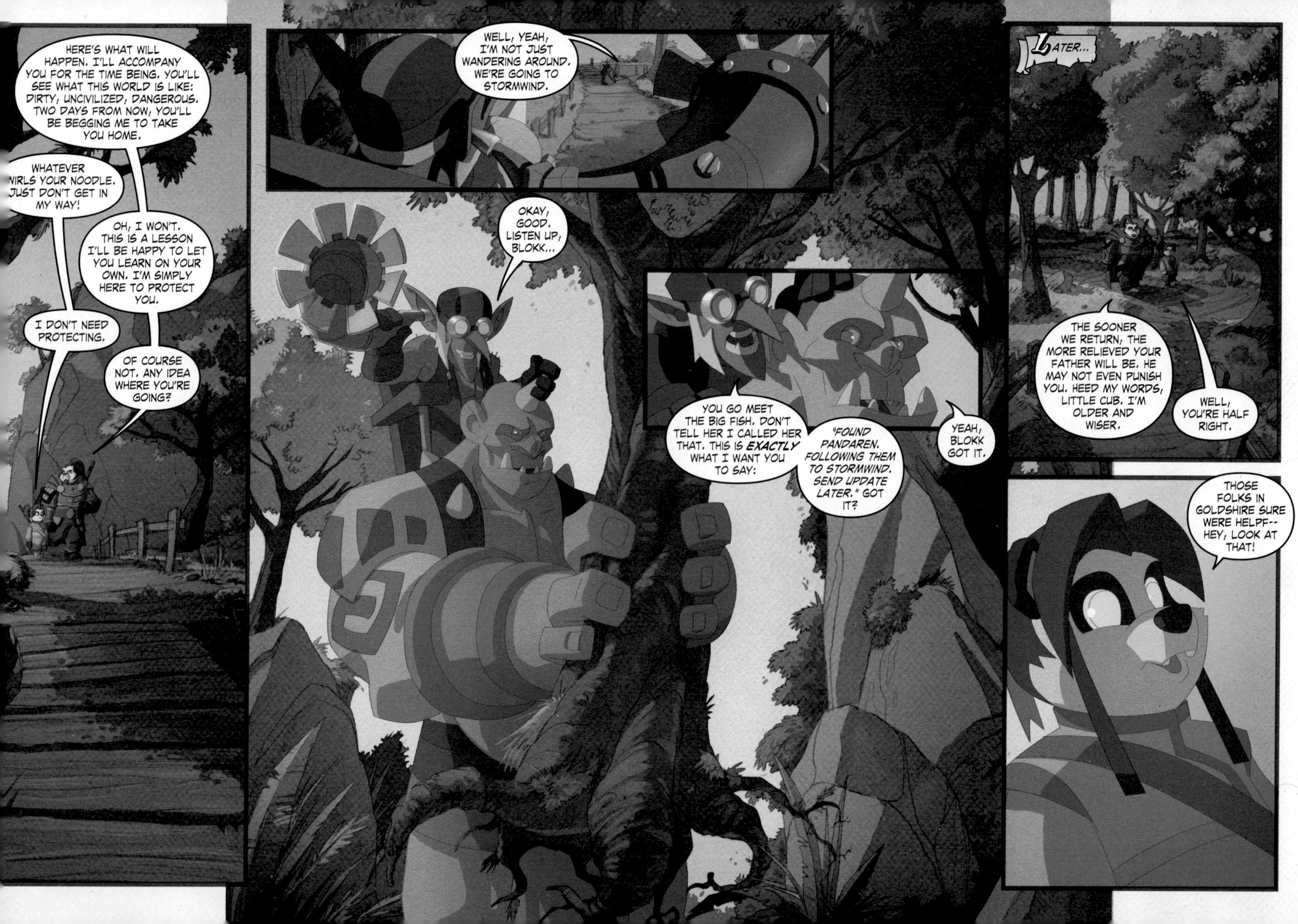
HERE'S WHAT WILL HAPPEN. I'LL ACCOMPANY YOU FOR THE TIME BEING. YOU'LL SEE WHAT THIS WORLD IS LIKE: DIRTY, UNCIVILIZED, DANGEROUS. TWO DAYS FROM NOW, YOU'LL BE BEGGING ME TO TAKE YOU HOME.
WHATEVER WIRLS YOUR NOODLE. JUST DON'T GET IN MY WAY!
OH, I WON'T. THIS IS A LESSON I'LL BE HAPPY TO LET YOU LEARN ON YOUR OWN. I'M SIMPLY HERE TO PROTECT YOU.
I DON'T NEED PROTECTING.
OF COURSE NOT. ANY IDEA WHERE YOU'RE GOING?
WELL, YEAH, I'M NOT JUST WANDERING AROUND. WE'RE GOING TO STORMWIND.
OKAY, GOOD. LISTEN UP, BLOKK...
YOU GO MEET THE BIG FISH. DON'T TELL HER I CALLED HER THAT. THIS IS **EXACTLY** WHAT I WANT YOU TO SAY:
"FOUND PANDAREN. FOLLOWING THEM TO STORMWIND. SEND UPDATE LATER." GOT IT?
YEAH, BLOKK GOT IT.
LATER...
THE SOONER WE RETURN, THE MORE RELIEVED YOUR FATHER WILL BE. HE MAY NOT EVEN PUNISH YOU. HEED MY WORDS, LITTLE CUB. I'M OLDER AND WISER.
WELL, YOU'RE HALF RIGHT.
THOSE FOLKS IN GOLDSHIRE SURE WERE HELPF-- HEY, LOOK AT THAT!

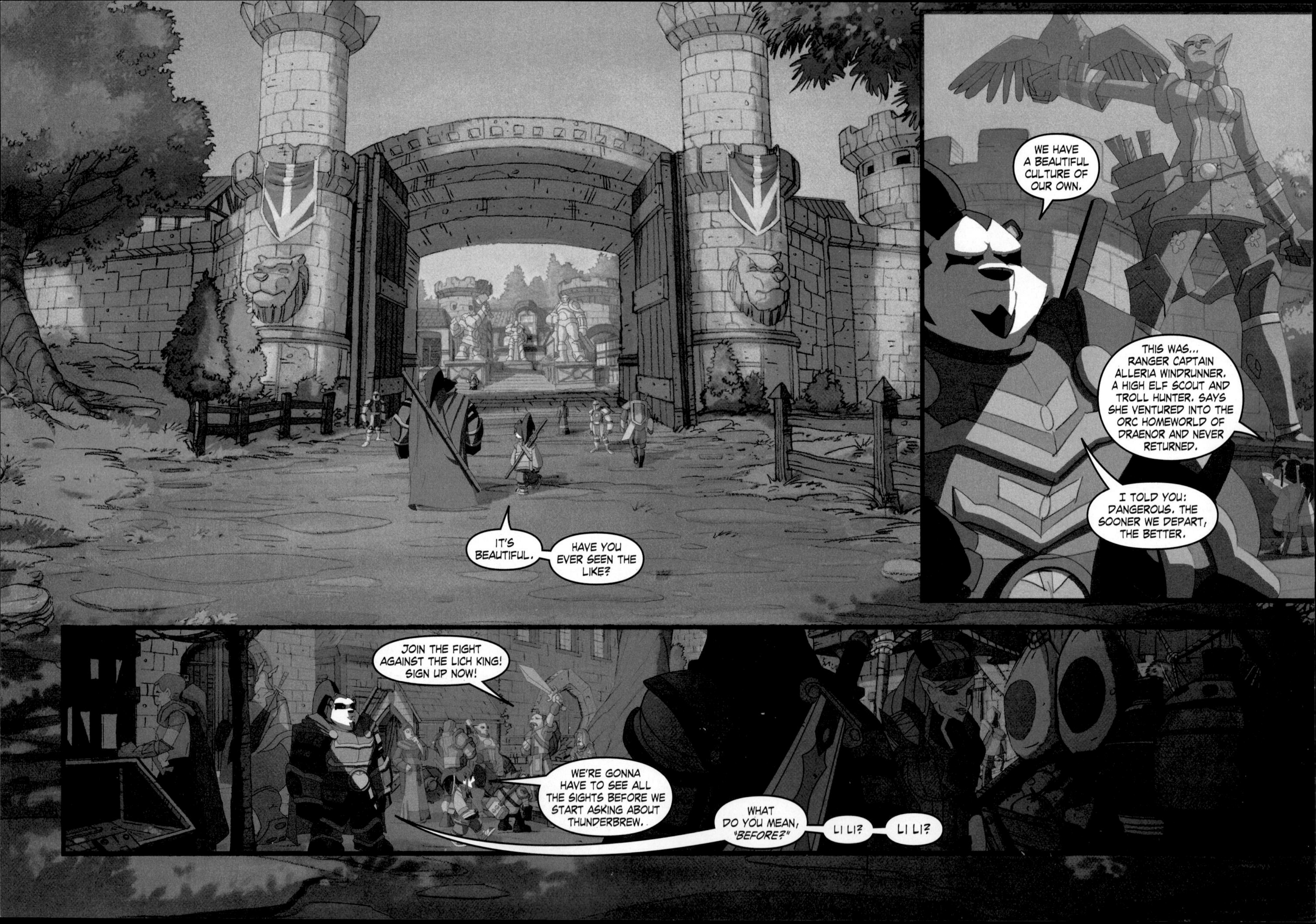
IT'S BEAUTIFUL.
HAVE YOU EVER SEEN THE LIKE?
WE HAVE A BEAUTIFUL CULTURE OF OUR OWN.
THIS WAS... RANGER CAPTAIN ALLERIA WINDRUNNER. A HIGH ELF SCOUT AND TROLL HUNTER. SAYS SHE VENTURED INTO THE ORC HOMEWORLD OF DRAENOR AND NEVER RETURNED.
I TOLD YOU: DANGEROUS. THE SOONER WE DEPART, THE BETTER.
JOIN THE FIGHT AGAINST THE LICH KING! SIGN UP NOW!
WE'RE GONNA HAVE TO SEE ALL THE SIGHTS BEFORE WE START ASKING ABOUT THUNDERBREW.
WHAT DO YOU MEAN, *"BEFORE?"*
LI LI?
LI LI?

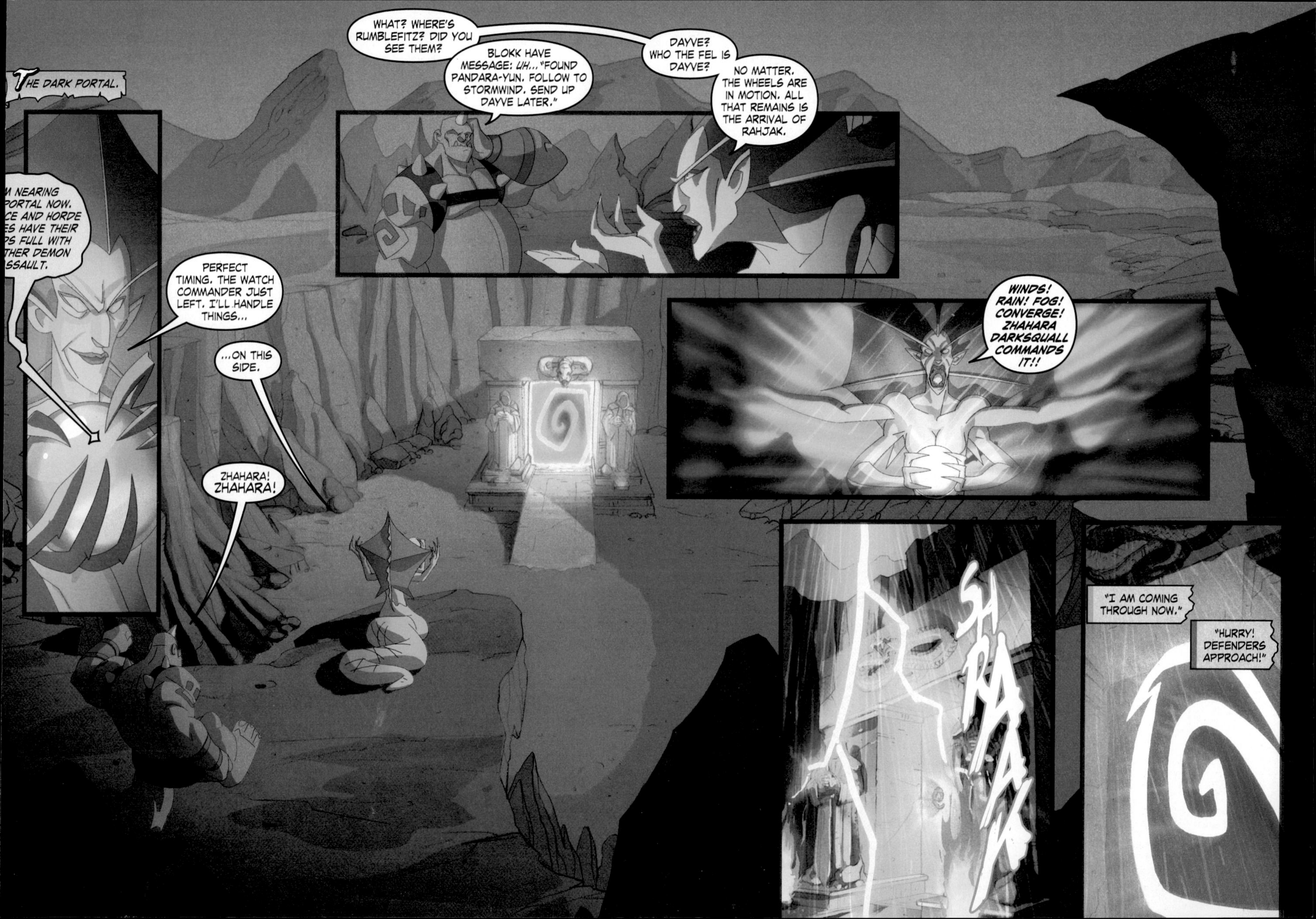
THE DARK PORTAL.
WHAT? WHERE'S RUMBLEFITZ? DID YOU SEE THEM?
BLOKK HAVE MESSAGE: UH... "FOUND PANDARA-YUN. FOLLOW TO STORMWIND. SEND UP DAYVE LATER."
DAYVE? WHO THE FEL IS DAYVE?
NO MATTER. THE WHEELS ARE IN MOTION. ALL THAT REMAINS IS THE ARRIVAL OF RAHJAK.
M NEARING PORTAL NOW. CE AND HORDE ES HAVE THEIR PS FULL WITH THER DEMON SSAULT.
PERFECT TIMING. THE WATCH COMMANDER JUST LEFT. I'LL HANDLE THINGS...
...ON THIS SIDE.
ZHAHARA! ZHAHARA!
WINDS! RAIN! FOG! CONVERGE! ZHAHARA DARKSQUALL COMMANDS IT!!
SHRAAK
"I AM COMING THROUGH NOW."
"HURRY! DEFENDERS APPROACH!"

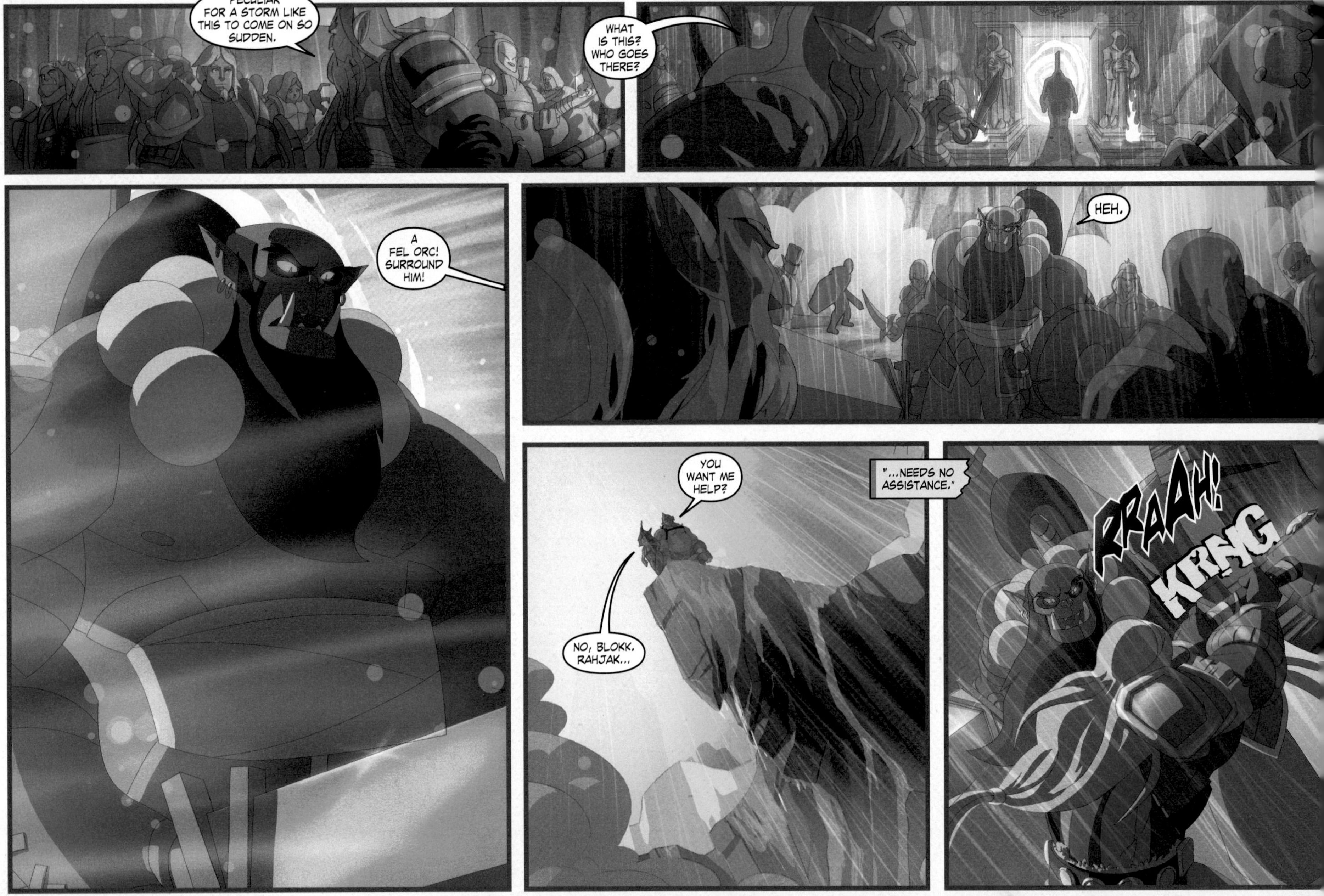
PECULIAR FOR A STORM LIKE THIS TO COME ON SO SUDDEN.
WHAT IS THIS? WHO GOES THERE?
A FEL ORC! SURROUND HIM!
HEH.
YOU WANT ME HELP?
NO, BLOKK. RAHJAK...
"...NEEDS NO ASSISTANCE."
RRAAH!
KRRNG

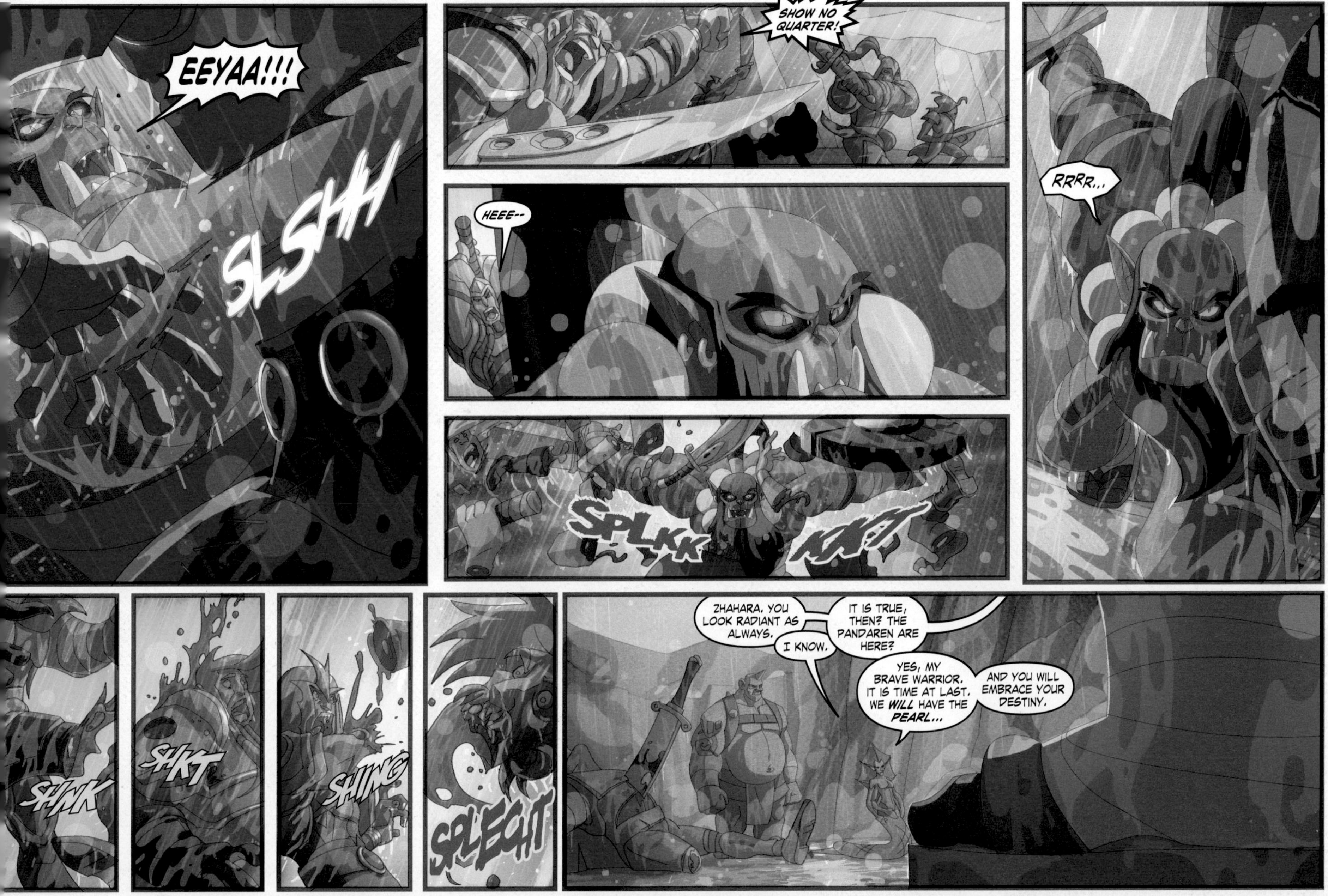

EEYAA!!!
SLSHH
SHOW NO QUARTER!
HEEE--
SPLKK
KKKT
RRRR...
SHNK
SHKT
SHING
SPLECHT
ZHAHARA. YOU LOOK RADIANT AS ALWAYS.
I KNOW.
IT IS TRUE, THEN? THE PANDAREN ARE HERE?
YES, MY BRAVE WARRIOR. IT IS TIME AT LAST. WE WILL HAVE THE PEARL...
AND YOU WILL EMBRACE YOUR DESTINY.

CHAPTER THREE

Thunderbrew

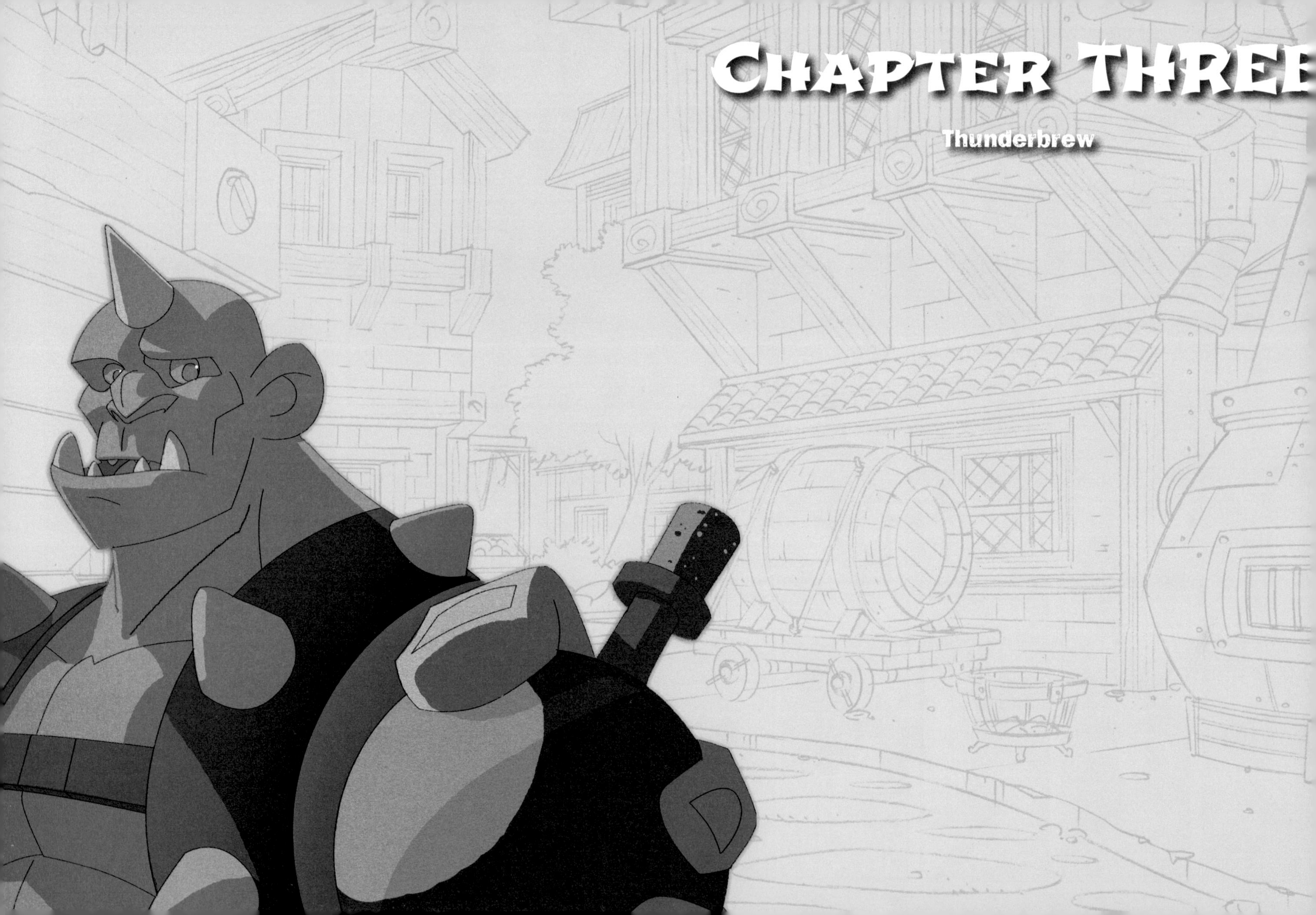

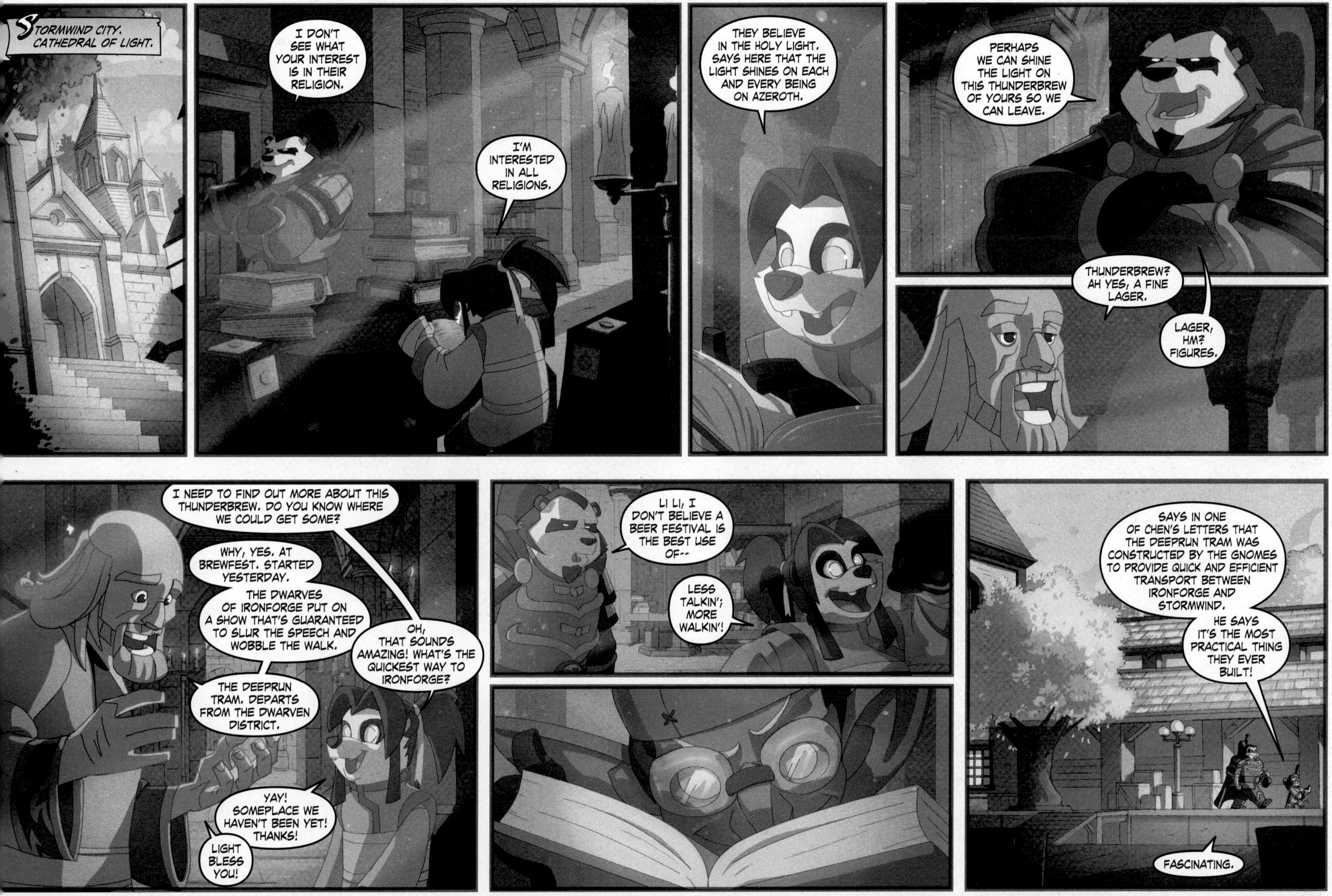
STORMWIND CITY. CATHEDRAL OF LIGHT.
I DON'T SEE WHAT YOUR INTEREST IS IN THEIR RELIGION.
I'M INTERESTED IN ALL RELIGIONS.
THEY BELIEVE IN THE HOLY LIGHT. SAYS HERE THAT THE LIGHT SHINES ON EACH AND EVERY BEING ON AZEROTH.
PERHAPS WE CAN SHINE THE LIGHT ON THIS THUNDERBREW OF YOURS SO WE CAN LEAVE.
THUNDERBREW? AH YES, A FINE LAGER.
LAGER, HM? FIGURES.
I NEED TO FIND OUT MORE ABOUT THIS THUNDERBREW. DO YOU KNOW WHERE WE COULD GET SOME?
WHY, YES. AT BREWFEST. STARTED YESTERDAY.
THE DWARVES OF IRONFORGE PUT ON A SHOW THAT'S GUARANTEED TO SLUR THE SPEECH AND WOBBLE THE WALK.
OH, THAT SOUNDS AMAZING! WHAT'S THE QUICKEST WAY TO IRONFORGE?
THE DEEPRUN TRAM. DEPARTS FROM THE DWARVEN DISTRICT.
YAY! SOMEPLACE WE HAVEN'T BEEN YET! THANKS!
LIGHT BLESS YOU!
LI LI, I DON'T BELIEVE A BEER FESTIVAL IS THE BEST USE OF--
LESS TALKIN'; MORE WALKIN'!
SAYS IN ONE OF CHEN'S LETTERS THAT THE DEEPRUN TRAM WAS CONSTRUCTED BY THE GNOMES TO PROVIDE QUICK AND EFFICIENT TRANSPORT BETWEEN IRONFORGE AND STORMWIND.
HE SAYS IT'S THE MOST PRACTICAL THING THEY EVER BUILT!
FASCINATING.

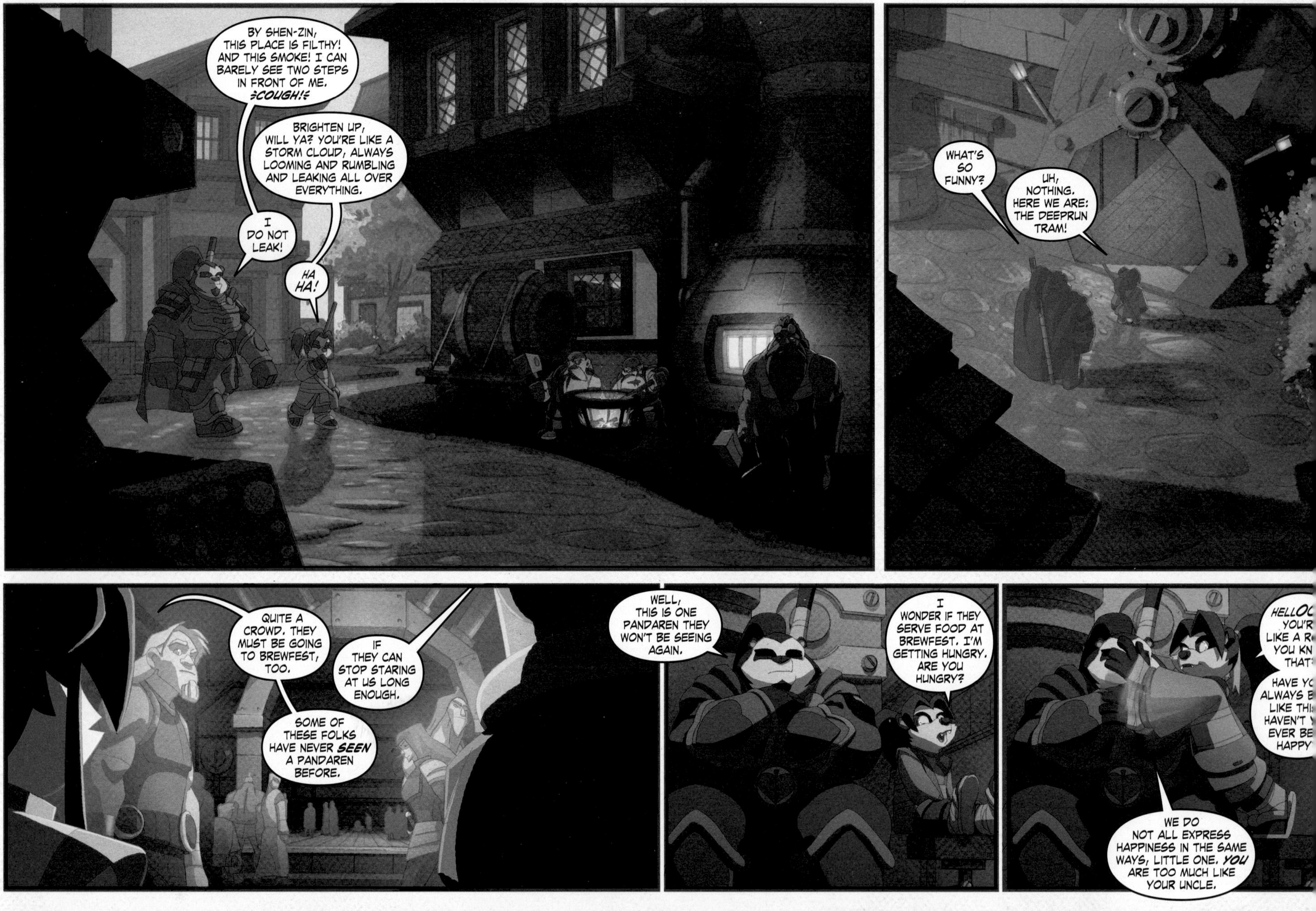

BY SHEN-ZIN, THIS PLACE IS FILTHY! AND THIS SMOKE! I CAN BARELY SEE TWO STEPS IN FRONT OF ME. *COUGH!*
BRIGHTEN UP, WILL YA? YOU'RE LIKE A STORM CLOUD, ALWAYS LOOMING AND RUMBLING AND LEAKING ALL OVER EVERYTHING.
I DO NOT LEAK!
HA HA!
WHAT'S SO FUNNY?
UH, NOTHING. HERE WE ARE: THE DEEPRUN TRAM!
QUITE A CROWD. THEY MUST BE GOING TO BREWFEST, TOO.
IF THEY CAN STOP STARING AT US LONG ENOUGH.
SOME OF THESE FOLKS HAVE NEVER SEEN A PANDAREN BEFORE.
WELL, THIS IS ONE PANDAREN THEY WON'T BE SEEING AGAIN.
I WONDER IF THEY SERVE FOOD AT BREWFEST. I'M GETTING HUNGRY. ARE YOU HUNGRY?
HELLO YOU'R LIKE A R YOU KN THAT
HAVE YO ALWAYS B LIKE THI HAVEN'T EVER BE HAPPY
WE DO NOT ALL EXPRESS HAPPINESS IN THE SAME WAYS, LITTLE ONE. YOU ARE TOO MUCH LIKE YOUR UNCLE.

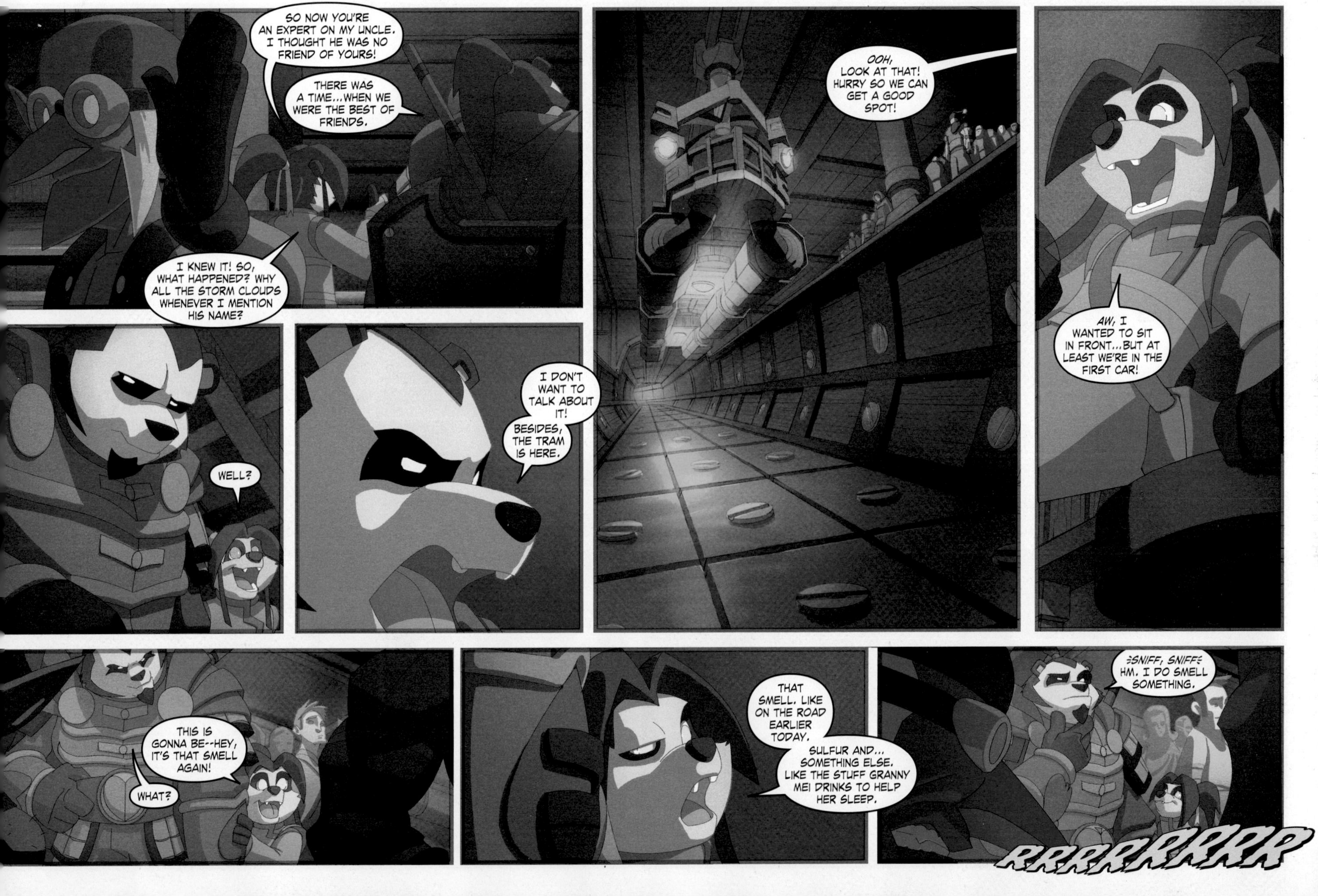
SO NOW YOU'RE AN EXPERT ON MY UNCLE. I THOUGHT HE WAS NO FRIEND OF YOURS!
THERE WAS A TIME...WHEN WE WERE THE BEST OF FRIENDS.
I KNEW IT! SO, WHAT HAPPENED? WHY ALL THE STORM CLOUDS WHENEVER I MENTION HIS NAME?
WELL?
I DON'T WANT TO TALK ABOUT IT!
BESIDES, THE TRAM IS HERE.
OOH, LOOK AT THAT! HURRY SO WE CAN GET A GOOD SPOT!
AW, I WANTED TO SIT IN FRONT...BUT AT LEAST WE'RE IN THE FIRST CAR!
THIS IS GONNA BE--HEY, IT'S THAT SMELL AGAIN!
WHAT?
THAT SMELL. LIKE ON THE ROAD EARLIER TODAY.
SULFUR AND... SOMETHING ELSE. LIKE THE STUFF GRANNY MEI DRINKS TO HELP HER SLEEP.
≈SNIFF, SNIFF≈ HM. I DO SMELL SOMETHING.
RRRRRRRRR

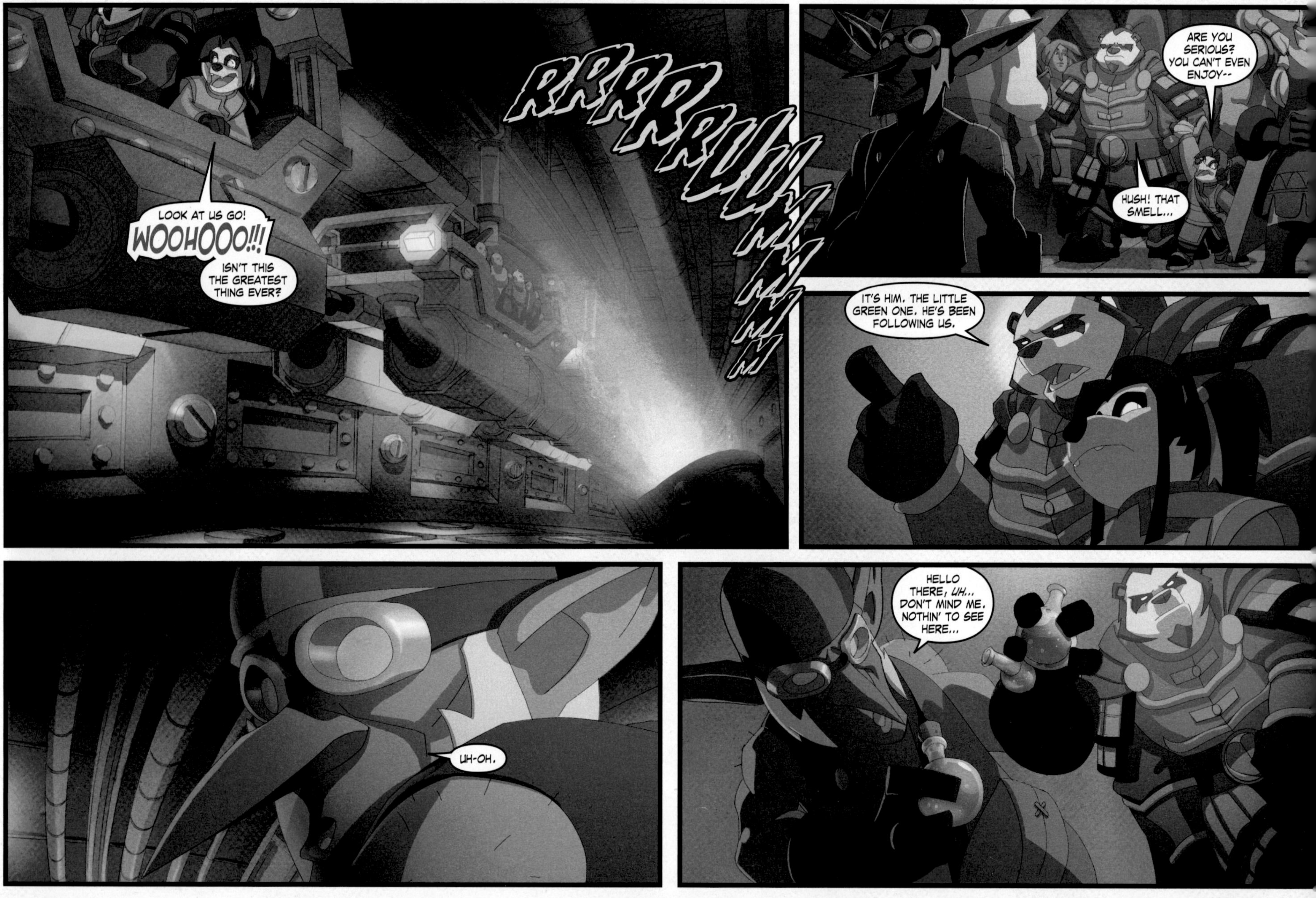
LOOK AT US GO!
WOOHOOO!!!
ISN'T THIS THE GREATEST THING EVER?
RRRRRUUMMMMMM
ARE YOU SERIOUS? YOU CAN'T EVEN ENJOY--
HUSH! THAT SMELL...
IT'S HIM. THE LITTLE GREEN ONE. HE'S BEEN FOLLOWING US.
UH-OH.
HELLO THERE, *UH*... DON'T MIND ME. NOTHIN' TO SEE HERE...

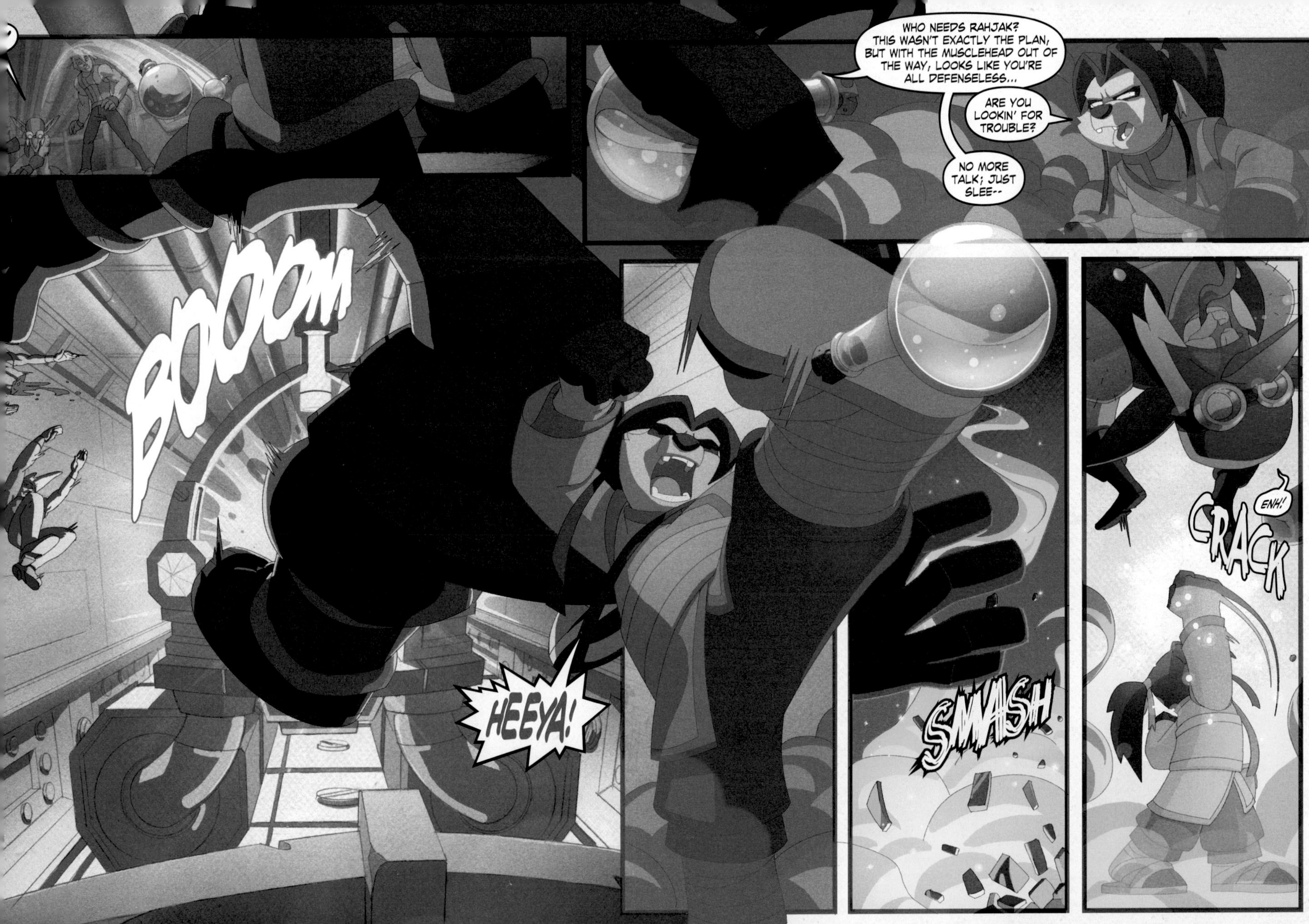

WHO NEEDS RAHJAK? THIS WASN'T EXACTLY THE PLAN, BUT WITH THE MUSCLEHEAD OUT OF THE WAY, LOOKS LIKE YOU'RE ALL DEFENSELESS...
ARE YOU LOOKIN' FOR TROUBLE?
NO MORE TALK; JUST SLEE--
BOOOM
HEEYA!
SMASH
ENH!
CRACK

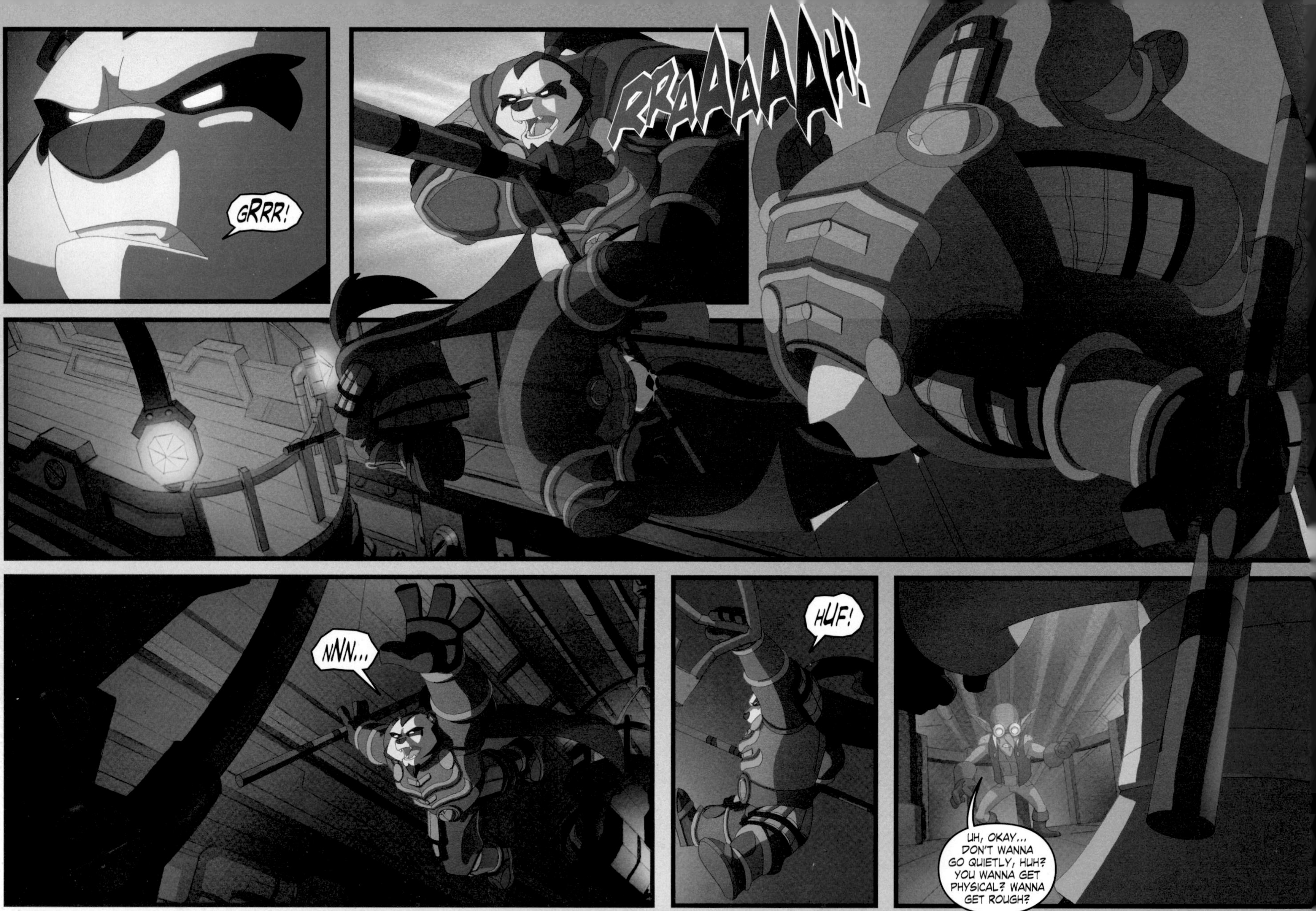
GRRR!
RRAAAAAH!
NNN...
HUF!
UH, OKAY... DON'T WANNA GO QUIETLY, HUH? YOU WANNA GET PHYSICAL? WANNA GET ROUGH?

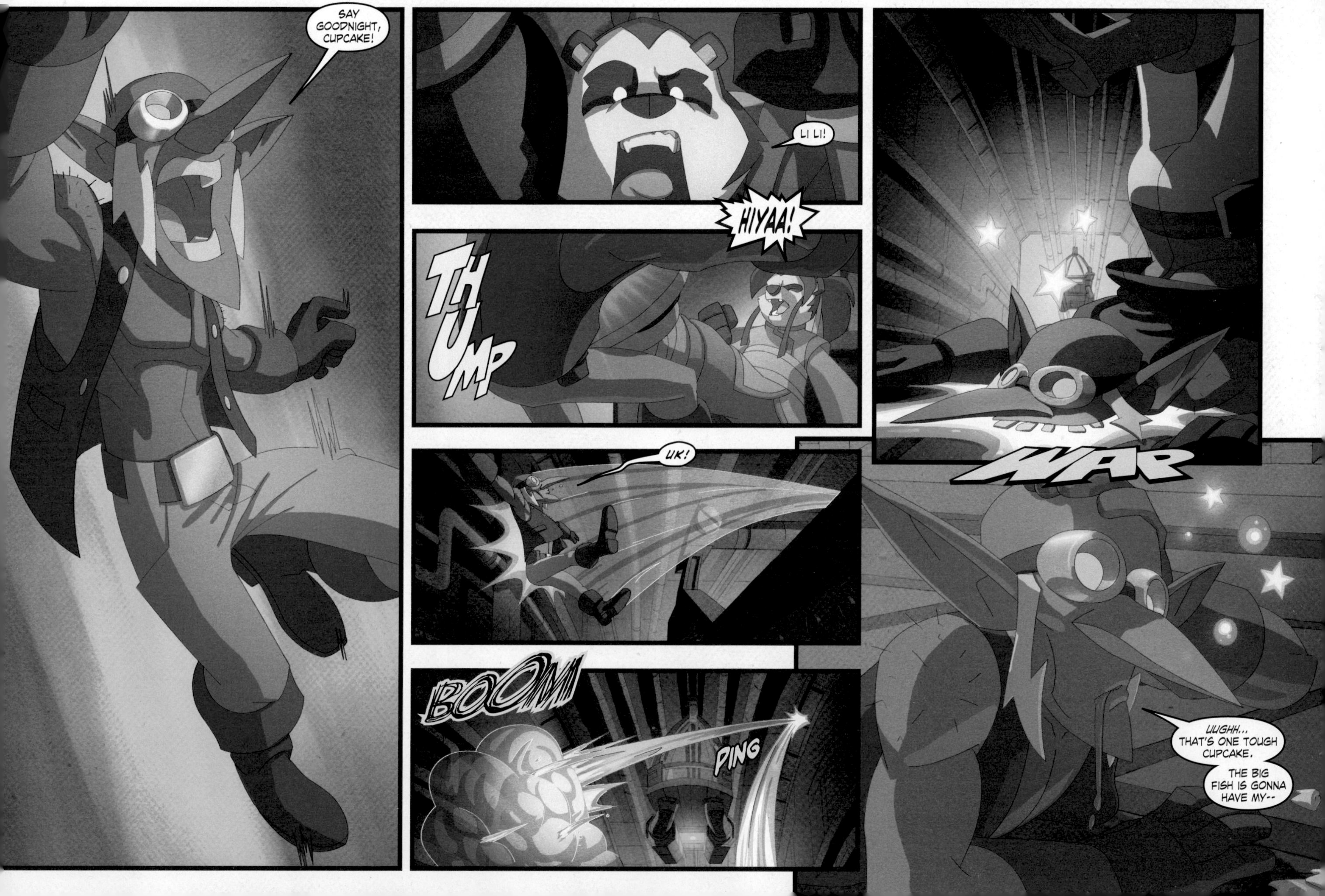
SAY GOODNIGHT, CUPCAKE!
LI LI!
HIYAA!
THUMP
UK!
BOOM
PING
WAR
UUGHH... THAT'S ONE TOUGH CUPCAKE.
THE BIG FISH IS GONNA HAVE MY--

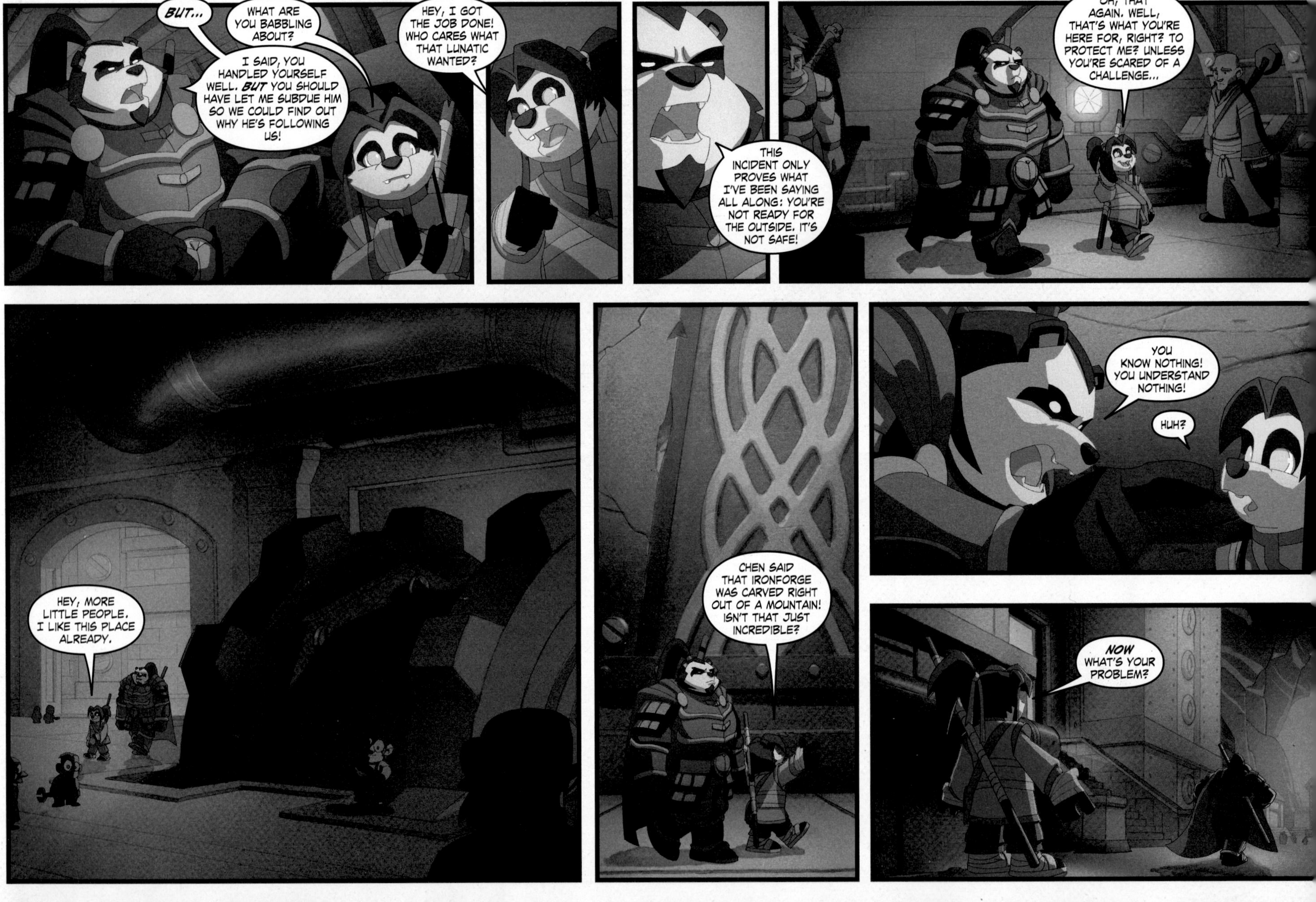
BUT...
WHAT ARE YOU BABBLING ABOUT?
I SAID, YOU HANDLED YOURSELF WELL. BUT YOU SHOULD HAVE LET ME SUBDUE HIM SO WE COULD FIND OUT WHY HE'S FOLLOWING US!
HEY, I GOT THE JOB DONE! WHO CARES WHAT THAT LUNATIC WANTED?
THIS INCIDENT ONLY PROVES WHAT I'VE BEEN SAYING ALL ALONG: YOU'RE NOT READY FOR THE OUTSIDE. IT'S NOT SAFE!
OH, THAT AGAIN. WELL, THAT'S WHAT YOU'RE HERE FOR, RIGHT? TO PROTECT ME? UNLESS YOU'RE SCARED OF A CHALLENGE...
HEY, MORE LITTLE PEOPLE. I LIKE THIS PLACE ALREADY.
CHEN SAID THAT IRONFORGE WAS CARVED RIGHT OUT OF A MOUNTAIN! ISN'T THAT JUST INCREDIBLE?
YOU KNOW NOTHING! YOU UNDERSTAND NOTHING!
HUH?
NOW WHAT'S YOUR PROBLEM?

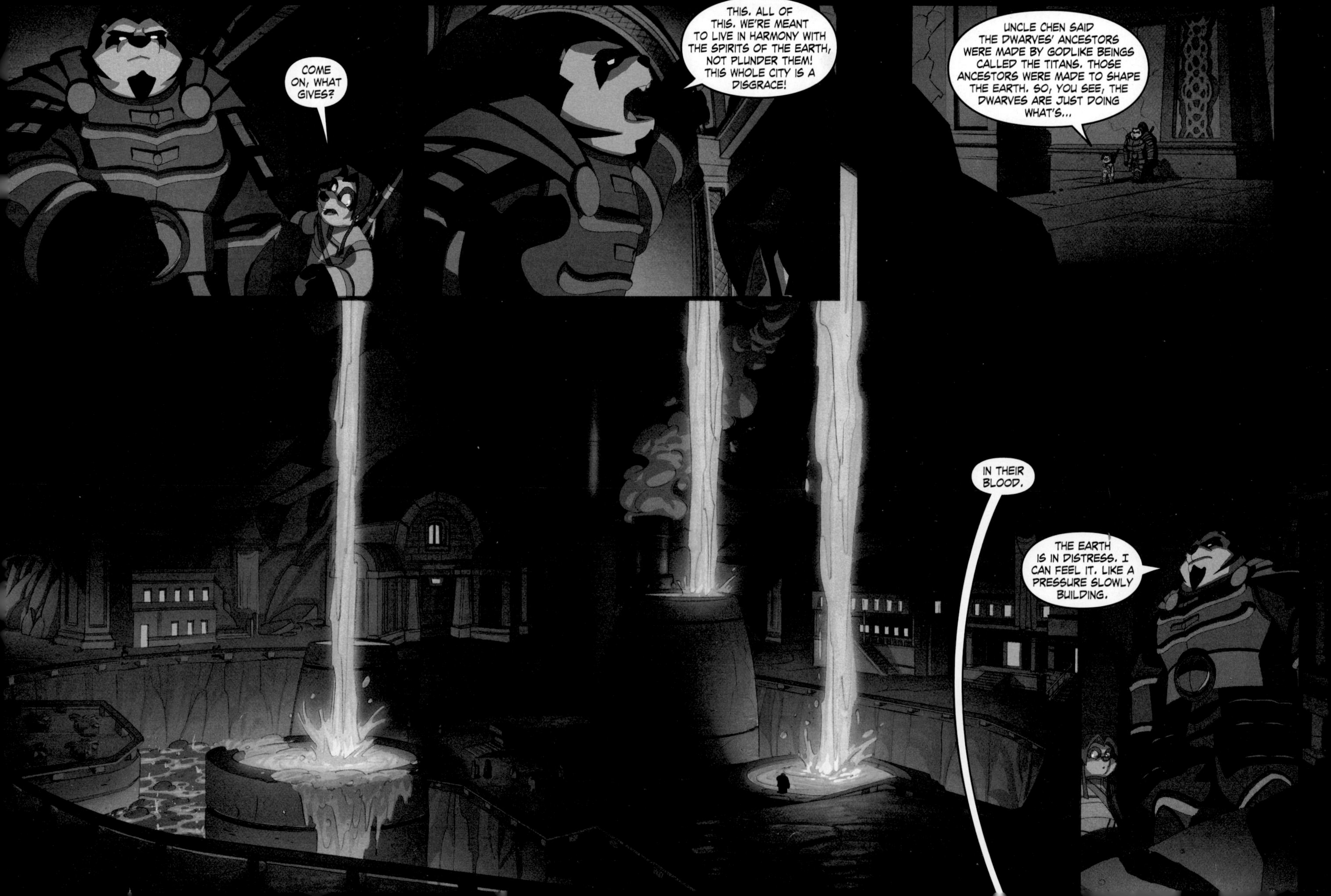
COME ON, WHAT GIVES?
THIS. ALL OF THIS. WE'RE MEANT TO LIVE IN HARMONY WITH THE SPIRITS OF THE EARTH, NOT PLUNDER THEM! THIS WHOLE CITY IS A DISGRACE!
UNCLE CHEN SAID THE DWARVES' ANCESTORS WERE MADE BY GODLIKE BEINGS CALLED THE TITANS. THOSE ANCESTORS WERE MADE TO SHAPE THE EARTH. SO, YOU SEE, THE DWARVES ARE JUST DOING WHAT'S...
IN THEIR BLOOD.
THE EARTH IS IN DISTRESS. I CAN FEEL IT. LIKE A PRESSURE SLOWLY BUILDING.

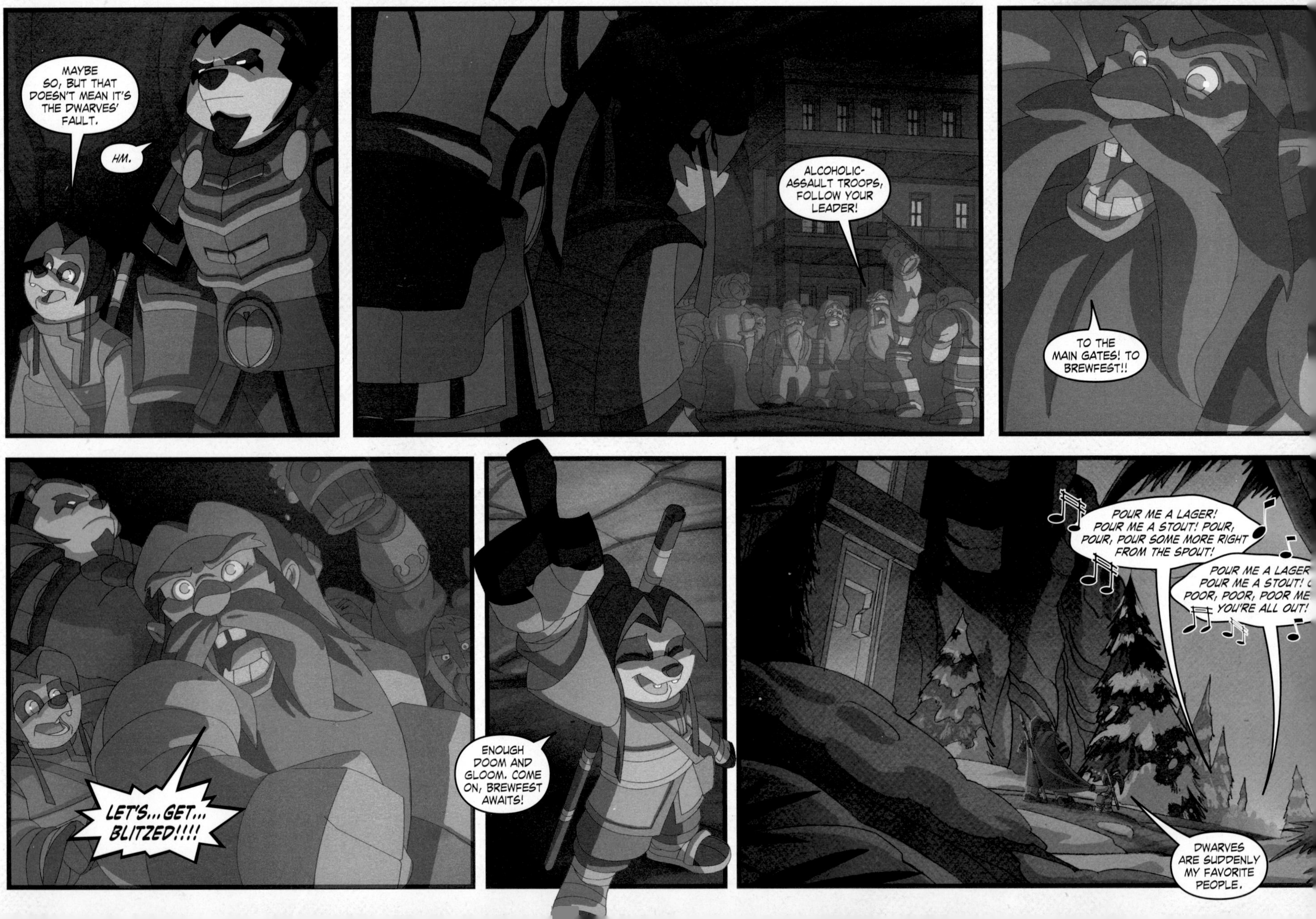
MAYBE SO, BUT THAT DOESN'T MEAN IT'S THE DWARVES' FAULT.
HM.
ALCOHOLIC-ASSAULT TROOPS, FOLLOW YOUR LEADER!
TO THE MAIN GATES! TO BREWFEST!!
LET'S...GET... BLITZED!!!!
ENOUGH DOOM AND GLOOM. COME ON, BREWFEST AWAITS!
POUR ME A LAGER! POUR ME A STOUT! POUR, POUR, POUR SOME MORE RIGHT FROM THE SPOUT!
POUR ME A LAGER POUR ME A STOUT! POOR, POOR, POOR ME YOU'RE ALL OUT!
DWARVES ARE SUDDENLY MY FAVORITE PEOPLE.

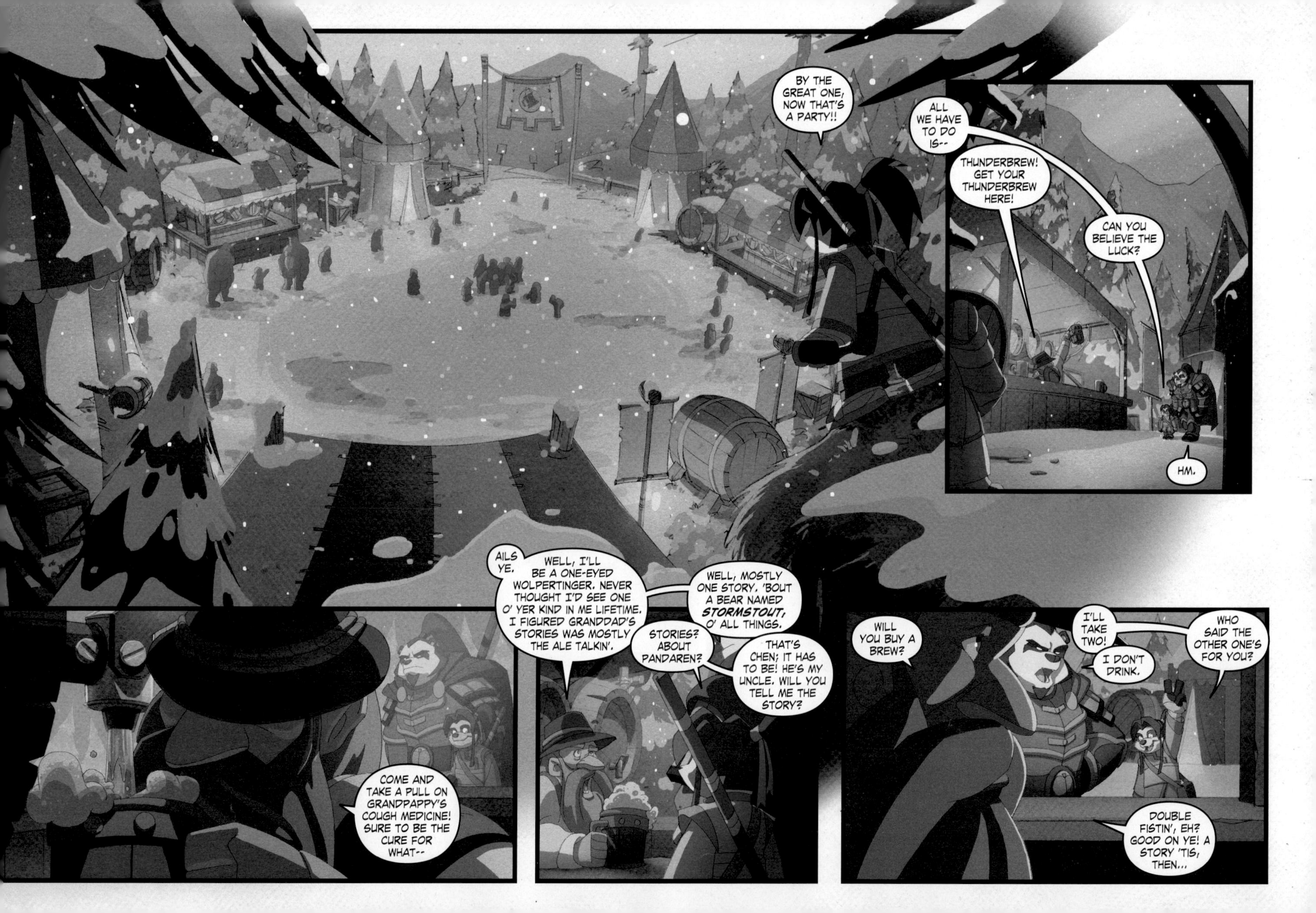
BY THE GREAT ONE, NOW THAT'S A PARTY!!
ALL WE HAVE TO DO IS--
THUNDERBREW! GET YOUR THUNDERBREW HERE!
CAN YOU BELIEVE THE LUCK?
HM.
COME AND TAKE A PULL ON GRANDPAPPY'S COUGH MEDICINE! SURE TO BE THE CURE FOR WHAT--
AILS YE.
WELL, I'LL BE A ONE-EYED WOLPERTINGER. NEVER THOUGHT I'D SEE ONE O' YER KIND IN ME LIFETIME. I FIGURED GRANDDAD'S STORIES WAS MOSTLY THE ALE TALKIN'.
STORIES? ABOUT PANDAREN?
WELL, MOSTLY ONE STORY. 'BOUT A BEAR NAMED **STORMSTOUT,** O' ALL THINGS.
THAT'S CHEN; IT HAS TO BE! HE'S MY UNCLE. WILL YOU TELL ME THE STORY?
WILL YOU BUY A BREW?
I'LL TAKE TWO!
I DON'T DRINK.
WHO SAID THE OTHER ONE'S FOR YOU?
DOUBLE FISTIN', EH? GOOD ON YE! A STORY 'TIS, THEN...

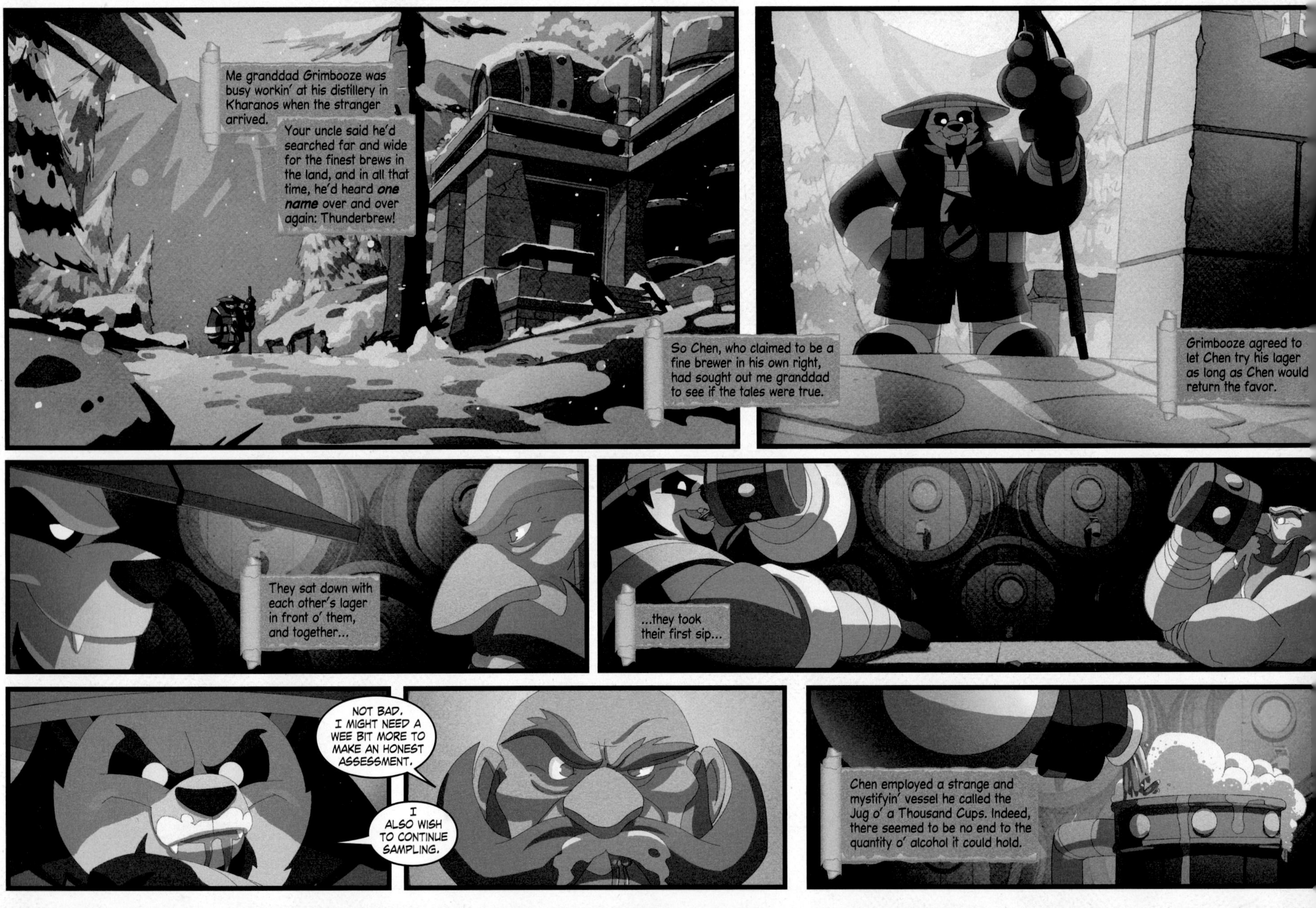
Me granddad Grimbooze was busy workin' at his distillery in Kharanos when the stranger arrived.
Your uncle said he'd searched far and wide for the finest brews in the land, and in all that time, he'd heard ***one name*** over and over again: Thunderbrew!
So Chen, who claimed to be a fine brewer in his own right, had sought out me granddad to see if the tales were true.
Grimbooze agreed to let Chen try his lager as long as Chen would return the favor.
They sat down with each other's lager in front o' them, and together...
...they took their first sip...
NOT BAD. I MIGHT NEED A WEE BIT MORE TO MAKE AN HONEST ASSESSMENT.
I ALSO WISH TO CONTINUE SAMPLING.
Chen employed a strange and mystifyin' vessel he called the Jug o' a Thousand Cups. Indeed, there seemed to be no end to the quantity o' alcohol it could hold.

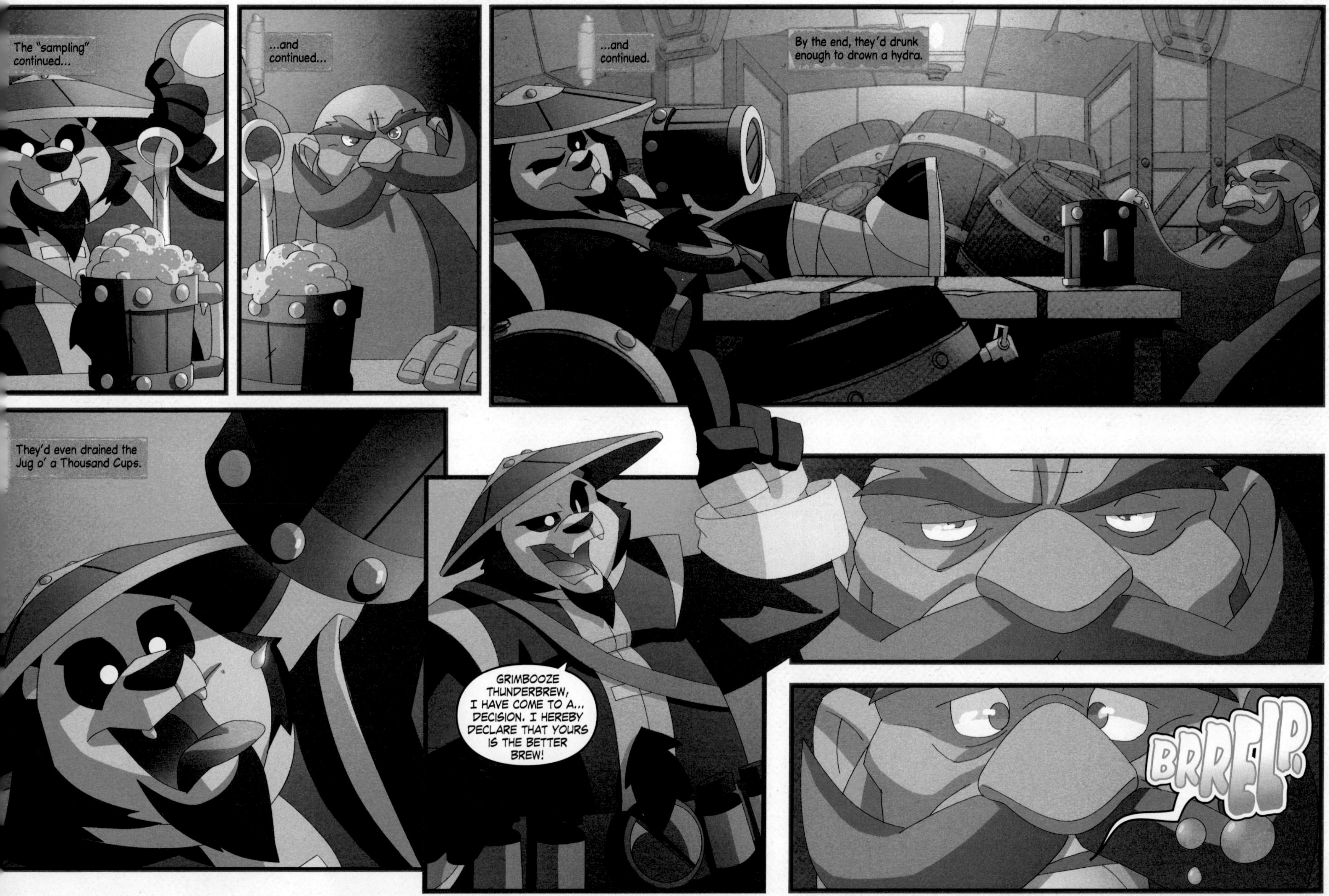
The "sampling" continued...
...and continued...
...and continued.
By the end, they'd drunk enough to drown a hydra.
They'd even drained the Jug o' a Thousand Cups.
GRIMBOOZE THUNDERBREW, I HAVE COME TO A... DECISION. I HEREBY DECLARE THAT YOURS IS THE BETTER BREW!
BRRELP!

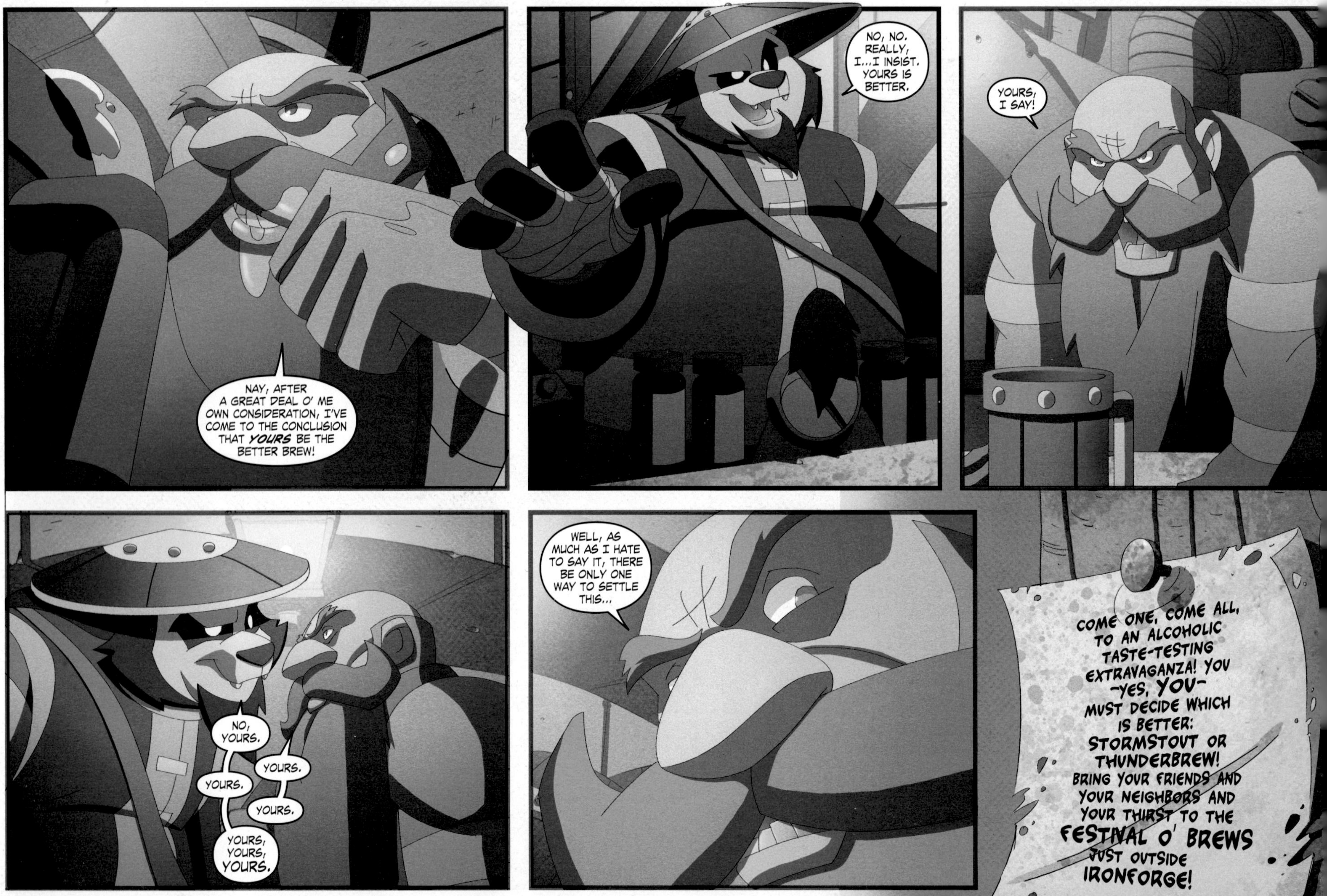
NAY, AFTER A GREAT DEAL O' ME OWN CONSIDERATION, I'VE COME TO THE CONCLUSION THAT *YOURS* BE THE BETTER BREW!
NO, NO. REALLY, I...I INSIST. YOURS IS BETTER.
YOURS, I SAY!
NO, YOURS.
YOURS.
YOURS.
YOURS.
YOURS, YOURS, YOURS.
WELL, AS MUCH AS I HATE TO SAY IT, THERE BE ONLY ONE WAY TO SETTLE THIS...
COME ONE, COME ALL, TO AN ALCOHOLIC TASTE-TESTING EXTRAVAGANZA! YOU -YES, YOU- MUST DECIDE WHICH IS BETTER: STORMSTOUT OR THUNDERBREW! BRING YOUR FRIENDS AND YOUR NEIGHBORS AND YOUR THIRST TO THE FESTIVAL O' BREWS JUST OUTSIDE IRONFORGE!

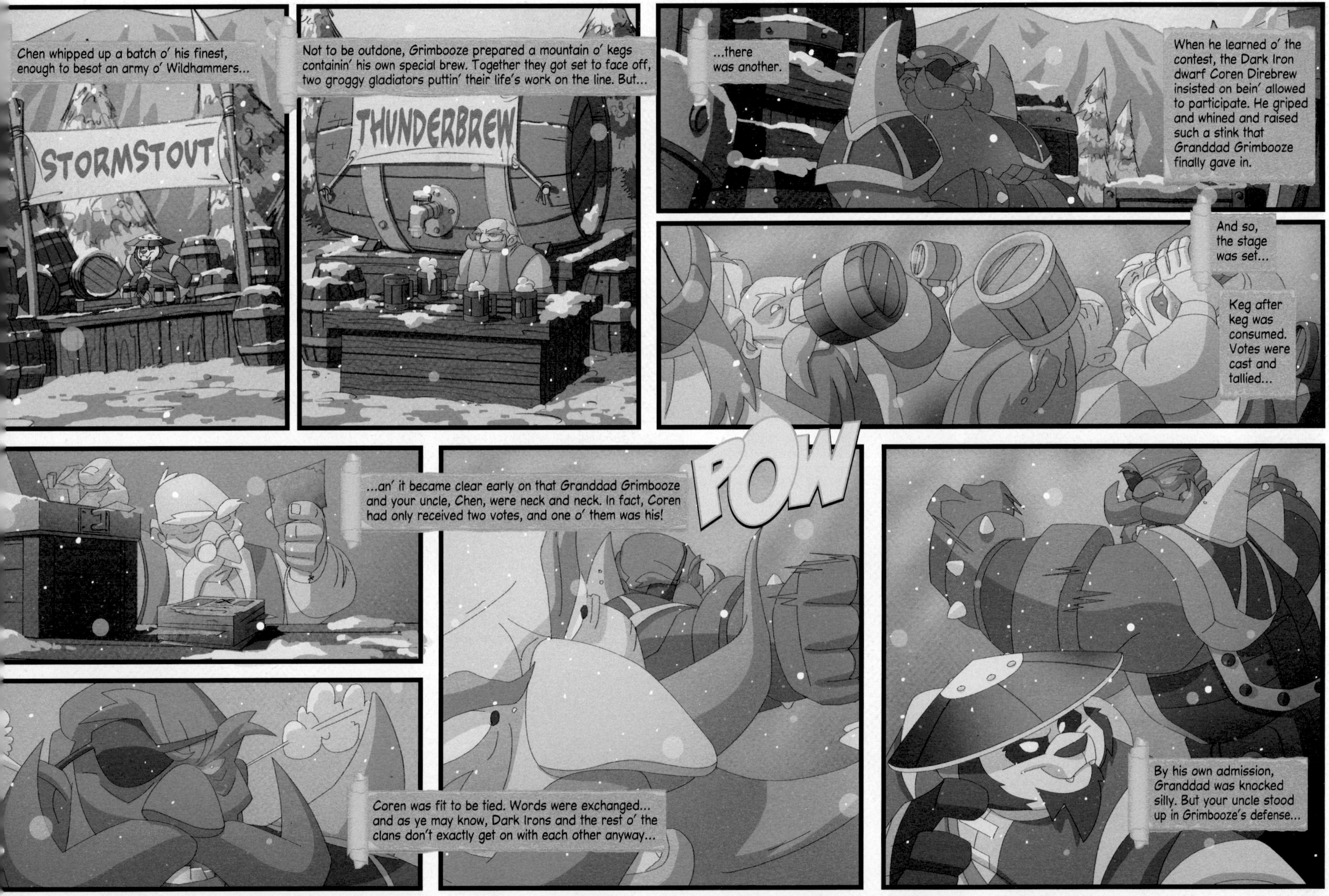
Chen whipped up a batch o' his finest, enough to besot an army o' Wildhammers...
STORMSTOUT
Not to be outdone, Grimbooze prepared a mountain o' kegs containin' his own special brew. Together they got set to face off, two groggy gladiators puttin' their life's work on the line. But...
THUNDERBREW
...there was another.
When he learned o' the contest, the Dark Iron dwarf Coren Direbrew insisted on bein' allowed to participate. He griped and whined and raised such a stink that Granddad Grimbooze finally gave in.
And so, the stage was set...
Keg after keg was consumed. Votes were cast and tallied...
...an' it became clear early on that Granddad Grimbooze and your uncle, Chen, were neck and neck. In fact, Coren had only received two votes, and one o' them was his!
Coren was fit to be tied. Words were exchanged... and as ye may know, Dark Irons and the rest o' the clans don't exactly get on with each other anyway...
POW
By his own admission, Granddad was knocked silly. But your uncle stood up in Grimbooze's defense...

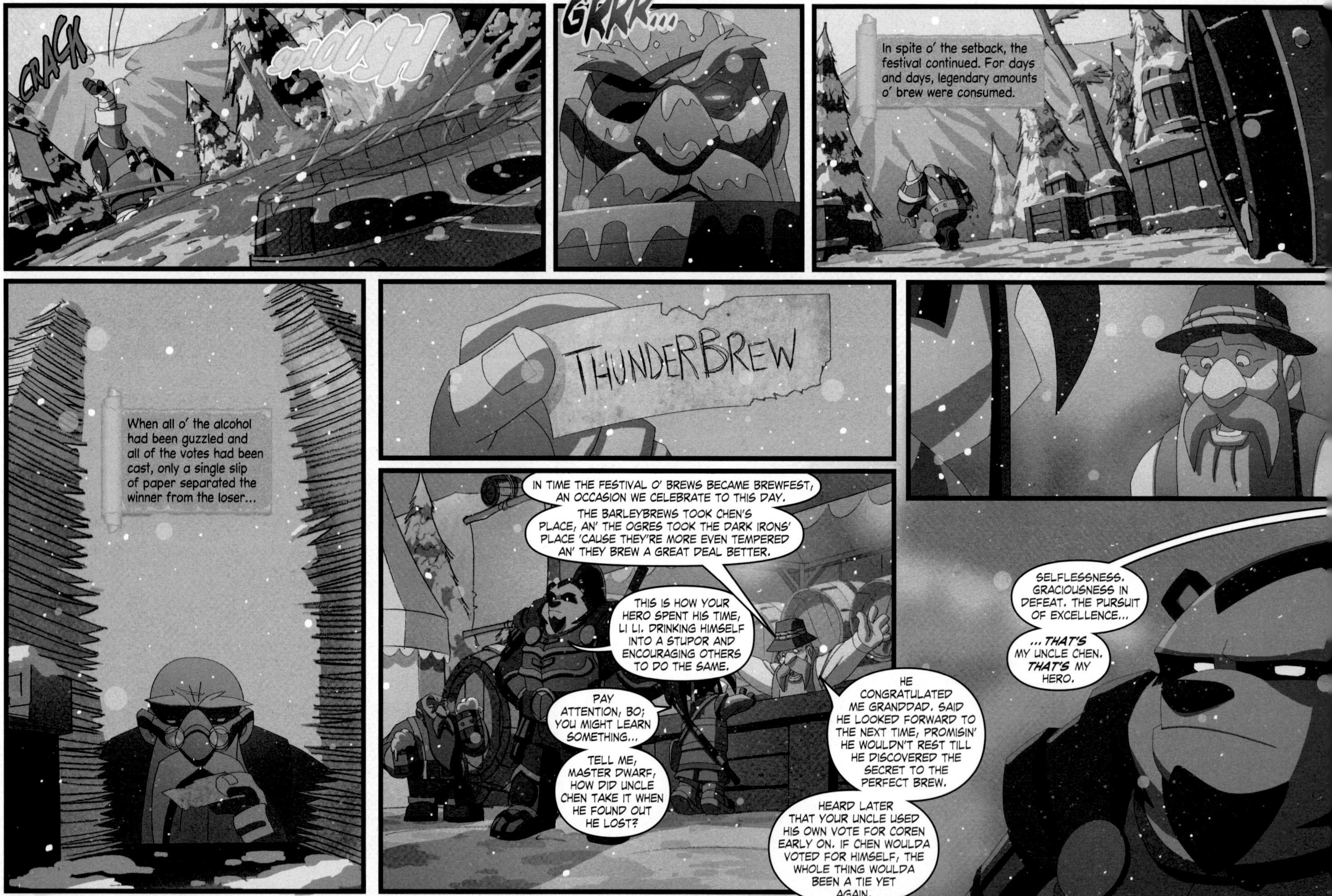

CRACK
SPLOOSH
GRRR...
In spite o' the setback, the festival continued. For days and days, legendary amounts o' brew were consumed.
When all o' the alcohol had been guzzled and all of the votes had been cast, only a single slip of paper separated the winner from the loser...
THUNDERBREW
IN TIME THE FESTIVAL O' BREWS BECAME BREWFEST, AN OCCASION WE CELEBRATE TO THIS DAY.
THE BARLEYBREWS TOOK CHEN'S PLACE, AN' THE OGRES TOOK THE DARK IRONS' PLACE 'CAUSE THEY'RE MORE EVEN TEMPERED AN' THEY BREW A GREAT DEAL BETTER.
THIS IS HOW YOUR HERO SPENT HIS TIME, LI LI. DRINKING HIMSELF INTO A STUPOR AND ENCOURAGING OTHERS TO DO THE SAME.
PAY ATTENTION, BO; YOU MIGHT LEARN SOMETHING...
TELL ME, MASTER DWARF, HOW DID UNCLE CHEN TAKE IT WHEN HE FOUND OUT HE LOST?
HE CONGRATULATED ME GRANDDAD. SAID HE LOOKED FORWARD TO THE NEXT TIME, PROMISIN' HE WOULDN'T REST TILL HE DISCOVERED THE SECRET TO THE PERFECT BREW.
HEARD LATER THAT YOUR UNCLE USED HIS OWN VOTE FOR COREN EARLY ON. IF CHEN WOULDA VOTED FOR HIMSELF, THE WHOLE THING WOULDA BEEN A TIE YET AGAIN.
SELFLESSNESS. GRACIOUSNESS IN DEFEAT. THE PURSUIT OF EXCELLENCE...
...*THAT'S* MY UNCLE CHEN. *THAT'S* MY HERO.

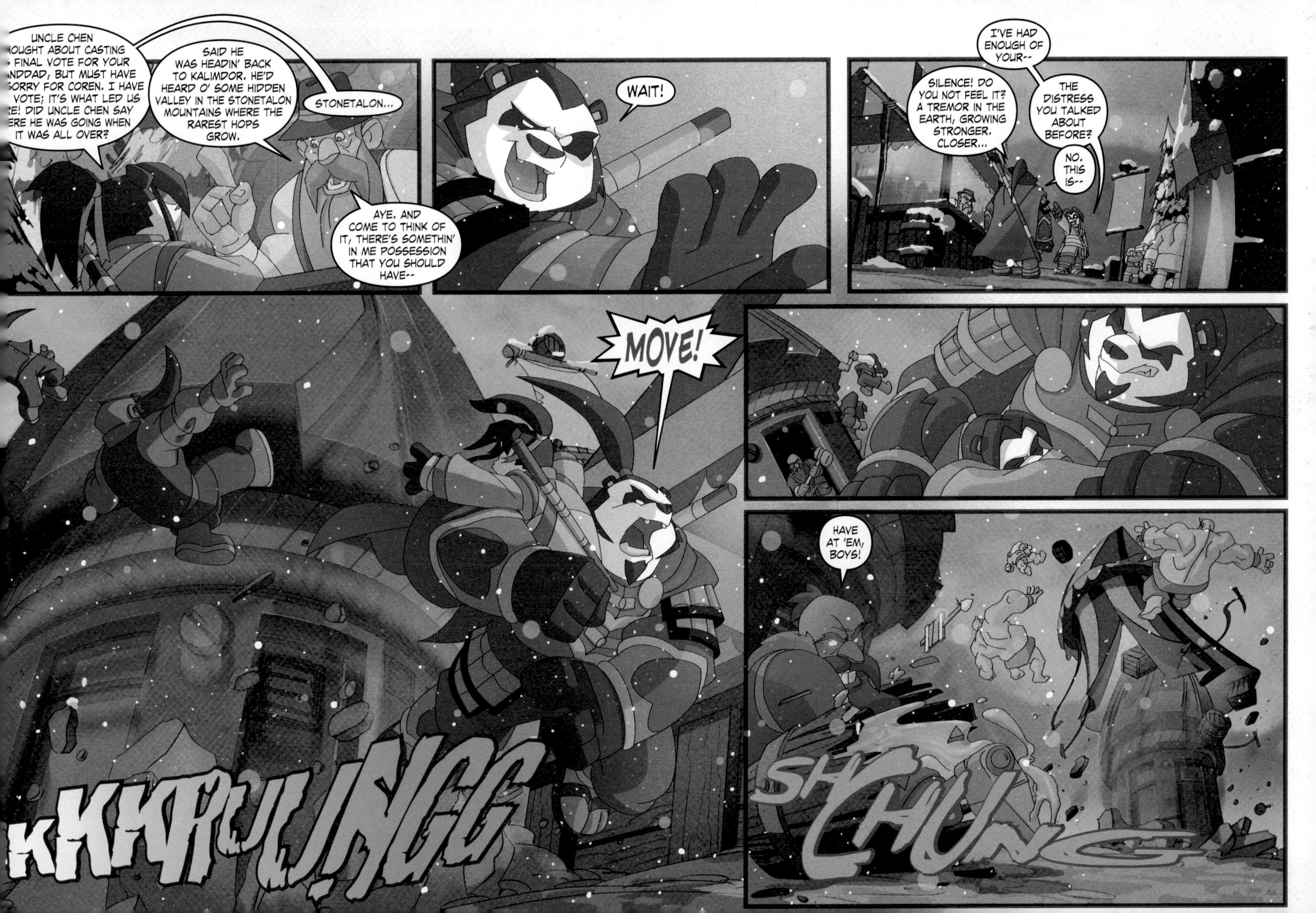

UNCLE CHEN HOUGHT ABOUT CASTING S FINAL VOTE FOR YOUR NDDAD, BUT MUST HAVE SORRY FOR COREN. I HAVE VOTE; IT'S WHAT LED US RE! DID UNCLE CHEN SAY ERE HE WAS GOING WHEN IT WAS ALL OVER?
STONETALON...
SAID HE WAS HEADIN' BACK TO KALIMDOR. HE'D HEARD O' SOME HIDDEN VALLEY IN THE STONETALON MOUNTAINS WHERE THE RAREST HOPS GROW.
AYE. AND COME TO THINK OF IT, THERE'S SOMETHIN' IN ME POSSESSION THAT YOU SHOULD HAVE--
WAIT!
SILENCE! DO YOU NOT FEEL IT? A TREMOR IN THE EARTH, GROWING STRONGER. CLOSER...
I'VE HAD ENOUGH OF YOUR--
THE DISTRESS YOU TALKED ABOUT BEFORE?
NO. THIS IS--
MOVE!
KKKRULNGG
HAVE AT 'EM, BOYS!
SHCHUNG

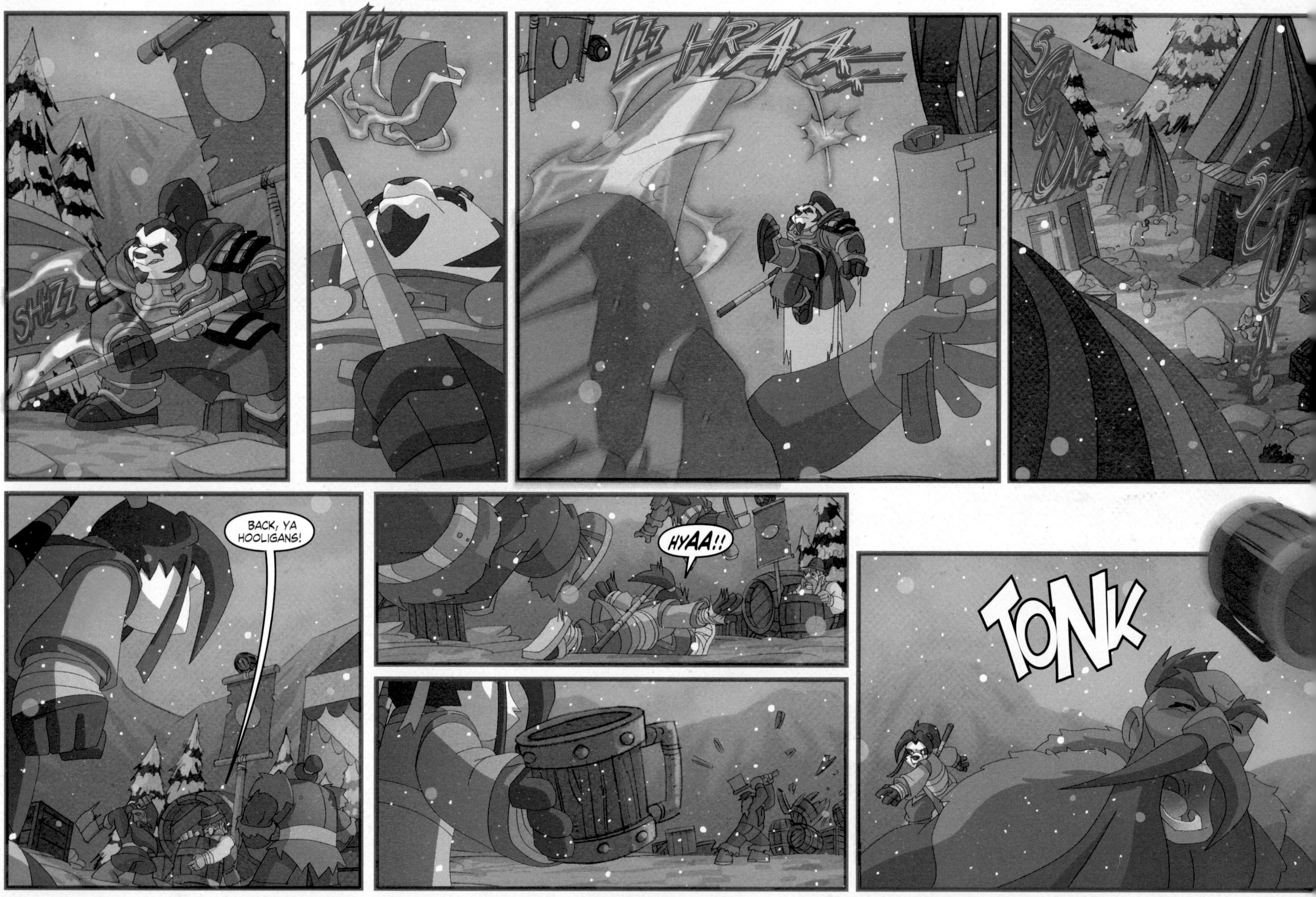
BACK, YA HOOLIGANS!
HYAA!!
TONK

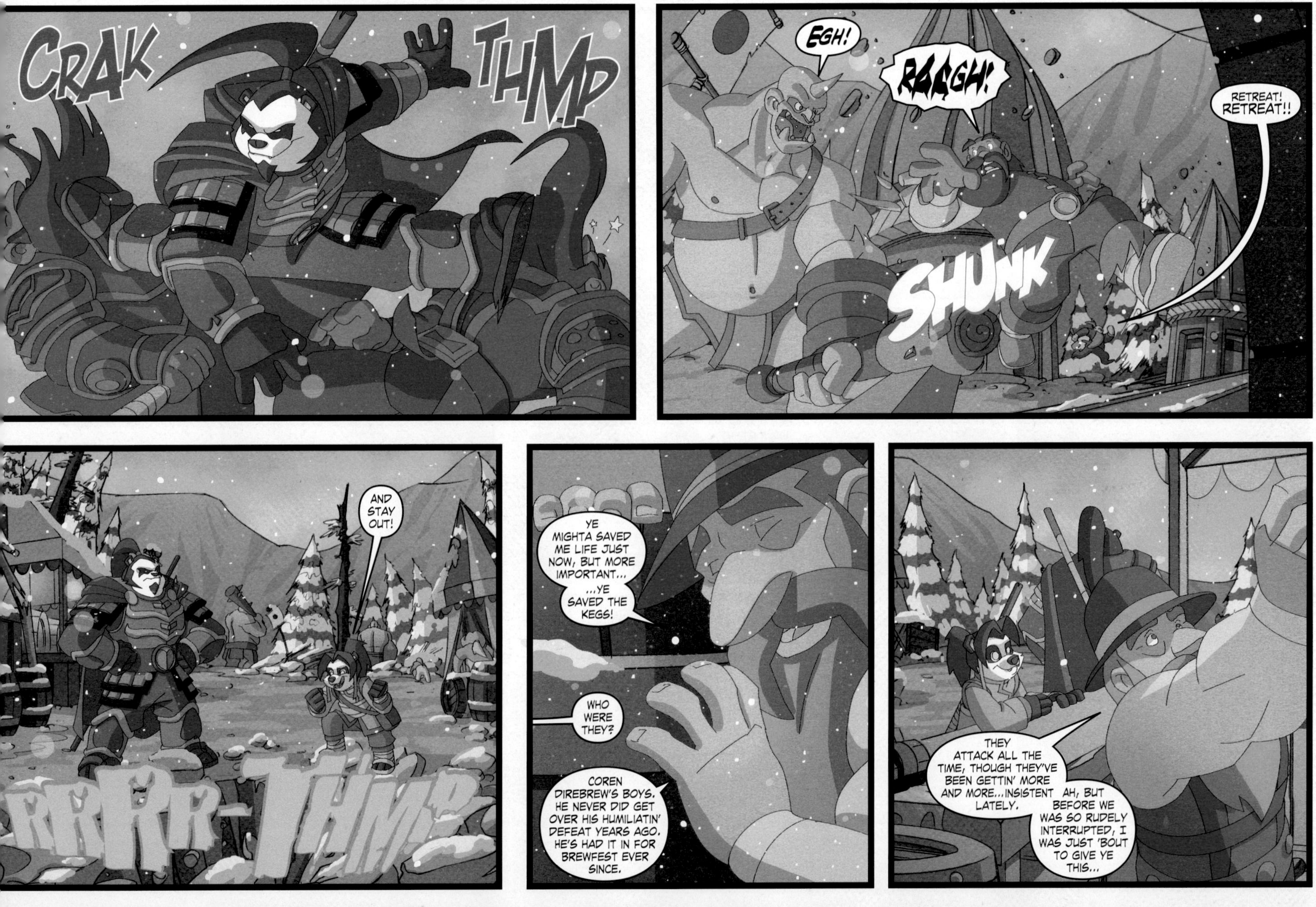
CRAK
THMP
EGH!
RAAGH!
RETREAT! RETREAT!!
SHUNK
AND STAY OUT!
RRRR-THMP
YE MIGHTA SAVED ME LIFE JUST NOW, BUT MORE IMPORTANT...
...YE SAVED THE KEGS!
WHO WERE THEY?
COREN DIREBREW'S BOYS. HE NEVER DID GET OVER HIS HUMILIATIN' DEFEAT YEARS AGO. HE'S HAD IT IN FOR BREWFEST EVER SINCE.
THEY ATTACK ALL THE TIME, THOUGH THEY'VE BEEN GETTIN' MORE AND MORE...INSISTENT LATELY.
AH, BUT BEFORE WE WAS SO RUDELY INTERRUPTED, I WAS JUST 'BOUT TO GIVE YE THIS...

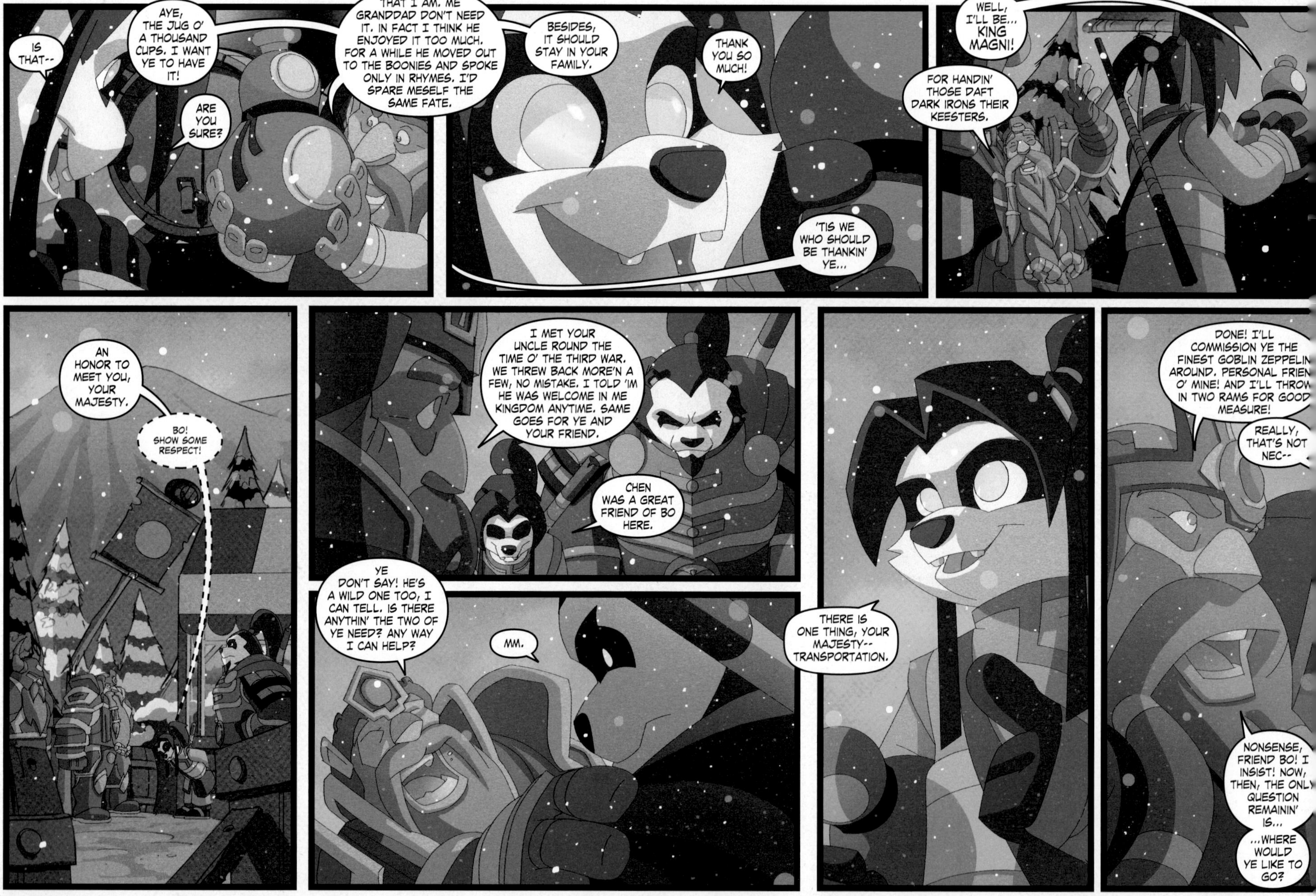

IS THAT--
AYE, THE JUG O' A THOUSAND CUPS. I WANT YE TO HAVE IT!
ARE YOU SURE?
THAT I AM. ME GRANDDAD DON'T NEED IT. IN FACT I THINK HE ENJOYED IT TOO MUCH. FOR A WHILE HE MOVED OUT TO THE BOONIES AND SPOKE ONLY IN RHYMES. I'D SPARE MESELF THE SAME FATE.
BESIDES, IT SHOULD STAY IN YOUR FAMILY.
THANK YOU SO MUCH!
'TIS WE WHO SHOULD BE THANKIN' YE...
WELL, I'LL BE... KING MAGNI!
FOR HANDIN' THOSE DAFT DARK IRONS THEIR KEESTERS.
AN HONOR TO MEET YOU, YOUR MAJESTY.
BO! SHOW SOME RESPECT!
I MET YOUR UNCLE ROUND THE TIME O' THE THIRD WAR. WE THREW BACK MORE'N A FEW, NO MISTAKE. I TOLD 'IM HE WAS WELCOME IN ME KINGDOM ANYTIME. SAME GOES FOR YE AND YOUR FRIEND.
CHEN WAS A GREAT FRIEND OF BO HERE.
YE DON'T SAY! HE'S A WILD ONE TOO, I CAN TELL. IS THERE ANYTHIN' THE TWO OF YE NEED? ANY WAY I CAN HELP?
MM.
THERE IS ONE THING, YOUR MAJESTY-- TRANSPORTATION.
DONE! I'LL COMMISSION YE THE FINEST GOBLIN ZEPPELIN AROUND. PERSONAL FRIEN O' MINE! AND I'LL THROW IN TWO RAMS FOR GOOD MEASURE!
REALLY, THAT'S NOT NEC--
NONSENSE, FRIEND BO! I INSIST! NOW, THEN, THE ONLY QUESTION REMAININ' IS...
...WHERE WOULD YE LIKE TO GO?

Chapter Four

Kalimdor

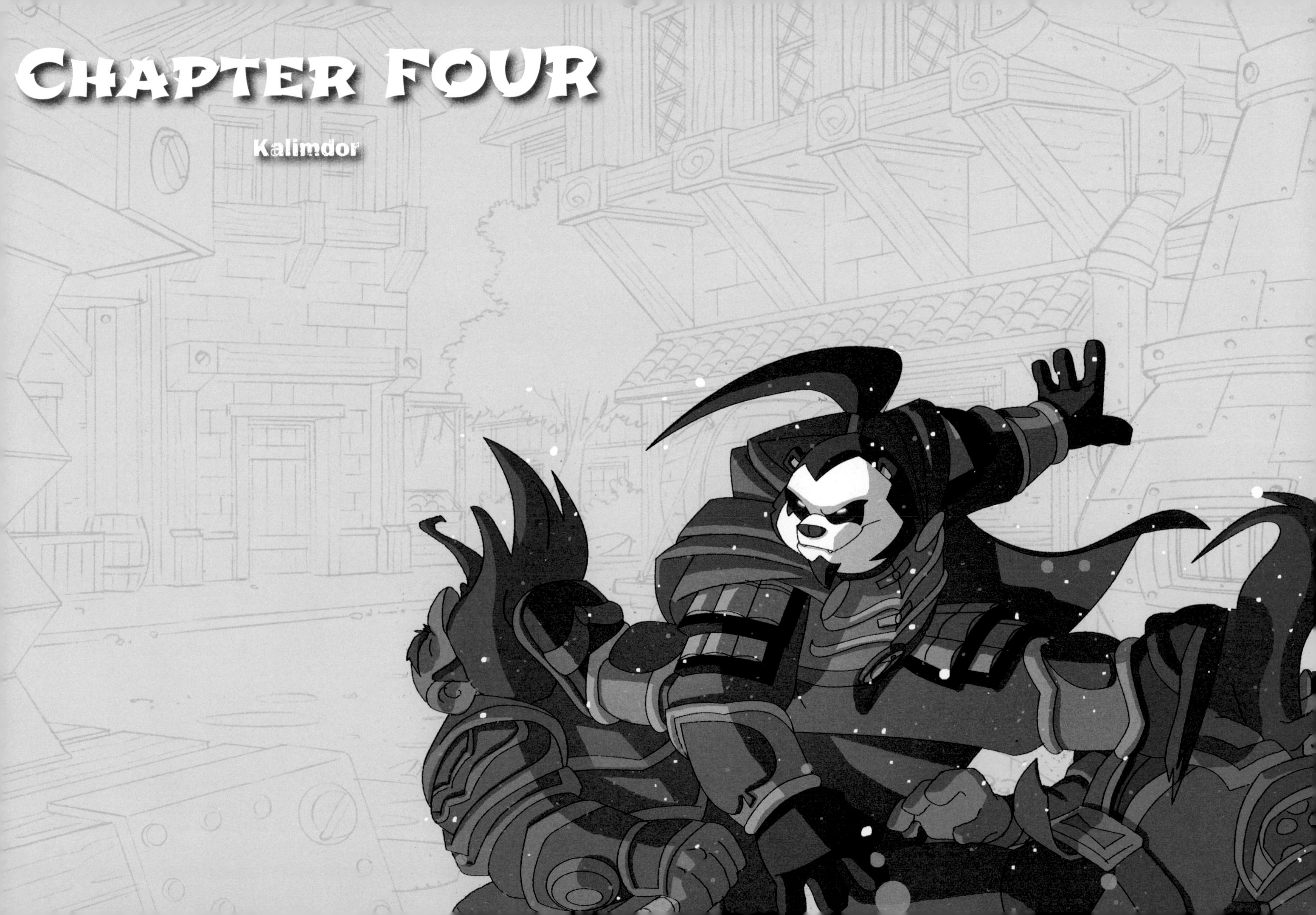

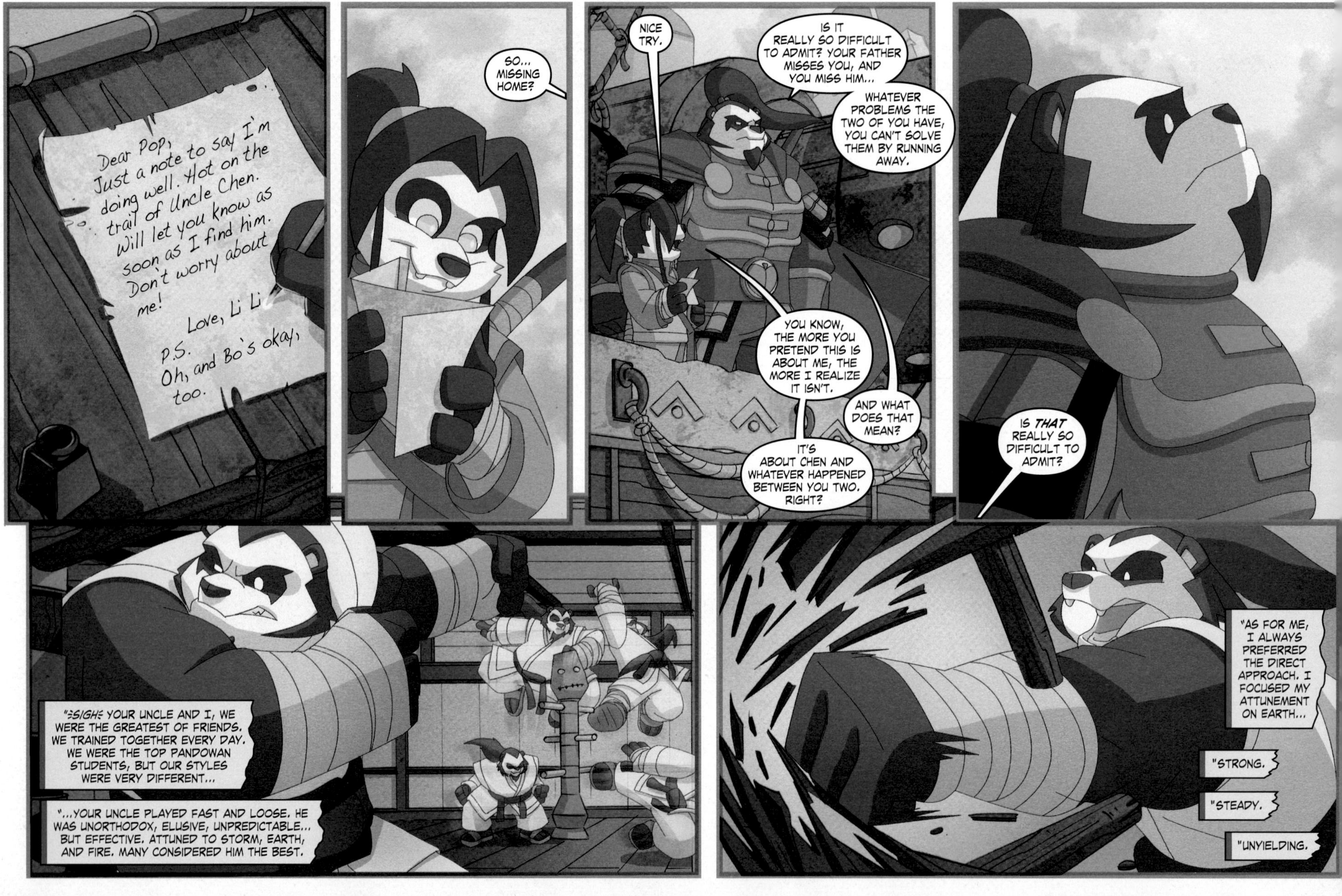

Dear Pop,
Just a note to say I'm doing well. Hot on the trail of Uncle Chen. Will let you know as soon as I find him. Don't worry about me!
Love, Li Li
P.S. Oh, and Bo's okay, too.
SO... MISSING HOME?
NICE TRY.
IS IT REALLY SO DIFFICULT TO ADMIT? YOUR FATHER MISSES YOU, AND YOU MISS HIM...
WHATEVER PROBLEMS THE TWO OF YOU HAVE, YOU CAN'T SOLVE THEM BY RUNNING AWAY.
YOU KNOW, THE MORE YOU PRETEND THIS IS ABOUT ME, THE MORE I REALIZE IT ISN'T.
AND WHAT DOES THAT MEAN?
IT'S ABOUT CHEN AND WHATEVER HAPPENED BETWEEN YOU TWO. RIGHT?
IS THAT REALLY SO DIFFICULT TO ADMIT?
"SIGH YOUR UNCLE AND I, WE WERE THE GREATEST OF FRIENDS. WE TRAINED TOGETHER EVERY DAY. WE WERE THE TOP PANDOWAN STUDENTS, BUT OUR STYLES WERE VERY DIFFERENT...
"...YOUR UNCLE PLAYED FAST AND LOOSE. HE WAS UNORTHODOX, ELUSIVE, UNPREDICTABLE... BUT EFFECTIVE. ATTUNED TO STORM, EARTH, AND FIRE. MANY CONSIDERED HIM THE BEST.
"AS FOR ME, I ALWAYS PREFERRED THE DIRECT APPROACH. I FOCUSED MY ATTUNEMENT ON EARTH...
"STRONG.
"STEADY.
"UNYIELDING.

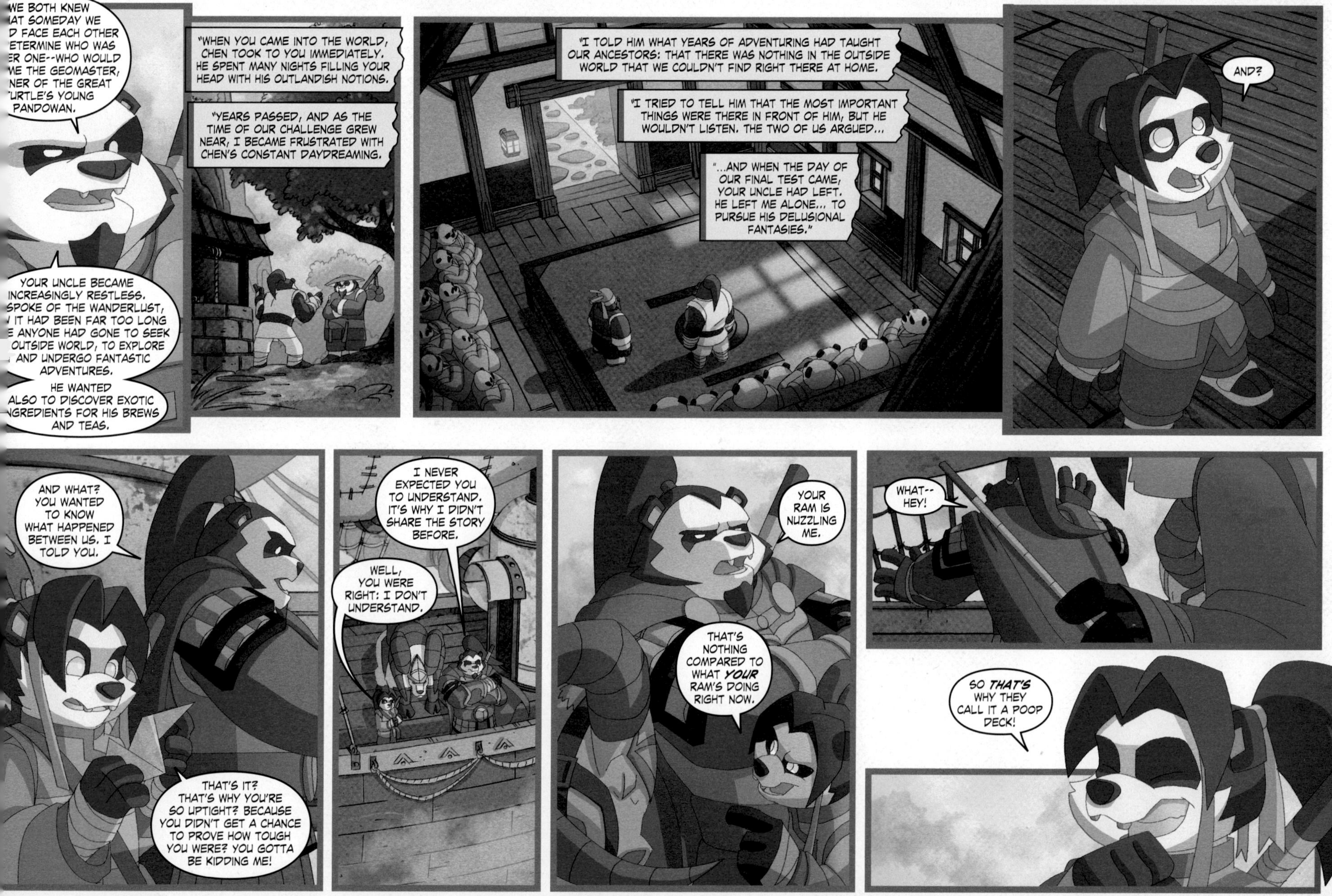
WE BOTH KNEW
IAT SOMEDAY WE
D FACE EACH OTHER
ETERMINE WHO WAS
ER ONE--WHO WOULD
ME THE GEOMASTER,
NER OF THE GREAT
URTLE'S YOUNG
PANDOWAN.
"WHEN YOU CAME INTO THE WORLD, CHEN TOOK TO YOU IMMEDIATELY. HE SPENT MANY NIGHTS FILLING YOUR HEAD WITH HIS OUTLANDISH NOTIONS.
"YEARS PASSED, AND AS THE TIME OF OUR CHALLENGE GREW NEAR, I BECAME FRUSTRATED WITH CHEN'S CONSTANT DAYDREAMING.
YOUR UNCLE BECAME INCREASINGLY RESTLESS. SPOKE OF THE WANDERLUST, IT HAD BEEN FAR TOO LONG E ANYONE HAD GONE TO SEEK OUTSIDE WORLD, TO EXPLORE AND UNDERGO FANTASTIC ADVENTURES.
HE WANTED ALSO TO DISCOVER EXOTIC NGREDIENTS FOR HIS BREWS AND TEAS.
"I TOLD HIM WHAT YEARS OF ADVENTURING HAD TAUGHT OUR ANCESTORS: THAT THERE WAS NOTHING IN THE OUTSIDE WORLD THAT WE COULDN'T FIND RIGHT THERE AT HOME.
"I TRIED TO TELL HIM THAT THE MOST IMPORTANT THINGS WERE THERE IN FRONT OF HIM, BUT HE WOULDN'T LISTEN. THE TWO OF US ARGUED...
"...AND WHEN THE DAY OF OUR FINAL TEST CAME, YOUR UNCLE HAD LEFT. HE LEFT ME ALONE... TO PURSUE HIS DELUSIONAL FANTASIES."
AND?
AND WHAT? YOU WANTED TO KNOW WHAT HAPPENED BETWEEN US. I TOLD YOU.
THAT'S IT? THAT'S WHY YOU'RE SO UPTIGHT? BECAUSE YOU DIDN'T GET A CHANCE TO PROVE HOW TOUGH YOU WERE? YOU GOTTA BE KIDDING ME!
I NEVER EXPECTED YOU TO UNDERSTAND. IT'S WHY I DIDN'T SHARE THE STORY BEFORE.
WELL, YOU WERE RIGHT: I DON'T UNDERSTAND.
YOUR RAM IS NUZZLING ME.
THAT'S NOTHING COMPARED TO WHAT *YOUR* RAM'S DOING RIGHT NOW.
WHAT-- HEY!
SO *THAT'S* WHY THEY CALL IT A POOP DECK!

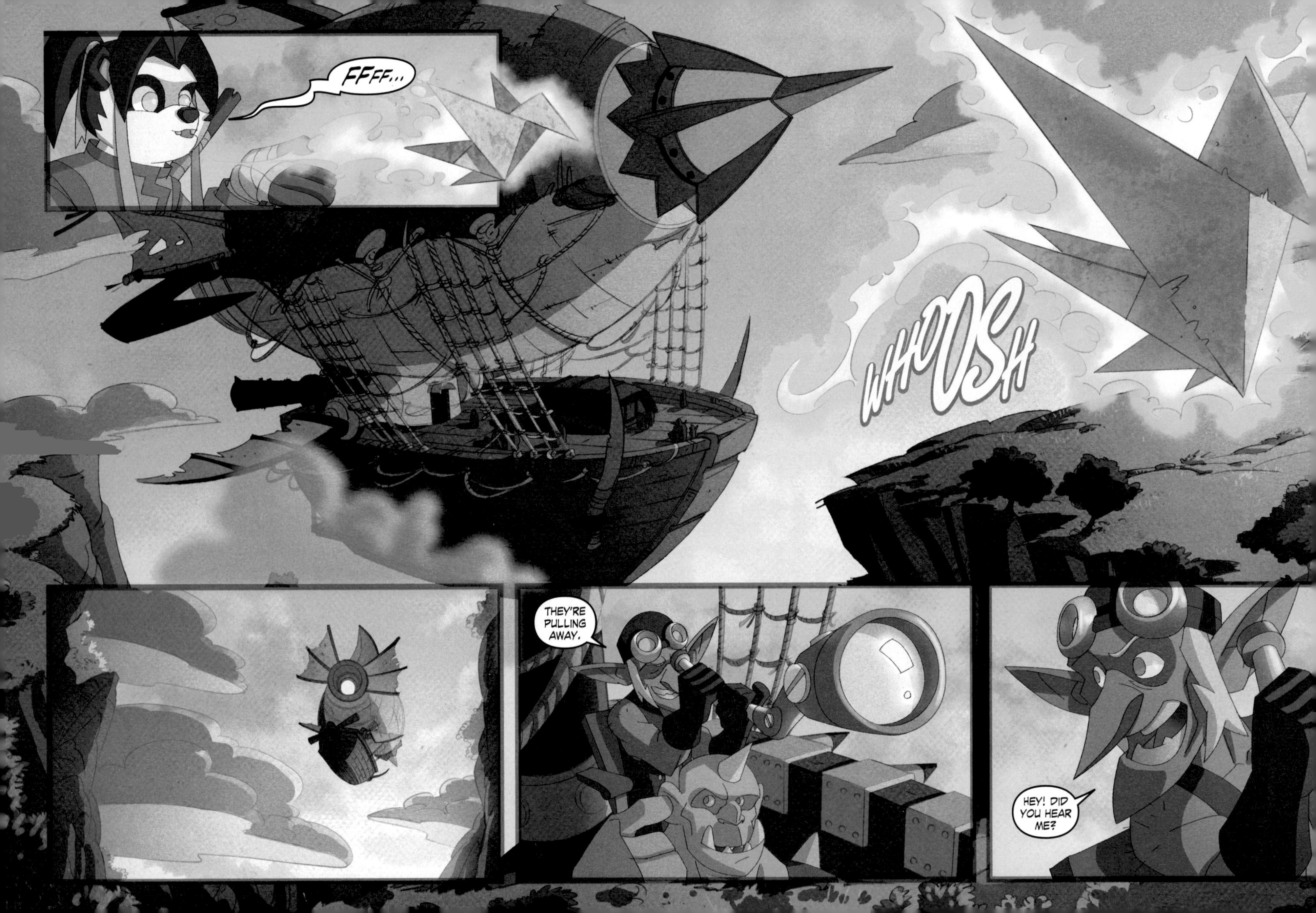
FFFF...
WHOOSH
THEY'RE PULLING AWAY.
HEY! DID YOU HEAR ME?

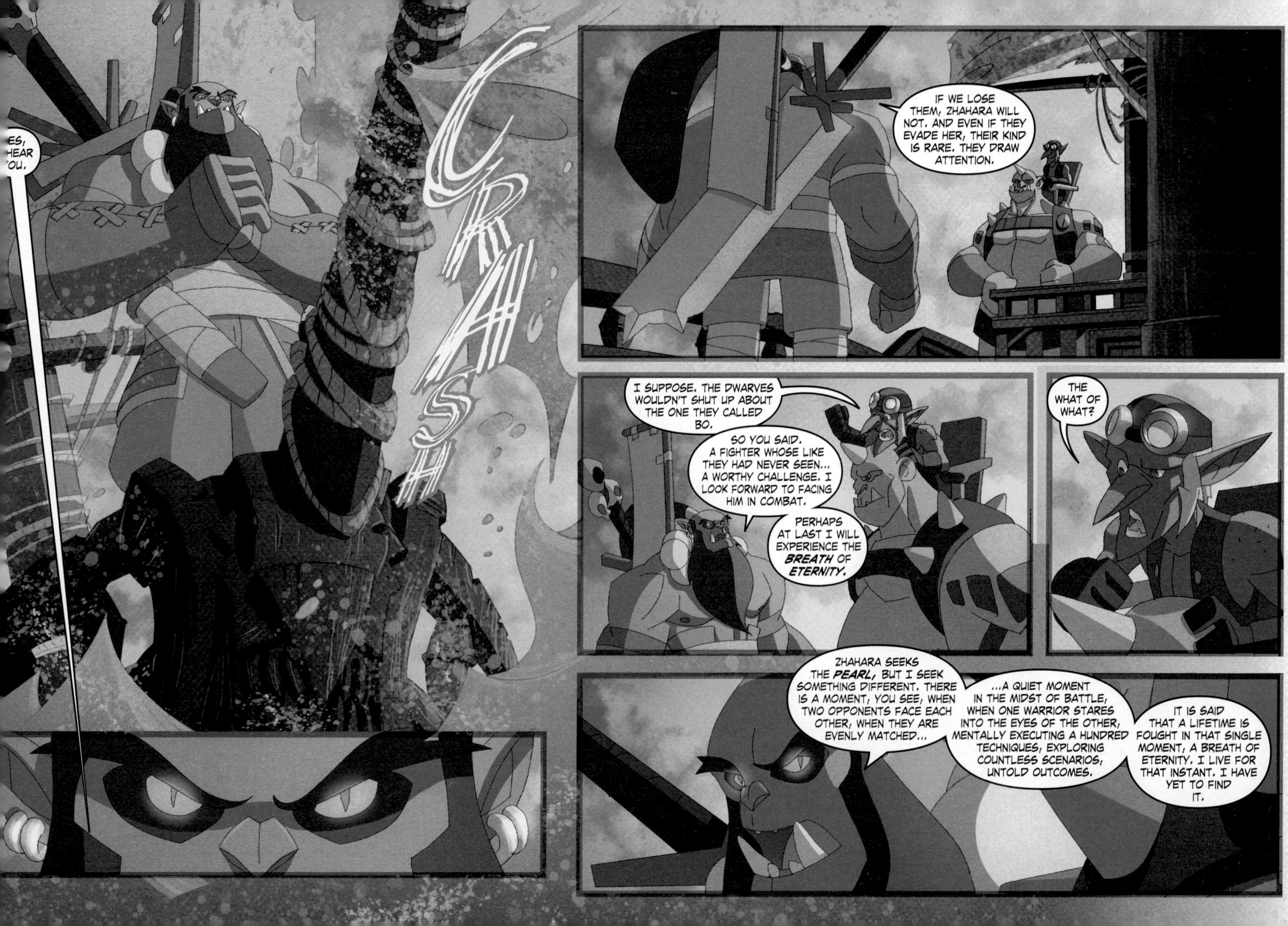
CRASH
IF WE LOSE THEM, ZHAHARA WILL NOT. AND EVEN IF THEY EVADE HER, THEIR KIND IS RARE. THEY DRAW ATTENTION.
I SUPPOSE. THE DWARVES WOULDN'T SHUT UP ABOUT THE ONE THEY CALLED BO.
SO YOU SAID. A FIGHTER WHOSE LIKE THEY HAD NEVER SEEN... A WORTHY CHALLENGE. I LOOK FORWARD TO FACING HIM IN COMBAT.
PERHAPS AT LAST I WILL EXPERIENCE THE ***BREATH*** OF ***ETERNITY.***
THE WHAT OF WHAT?
ZHAHARA SEEKS THE ***PEARL,*** BUT I SEEK SOMETHING DIFFERENT. THERE IS A MOMENT, YOU SEE, WHEN TWO OPPONENTS FACE EACH OTHER, WHEN THEY ARE EVENLY MATCHED...
...A QUIET MOMENT IN THE MIDST OF BATTLE, WHEN ONE WARRIOR STARES INTO THE EYES OF THE OTHER, MENTALLY EXECUTING A HUNDRED TECHNIQUES, EXPLORING COUNTLESS SCENARIOS, UNTOLD OUTCOMES.
IT IS SAID THAT A LIFETIME IS FOUGHT IN THAT SINGLE MOMENT, A BREATH OF ETERNITY. I LIVE FOR THAT INSTANT. I HAVE YET TO FIND IT.

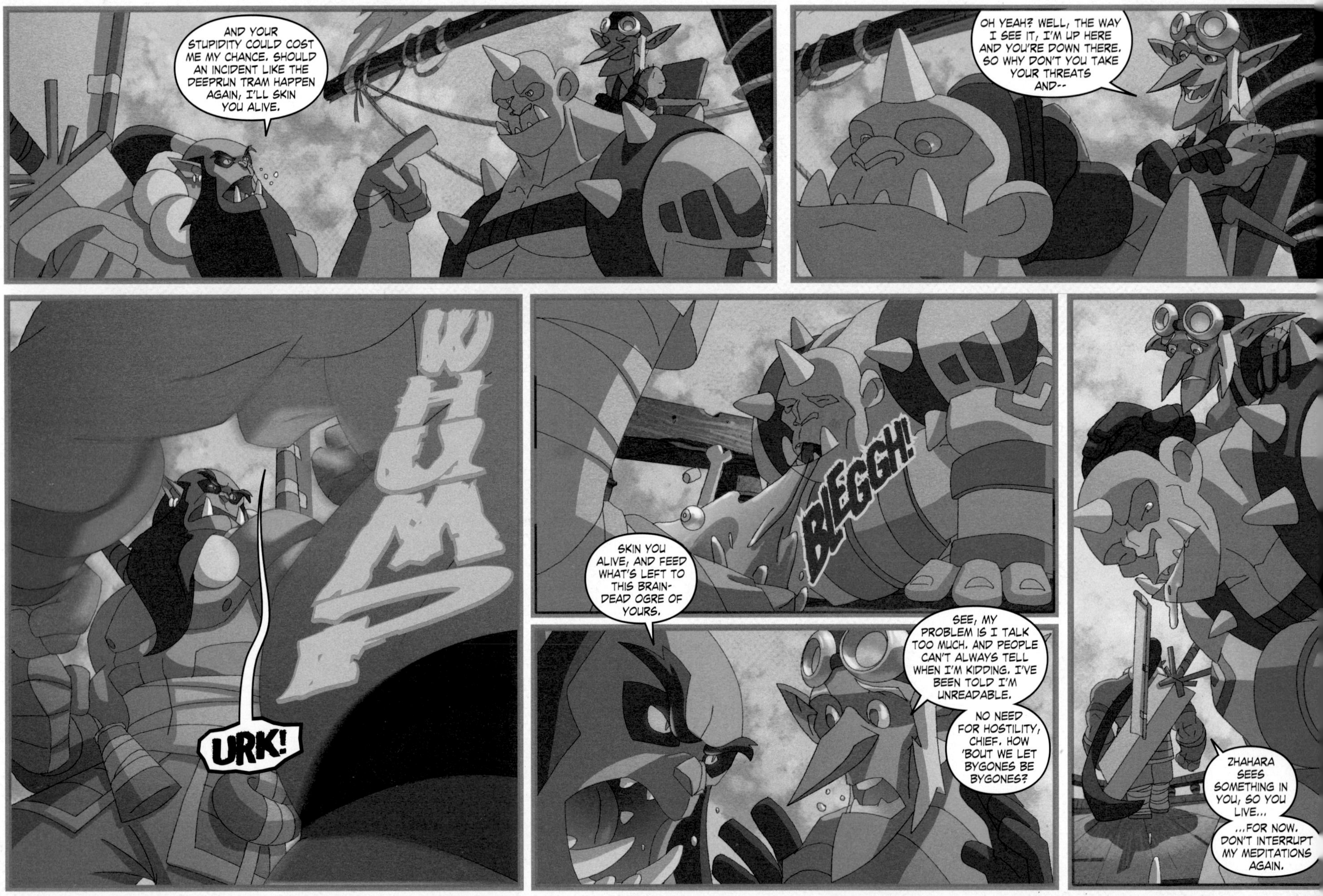
AND YOUR STUPIDITY COULD COST ME MY CHANCE. SHOULD AN INCIDENT LIKE THE DEEPRUN TRAM HAPPEN AGAIN, I'LL SKIN YOU ALIVE.
OH YEAH? WELL, THE WAY I SEE IT, I'M UP HERE AND YOU'RE DOWN THERE. SO WHY DON'T YOU TAKE YOUR THREATS AND--
WHUMP
URK!
BLEGGH!
SKIN YOU ALIVE, AND FEED WHAT'S LEFT TO THIS BRAIN-DEAD OGRE OF YOURS.
SEE, MY PROBLEM IS I TALK TOO MUCH. AND PEOPLE CAN'T ALWAYS TELL WHEN I'M KIDDING. I'VE BEEN TOLD I'M UNREADABLE.
NO NEED FOR HOSTILITY, CHIEF. HOW 'BOUT WE LET BYGONES BE BYGONES?
ZHAHARA SEES SOMETHING IN YOU, SO YOU LIVE...
...FOR NOW. DON'T INTERRUPT MY MEDITATIONS AGAIN.

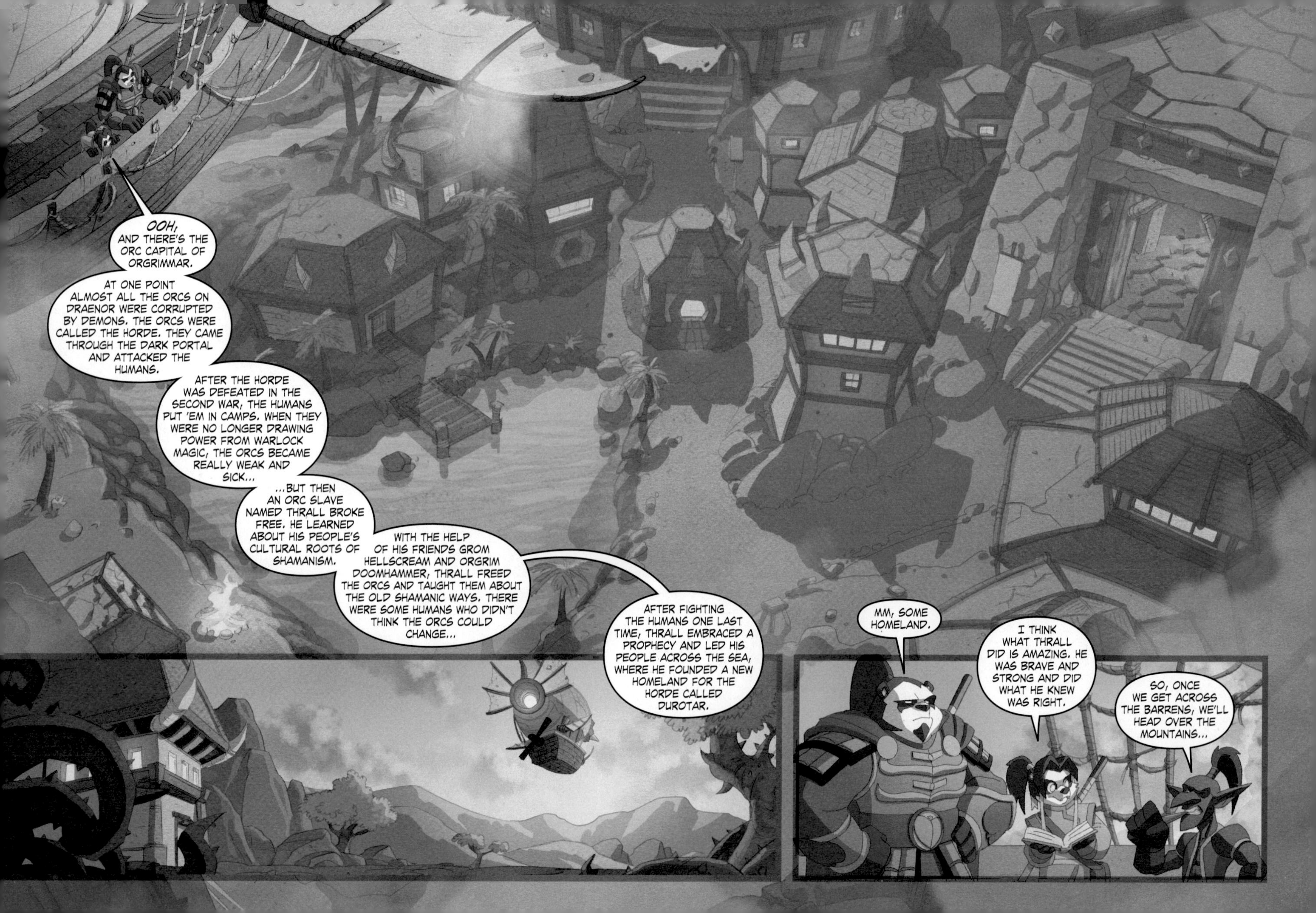
OOH, AND THERE'S THE ORC CAPITAL OF ORGRIMMAR.
AT ONE POINT ALMOST ALL THE ORCS ON DRAENOR WERE CORRUPTED BY DEMONS. THE ORCS WERE CALLED THE HORDE. THEY CAME THROUGH THE DARK PORTAL AND ATTACKED THE HUMANS.
AFTER THE HORDE WAS DEFEATED IN THE SECOND WAR, THE HUMANS PUT 'EM IN CAMPS. WHEN THEY WERE NO LONGER DRAWING POWER FROM WARLOCK MAGIC, THE ORCS BECAME REALLY WEAK AND SICK...
...BUT THEN AN ORC SLAVE NAMED THRALL BROKE FREE. HE LEARNED ABOUT HIS PEOPLE'S CULTURAL ROOTS OF SHAMANISM.
WITH THE HELP OF HIS FRIENDS GROM HELLSCREAM AND ORGRIM DOOMHAMMER, THRALL FREED THE ORCS AND TAUGHT THEM ABOUT THE OLD SHAMANIC WAYS. THERE WERE SOME HUMANS WHO DIDN'T THINK THE ORCS COULD CHANGE...
AFTER FIGHTING THE HUMANS ONE LAST TIME, THRALL EMBRACED A PROPHECY AND LED HIS PEOPLE ACROSS THE SEA, WHERE HE FOUNDED A NEW HOMELAND FOR THE HORDE CALLED DUROTAR.
MM, SOME HOMELAND.
I THINK WHAT THRALL DID IS AMAZING. HE WAS BRAVE AND STRONG AND DID WHAT HE KNEW WAS RIGHT.
SO, ONCE WE GET ACROSS THE BARRENS, WE'LL HEAD OVER THE MOUNTAINS...

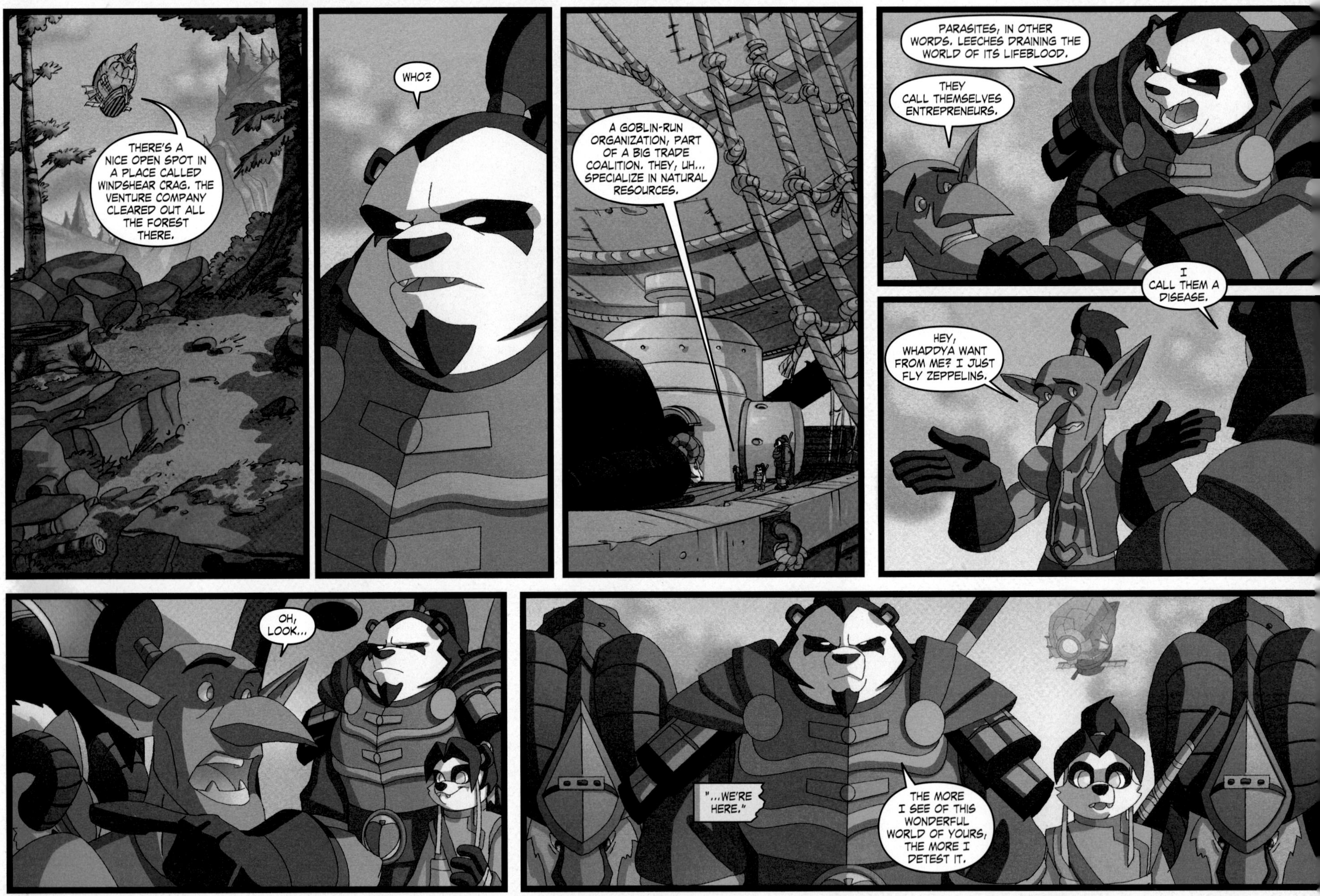

THERE'S A NICE OPEN SPOT IN A PLACE CALLED WINDSHEAR CRAG. THE VENTURE COMPANY CLEARED OUT ALL THE FOREST THERE.
WHO?
A GOBLIN-RUN ORGANIZATION, PART OF A BIG TRADE COALITION. THEY, UH... SPECIALIZE IN NATURAL RESOURCES.
THEY CALL THEMSELVES ENTREPRENEURS.
PARASITES, IN OTHER WORDS. LEECHES DRAINING THE WORLD OF ITS LIFEBLOOD.
I CALL THEM A DISEASE.
HEY, WHADDYA WANT FROM ME? I JUST FLY ZEPPELINS.
OH, LOOK...
"...WE'RE HERE."
THE MORE I SEE OF THIS WONDERFUL WORLD OF YOURS, THE MORE I DETEST IT.

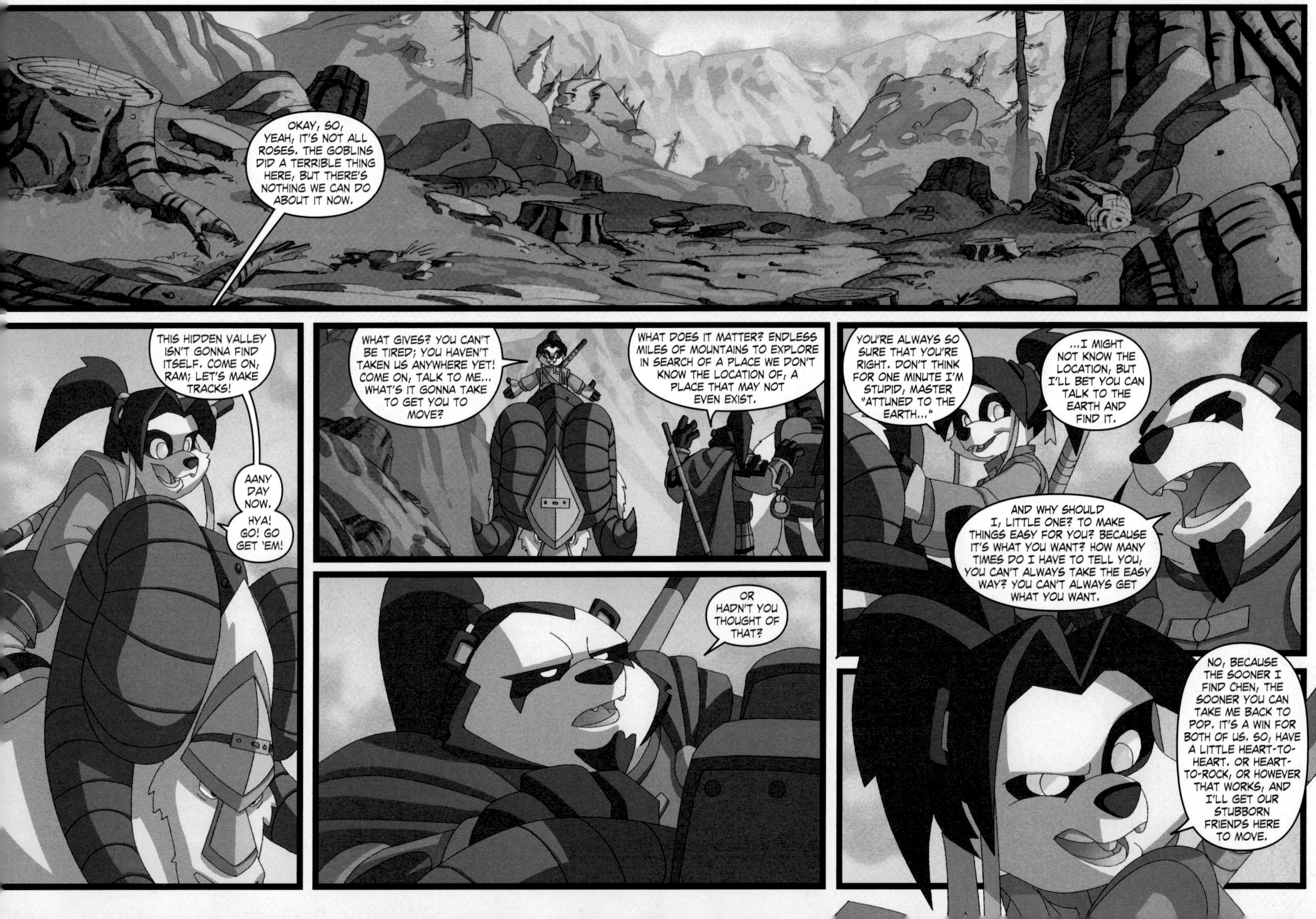
OKAY, SO, YEAH, IT'S NOT ALL ROSES. THE GOBLINS DID A TERRIBLE THING HERE, BUT THERE'S NOTHING WE CAN DO ABOUT IT NOW.
THIS HIDDEN VALLEY ISN'T GONNA FIND ITSELF. COME ON, RAM; LET'S MAKE TRACKS!
AANY DAY NOW.
HYA! GO! GO GET 'EM!
WHAT GIVES? YOU CAN'T BE TIRED; YOU HAVEN'T TAKEN US ANYWHERE YET! COME ON, TALK TO ME... WHAT'S IT GONNA TAKE TO GET YOU TO MOVE?
WHAT DOES IT MATTER? ENDLESS MILES OF MOUNTAINS TO EXPLORE IN SEARCH OF A PLACE WE DON'T KNOW THE LOCATION OF, A PLACE THAT MAY NOT EVEN EXIST.
OR HADN'T YOU THOUGHT OF THAT?
YOU'RE ALWAYS SO SURE THAT YOU'RE RIGHT. DON'T THINK FOR ONE MINUTE I'M STUPID, MASTER "ATTUNED TO THE EARTH..."
...I MIGHT NOT KNOW THE LOCATION, BUT I'LL BET YOU CAN TALK TO THE EARTH AND FIND IT.
AND WHY SHOULD I, LITTLE ONE? TO MAKE THINGS EASY FOR YOU? BECAUSE IT'S WHAT YOU WANT? HOW MANY TIMES DO I HAVE TO TELL YOU, YOU CAN'T ALWAYS TAKE THE EASY WAY? YOU CAN'T ALWAYS GET WHAT YOU WANT.
NO, BECAUSE THE SOONER I FIND CHEN, THE SOONER YOU CAN TAKE ME BACK TO POP. IT'S A WIN FOR BOTH OF US. SO, HAVE A LITTLE HEART-TO-HEART. OR HEART-TO-ROCK, OR HOWEVER THAT WORKS, AND I'LL GET OUR STUBBORN FRIENDS HERE TO MOVE.

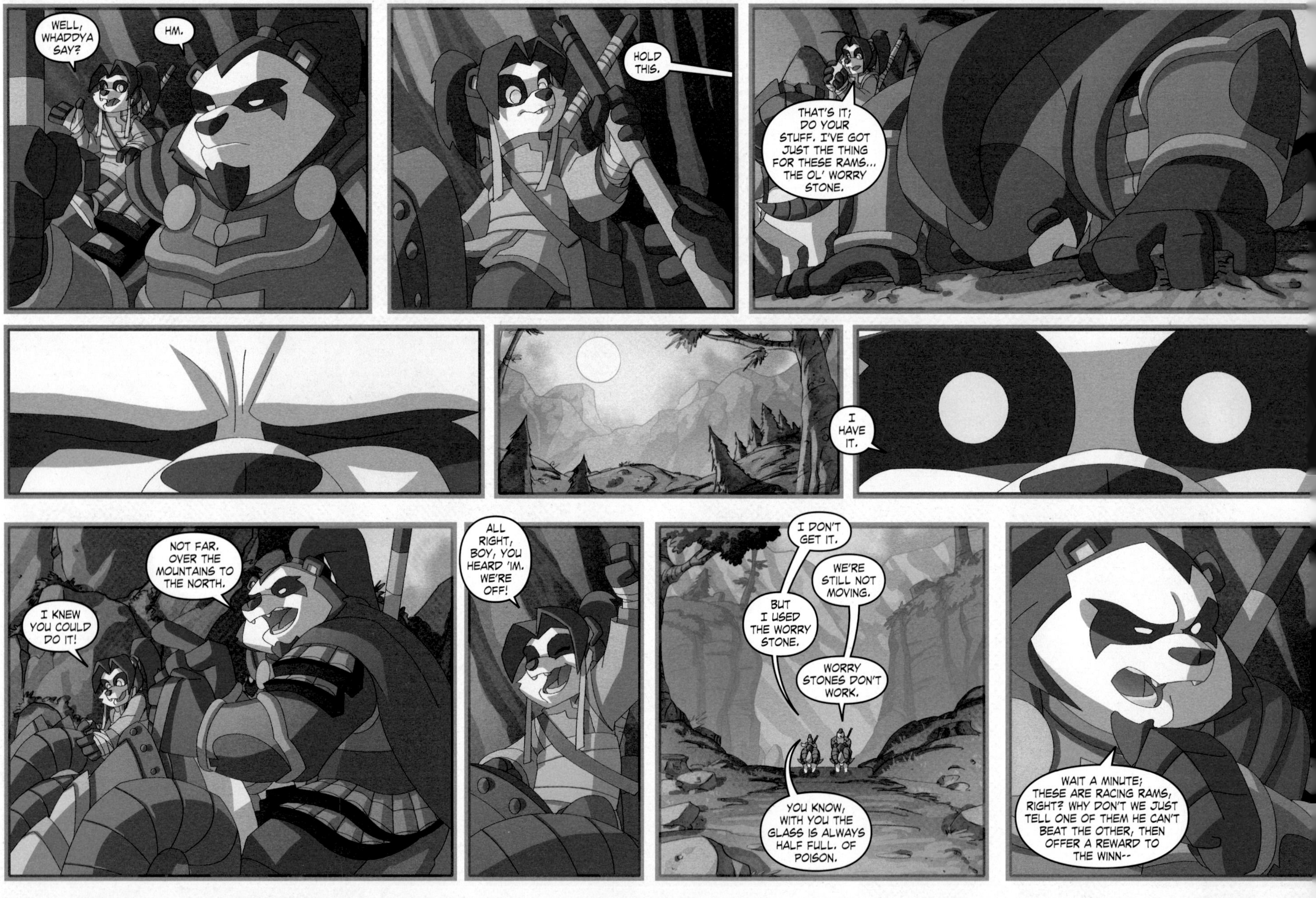

WELL, WHADDYA SAY?
HM.
HOLD THIS.
THAT'S IT; DO YOUR STUFF. I'VE GOT JUST THE THING FOR THESE RAMS... THE OL' WORRY STONE.
I HAVE IT.
I KNEW YOU COULD DO IT!
NOT FAR. OVER THE MOUNTAINS TO THE NORTH.
ALL RIGHT, BOY, YOU HEARD 'IM. WE'RE OFF!
I DON'T GET IT.
WE'RE STILL NOT MOVING.
BUT I USED THE WORRY STONE.
WORRY STONES DON'T WORK.
YOU KNOW, WITH YOU THE GLASS IS ALWAYS HALF FULL. OF POISON.
WAIT A MINUTE; THESE ARE RACING RAMS, RIGHT? WHY DON'T WE JUST TELL ONE OF THEM HE CAN'T BEAT THE OTHER, THEN OFFER A REWARD TO THE WINN--

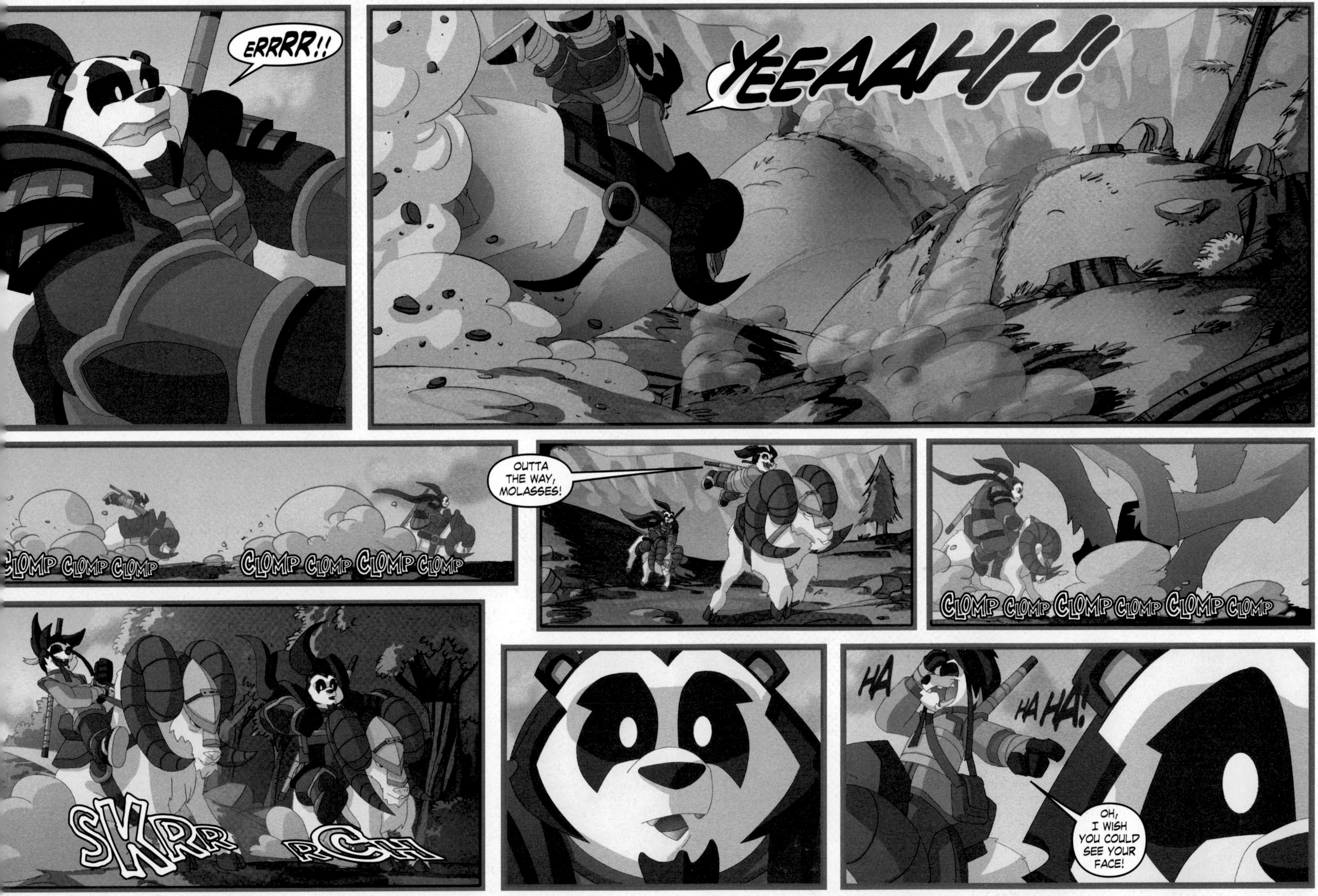

ERRRR!!
YEEAAHH!
CLOMP CLOMP CLOMP CLOMP CLOMP CLOMP CLOMP
OUTTA THE WAY, MOLASSES!
CLOMP CLOMP CLOMP CLOMP CLOMP CLOMP
SKRR RCH
HA HA HA!
OH, I WISH YOU COULD SEE YOUR FACE!

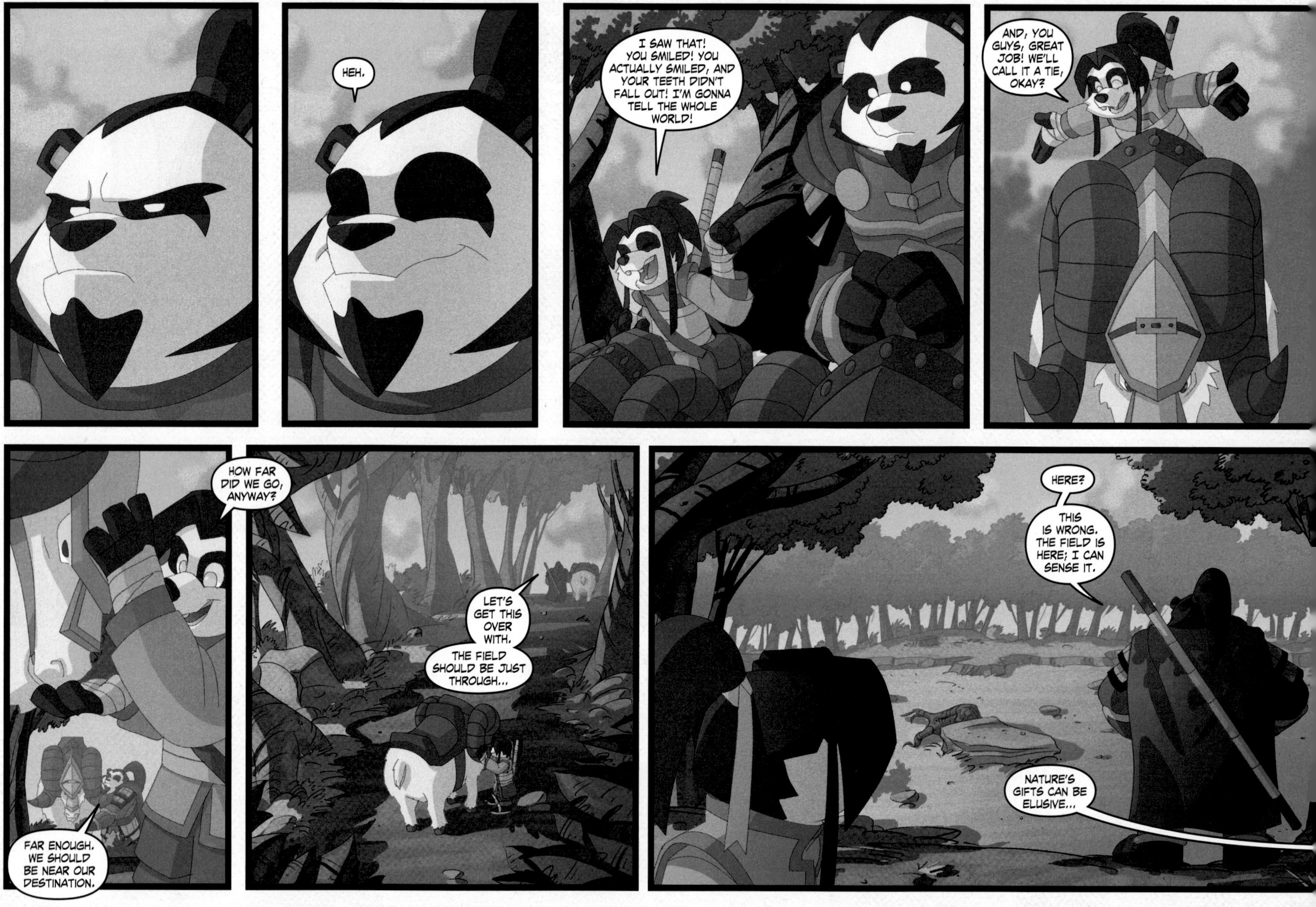
HEH.
I SAW THAT! YOU SMILED! YOU ACTUALLY SMILED, AND YOUR TEETH DIDN'T FALL OUT! I'M GONNA TELL THE WHOLE WORLD!
AND, YOU GUYS, GREAT JOB! WE'LL CALL IT A TIE, OKAY?
HOW FAR DID WE GO, ANYWAY?
FAR ENOUGH. WE SHOULD BE NEAR OUR DESTINATION.
LET'S GET THIS OVER WITH.
THE FIELD SHOULD BE JUST THROUGH...
HERE?
THIS IS WRONG. THE FIELD IS HERE; I CAN SENSE IT.
NATURE'S GIFTS CAN BE ELUSIVE...

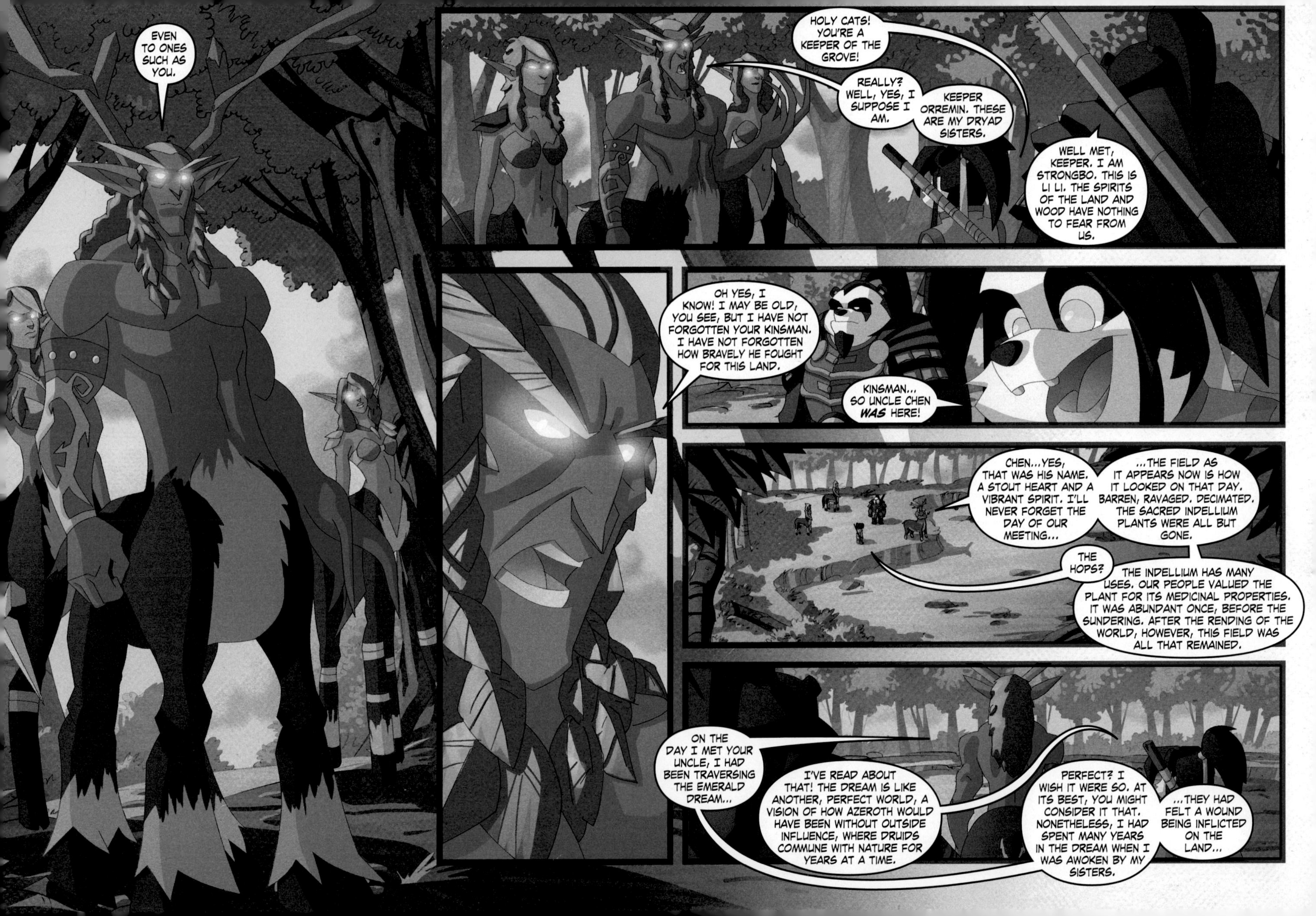
EVEN TO ONES SUCH AS YOU.
HOLY CATS! YOU'RE A KEEPER OF THE GROVE!
REALLY? WELL, YES, I SUPPOSE I AM.
KEEPER ORREMIN. THESE ARE MY DRYAD SISTERS.
WELL MET, KEEPER. I AM STRONGBO. THIS IS LI LI. THE SPIRITS OF THE LAND AND WOOD HAVE NOTHING TO FEAR FROM US.
OH YES, I KNOW! I MAY BE OLD, YOU SEE, BUT I HAVE NOT FORGOTTEN YOUR KINSMAN. I HAVE NOT FORGOTTEN HOW BRAVELY HE FOUGHT FOR THIS LAND.
KINSMAN... SO UNCLE CHEN WAS HERE!
CHEN...YES, THAT WAS HIS NAME. A STOUT HEART AND A VIBRANT SPIRIT. I'LL NEVER FORGET THE DAY OF OUR MEETING...
...THE FIELD AS IT APPEARS NOW IS HOW IT LOOKED ON THAT DAY. BARREN, RAVAGED. DECIMATED. THE SACRED INDELLIUM PLANTS WERE ALL BUT GONE.
THE HOPS?
THE INDELLIUM HAS MANY USES. OUR PEOPLE VALUED THE PLANT FOR ITS MEDICINAL PROPERTIES. IT WAS ABUNDANT ONCE, BEFORE THE SUNDERING. AFTER THE RENDING OF THE WORLD, HOWEVER, THIS FIELD WAS ALL THAT REMAINED.
ON THE DAY I MET YOUR UNCLE, I HAD BEEN TRAVERSING THE EMERALD DREAM...
I'VE READ ABOUT THAT! THE DREAM IS LIKE ANOTHER, PERFECT WORLD, A VISION OF HOW AZEROTH WOULD HAVE BEEN WITHOUT OUTSIDE INFLUENCE, WHERE DRUIDS COMMUNE WITH NATURE FOR YEARS AT A TIME.
PERFECT? I WISH IT WERE SO. AT ITS BEST, YOU MIGHT CONSIDER IT THAT. NONETHELESS, I HAD SPENT MANY YEARS IN THE DREAM WHEN I WAS AWOKEN BY MY SISTERS.
...THEY HAD FELT A WOUND BEING INFLICTED ON THE LAND...

"...I RUSHED AS QUICKLY AS I COULD, BUT I WAS WOEFULLY UNPREPARED FOR THE SIGHT THAT GREETED ME..."

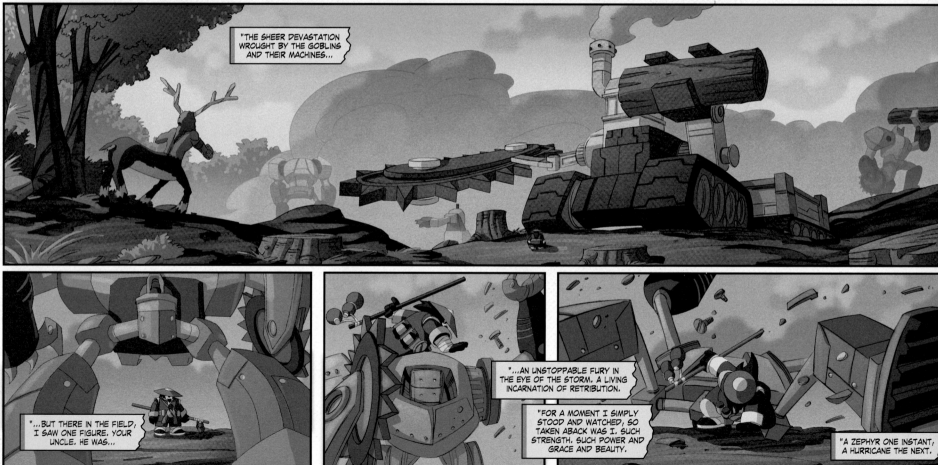

"THE SHEER DEVASTATION WROUGHT BY THE GOBLINS AND THEIR MACHINES...

"...BUT THERE IN THE FIELD, I SAW ONE FIGURE. YOUR UNCLE. HE WAS...

"...AN UNSTOPPABLE FURY IN THE EYE OF THE STORM. A LIVING INCARNATION OF RETRIBUTION.

"FOR A MOMENT I SIMPLY STOOD AND WATCHED, SO TAKEN ABACK WAS I. SUCH STRENGTH. SUCH POWER AND GRACE AND BEAUTY.

"A ZEPHYR ONE INSTANT, A HURRICANE THE NEXT.

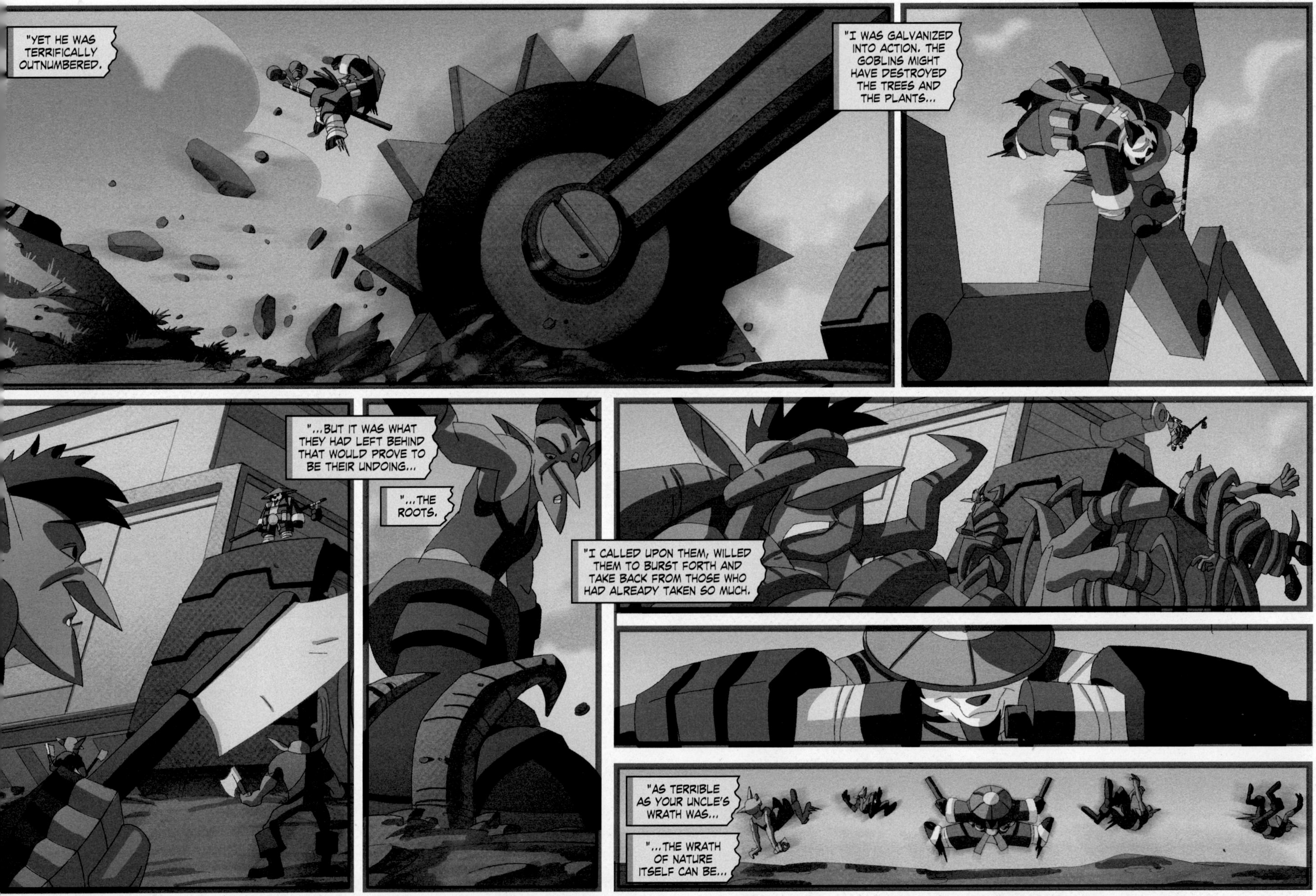
"YET HE WAS TERRIFICALLY OUTNUMBERED.
"I WAS GALVANIZED INTO ACTION. THE GOBLINS MIGHT HAVE DESTROYED THE TREES AND THE PLANTS...
"...BUT IT WAS WHAT THEY HAD LEFT BEHIND THAT WOULD PROVE TO BE THEIR UNDOING...
"...THE ROOTS.
"I CALLED UPON THEM, WILLED THEM TO BURST FORTH AND TAKE BACK FROM THOSE WHO HAD ALREADY TAKEN SO MUCH.
"AS TERRIBLE AS YOUR UNCLE'S WRATH WAS...
"...THE WRATH OF NATURE ITSELF CAN BE...

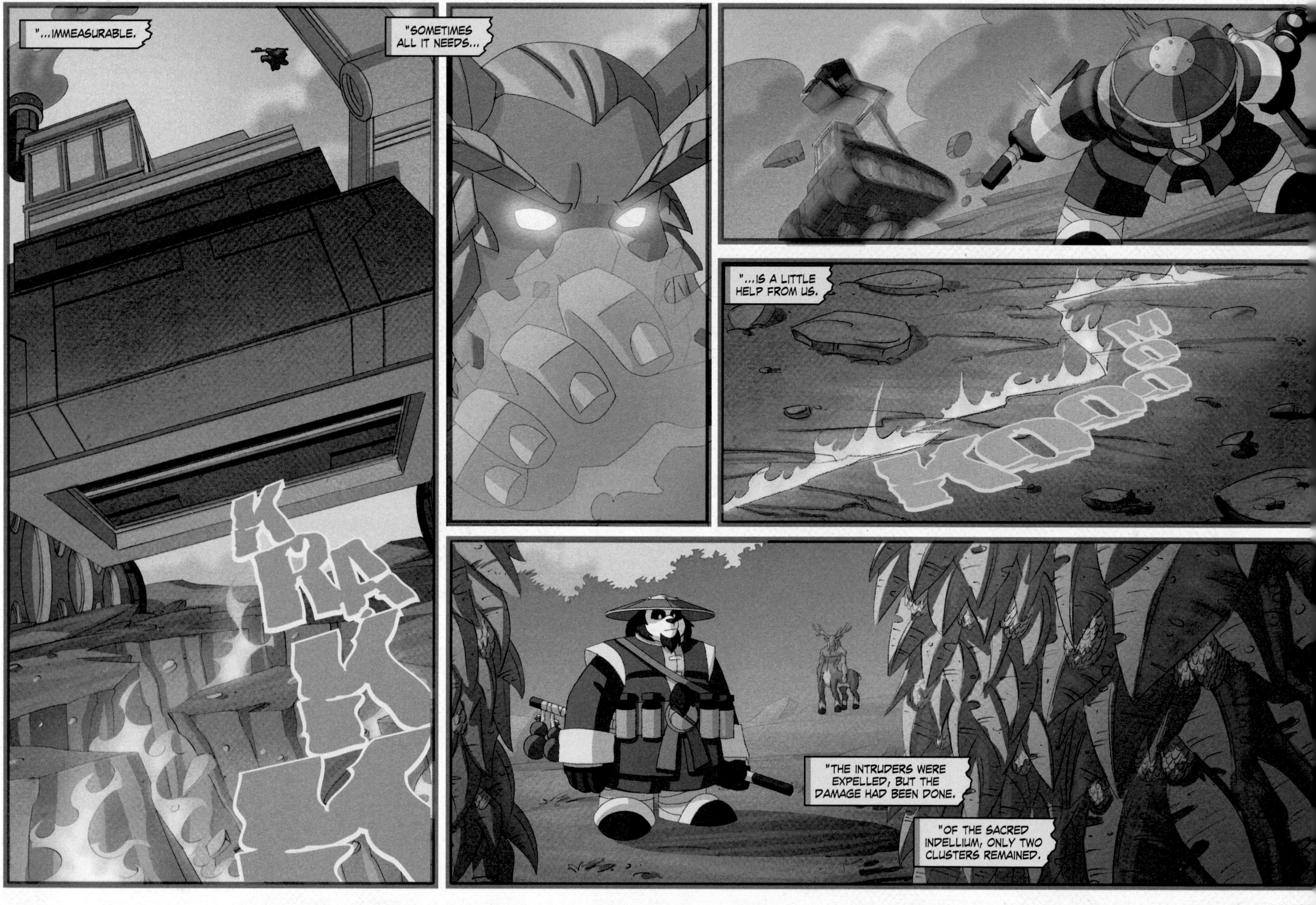
"...IMMEASURABLE.
KRAKK
"SOMETIMES ALL IT NEEDS...
"...IS A LITTLE HELP FROM US.
KOOOOM
"THE INTRUDERS WERE EXPELLED, BUT THE DAMAGE HAD BEEN DONE.
"OF THE SACRED INDELLIUM, ONLY TWO CLUSTERS REMAINED.

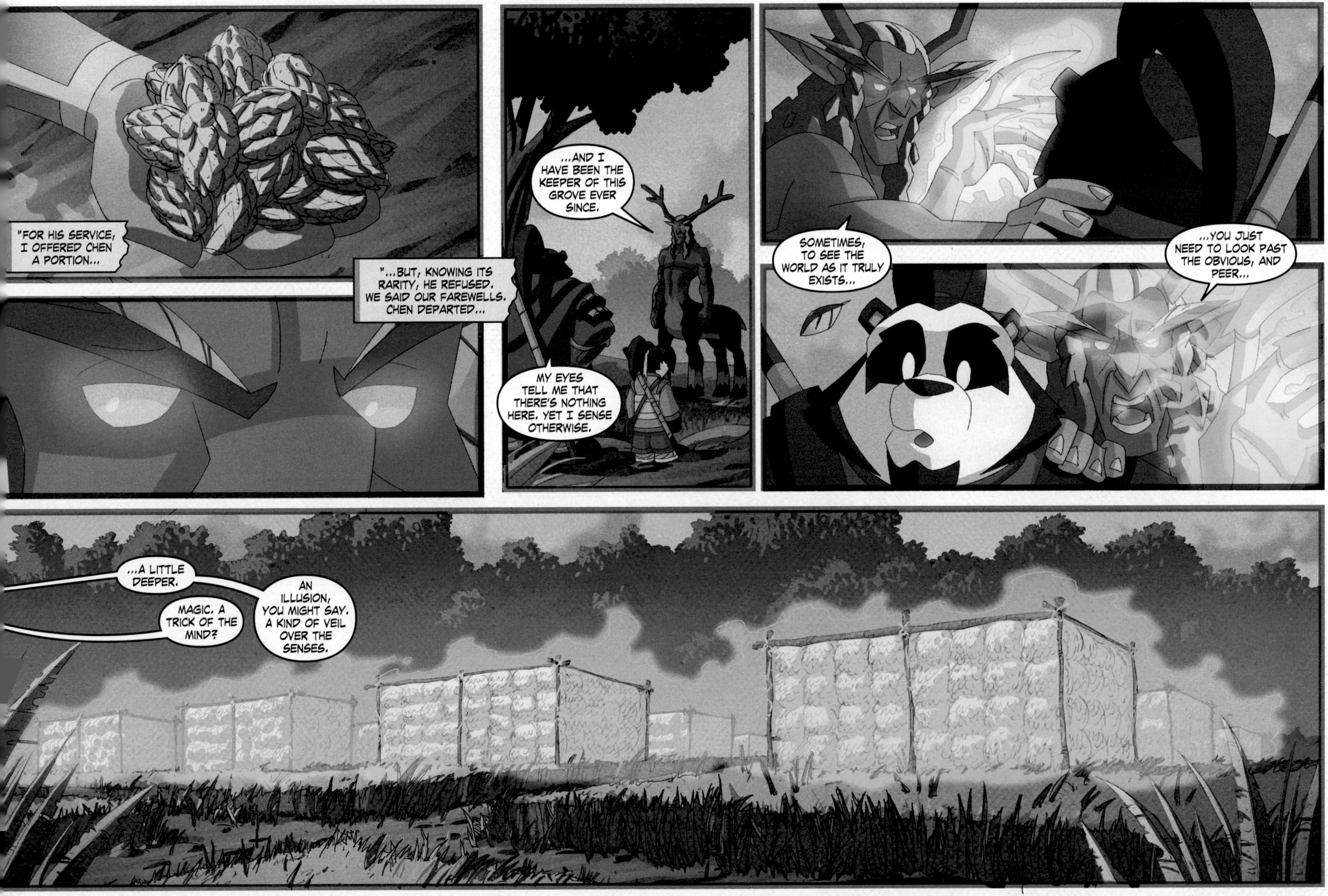
"FOR HIS SERVICE, I OFFERED CHEN A PORTION...
"...BUT, KNOWING ITS RARITY, HE REFUSED. WE SAID OUR FAREWELLS. CHEN DEPARTED...
...AND I HAVE BEEN THE KEEPER OF THIS GROVE EVER SINCE.
MY EYES TELL ME THAT THERE'S NOTHING HERE. YET I SENSE OTHERWISE.
SOMETIMES, TO SEE THE WORLD AS IT TRULY EXISTS...
...YOU JUST NEED TO LOOK PAST THE OBVIOUS, AND PEER...
...A LITTLE DEEPER.
MAGIC. A TRICK OF THE MIND?
AN ILLUSION, YOU MIGHT SAY. A KIND OF VEIL OVER THE SENSES.

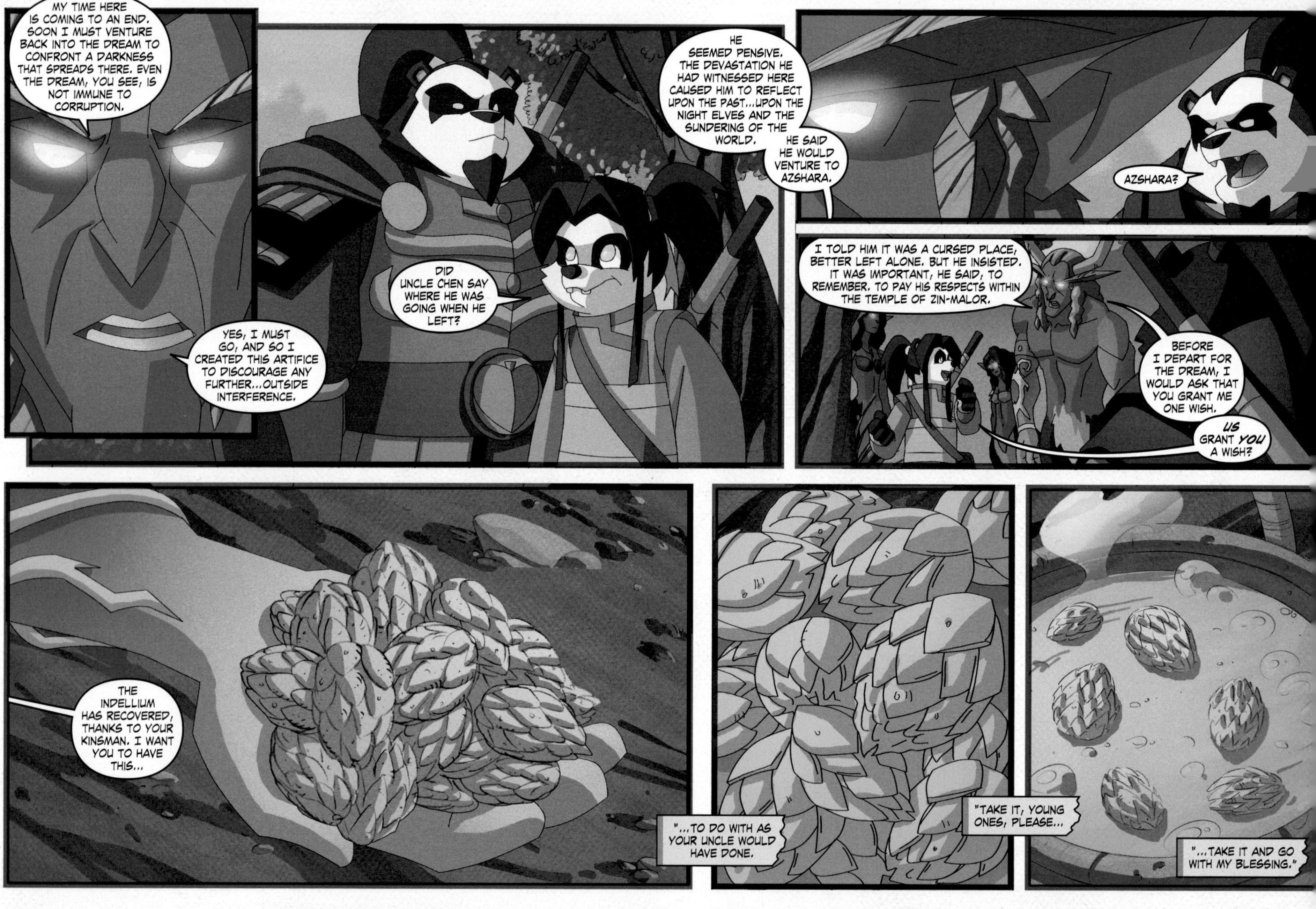
MY TIME HERE IS COMING TO AN END. SOON I MUST VENTURE BACK INTO THE DREAM TO CONFRONT A DARKNESS THAT SPREADS THERE. EVEN THE DREAM, YOU SEE, IS NOT IMMUNE TO CORRUPTION.
YES, I MUST GO, AND SO I CREATED THIS ARTIFICE TO DISCOURAGE ANY FURTHER...OUTSIDE INTERFERENCE.
DID UNCLE CHEN SAY WHERE HE WAS GOING WHEN HE LEFT?
HE SEEMED PENSIVE. THE DEVASTATION HE HAD WITNESSED HERE CAUSED HIM TO REFLECT UPON THE PAST...UPON THE NIGHT ELVES AND THE SUNDERING OF THE WORLD.
HE SAID HE WOULD VENTURE TO AZSHARA.
AZSHARA?
I TOLD HIM IT WAS A CURSED PLACE, BETTER LEFT ALONE. BUT HE INSISTED. IT WAS IMPORTANT, HE SAID, TO REMEMBER. TO PAY HIS RESPECTS WITHIN THE TEMPLE OF ZIN-MALOR.
BEFORE I DEPART FOR THE DREAM, I WOULD ASK THAT YOU GRANT ME ONE WISH.
US GRANT YOU A WISH?
THE INDELLIUM HAS RECOVERED, THANKS TO YOUR KINSMAN. I WANT YOU TO HAVE THIS...
"...TO DO WITH AS YOUR UNCLE WOULD HAVE DONE.
"TAKE IT, YOUNG ONES, PLEASE...
"...TAKE IT AND GO WITH MY BLESSING."

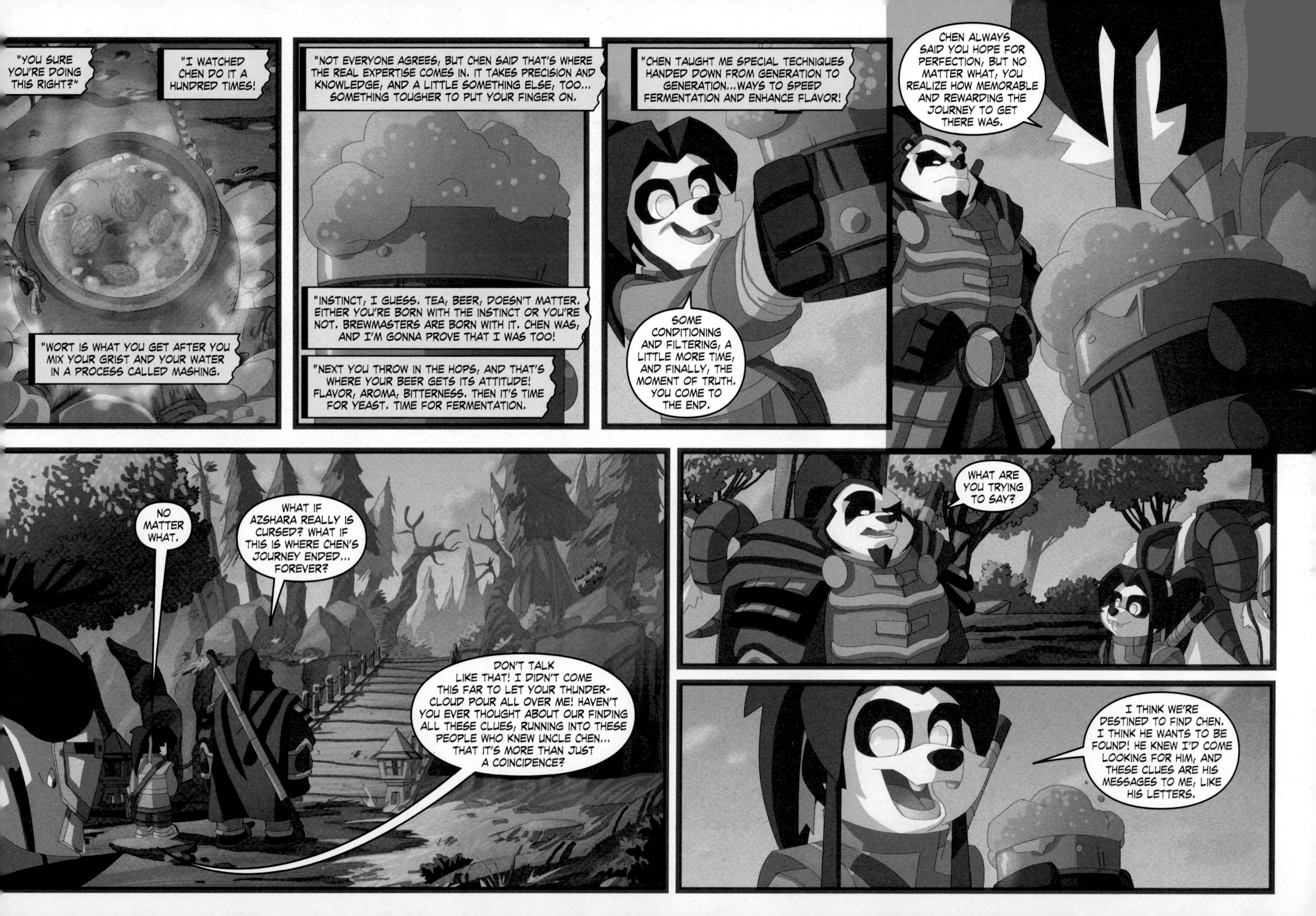
"YOU SURE YOU'RE DOING THIS RIGHT?"
"I WATCHED CHEN DO IT A HUNDRED TIMES!
"WORT IS WHAT YOU GET AFTER YOU MIX YOUR GRIST AND YOUR WATER IN A PROCESS CALLED MASHING.
"NOT EVERYONE AGREES, BUT CHEN SAID THAT'S WHERE THE REAL EXPERTISE COMES IN. IT TAKES PRECISION AND KNOWLEDGE, AND A LITTLE SOMETHING ELSE, TOO... SOMETHING TOUGHER TO PUT YOUR FINGER ON.
"INSTINCT, I GUESS. TEA, BEER, DOESN'T MATTER. EITHER YOU'RE BORN WITH THE INSTINCT OR YOU'RE NOT. BREWMASTERS ARE BORN WITH IT. CHEN WAS, AND I'M GONNA PROVE THAT I WAS TOO!
"NEXT YOU THROW IN THE HOPS, AND THAT'S WHERE YOUR BEER GETS ITS ATTITUDE! FLAVOR, AROMA, BITTERNESS. THEN IT'S TIME FOR YEAST. TIME FOR FERMENTATION.
"CHEN TAUGHT ME SPECIAL TECHNIQUES HANDED DOWN FROM GENERATION TO GENERATION...WAYS TO SPEED FERMENTATION AND ENHANCE FLAVOR!
SOME CONDITIONING AND FILTERING, A LITTLE MORE TIME, AND FINALLY, THE MOMENT OF TRUTH. YOU COME TO THE END.
CHEN ALWAYS SAID YOU HOPE FOR PERFECTION, BUT NO MATTER WHAT, YOU REALIZE HOW MEMORABLE AND REWARDING THE JOURNEY TO GET THERE WAS.
NO MATTER WHAT.
WHAT IF AZSHARA REALLY IS CURSED? WHAT IF THIS IS WHERE CHEN'S JOURNEY ENDED... FOREVER?
DON'T TALK LIKE THAT! I DIDN'T COME THIS FAR TO LET YOUR THUNDER-CLOUD POUR ALL OVER ME! HAVEN'T YOU EVER THOUGHT ABOUT OUR FINDING ALL THESE CLUES, RUNNING INTO THESE PEOPLE WHO KNEW UNCLE CHEN... THAT IT'S MORE THAN JUST A COINCIDENCE?
WHAT ARE YOU TRYING TO SAY?
I THINK WE'RE DESTINED TO FIND CHEN. I THINK HE WANTS TO BE FOUND! HE KNEW I'D COME LOOKING FOR HIM, AND THESE CLUES ARE HIS MESSAGES TO ME, LIKE HIS LETTERS.

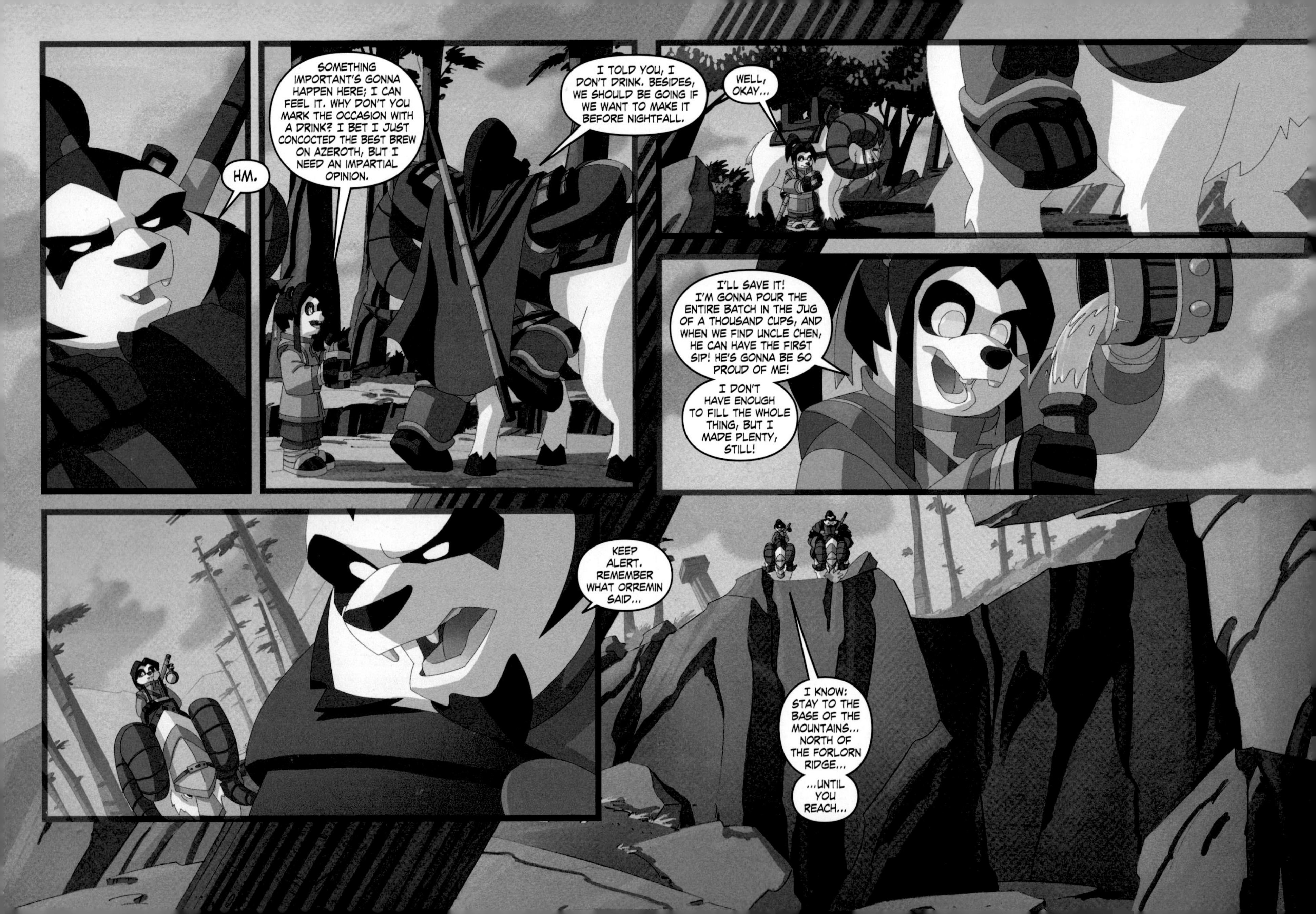
HM.
SOMETHING IMPORTANT'S GONNA HAPPEN HERE; I CAN FEEL IT. WHY DON'T YOU MARK THE OCCASION WITH A DRINK? I BET I JUST CONCOCTED THE BEST BREW ON AZEROTH, BUT I NEED AN IMPARTIAL OPINION.
I TOLD YOU, I DON'T DRINK. BESIDES, WE SHOULD BE GOING IF WE WANT TO MAKE IT BEFORE NIGHTFALL.
WELL, OKAY...
I'LL SAVE IT! I'M GONNA POUR THE ENTIRE BATCH IN THE JUG OF A THOUSAND CUPS, AND WHEN WE FIND UNCLE CHEN, HE CAN HAVE THE FIRST SIP! HE'S GONNA BE SO PROUD OF ME!
I DON'T HAVE ENOUGH TO FILL THE WHOLE THING, BUT I MADE PLENTY, STILL!
KEEP ALERT. REMEMBER WHAT ORREMIN SAID...
I KNOW: STAY TO THE BASE OF THE MOUNTAINS... NORTH OF THE FORLORN RIDGE...
...UNTIL YOU REACH...

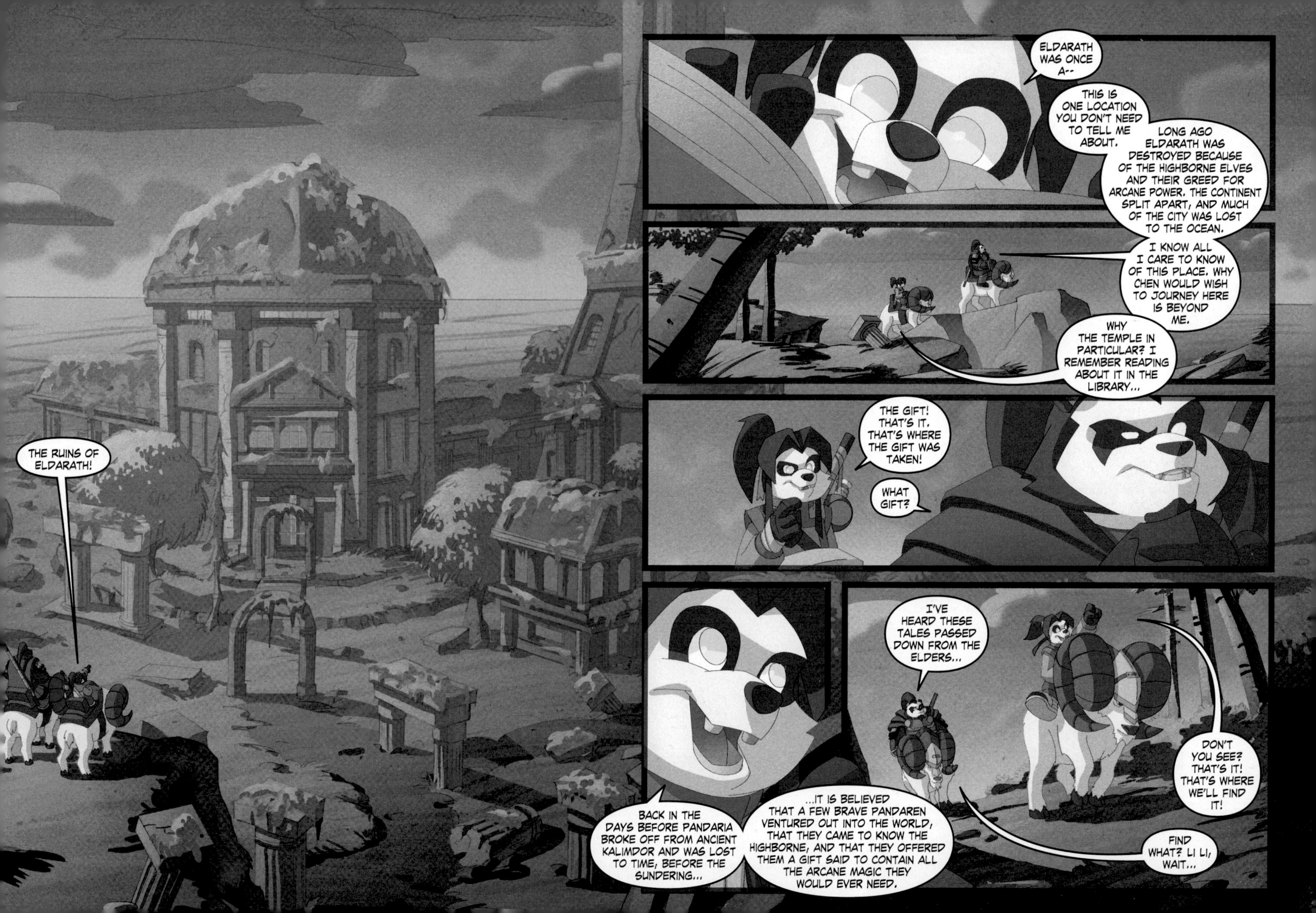

THE RUINS OF ELDARATH!
ELDARATH WAS ONCE A--
THIS IS ONE LOCATION YOU DON'T NEED TO TELL ME ABOUT.
LONG AGO ELDARATH WAS DESTROYED BECAUSE OF THE HIGHBORNE ELVES AND THEIR GREED FOR ARCANE POWER. THE CONTINENT SPLIT APART, AND MUCH OF THE CITY WAS LOST TO THE OCEAN.
I KNOW ALL I CARE TO KNOW OF THIS PLACE. WHY CHEN WOULD WISH TO JOURNEY HERE IS BEYOND ME.
WHY THE TEMPLE IN PARTICULAR? I REMEMBER READING ABOUT IT IN THE LIBRARY...
THE GIFT! THAT'S IT. THAT'S WHERE THE GIFT WAS TAKEN!
WHAT GIFT?
BACK IN THE DAYS BEFORE PANDARIA BROKE OFF FROM ANCIENT KALIMDOR AND WAS LOST TO TIME, BEFORE THE SUNDERING...
...IT IS BELIEVED THAT A FEW BRAVE PANDAREN VENTURED OUT INTO THE WORLD, THAT THEY CAME TO KNOW THE HIGHBORNE, AND THAT THEY OFFERED THEM A GIFT SAID TO CONTAIN ALL THE ARCANE MAGIC THEY WOULD EVER NEED.
I'VE HEARD THESE TALES PASSED DOWN FROM THE ELDERS...
DON'T YOU SEE? THAT'S IT! THAT'S WHERE WE'LL FIND IT!
FIND WHAT? LI LI, WAIT...

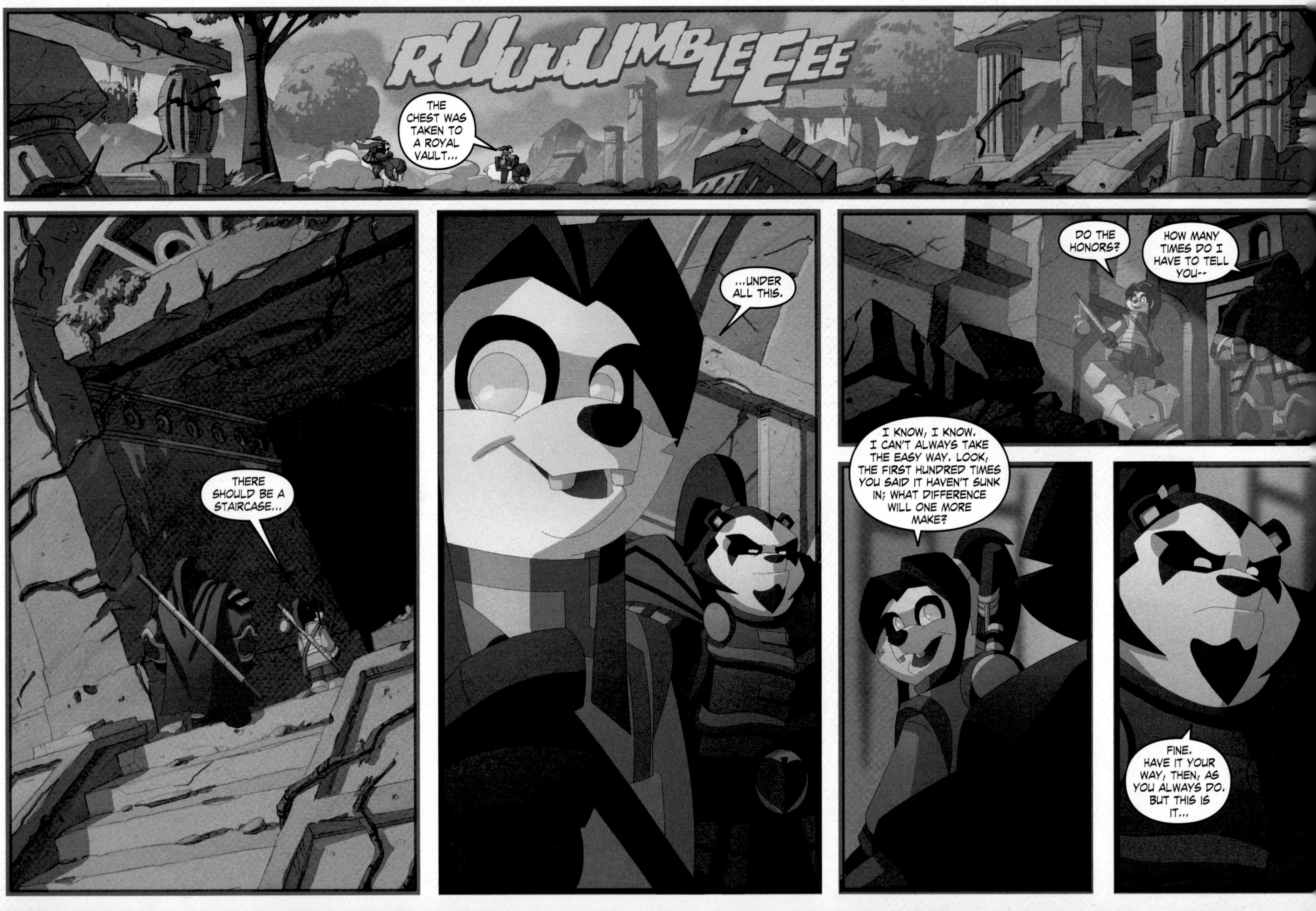
RUUUUMBLEEEE
THE CHEST WAS TAKEN TO A ROYAL VAULT...
THERE SHOULD BE A STAIRCASE...
...UNDER ALL THIS.
DO THE HONORS?
HOW MANY TIMES DO I HAVE TO TELL YOU--
I KNOW, I KNOW. I CAN'T ALWAYS TAKE THE EASY WAY. LOOK, THE FIRST HUNDRED TIMES YOU SAID IT HAVEN'T SUNK IN; WHAT DIFFERENCE WILL ONE MORE MAKE?
FINE. HAVE IT YOUR WAY, THEN, AS YOU ALWAYS DO. BUT THIS IS IT...

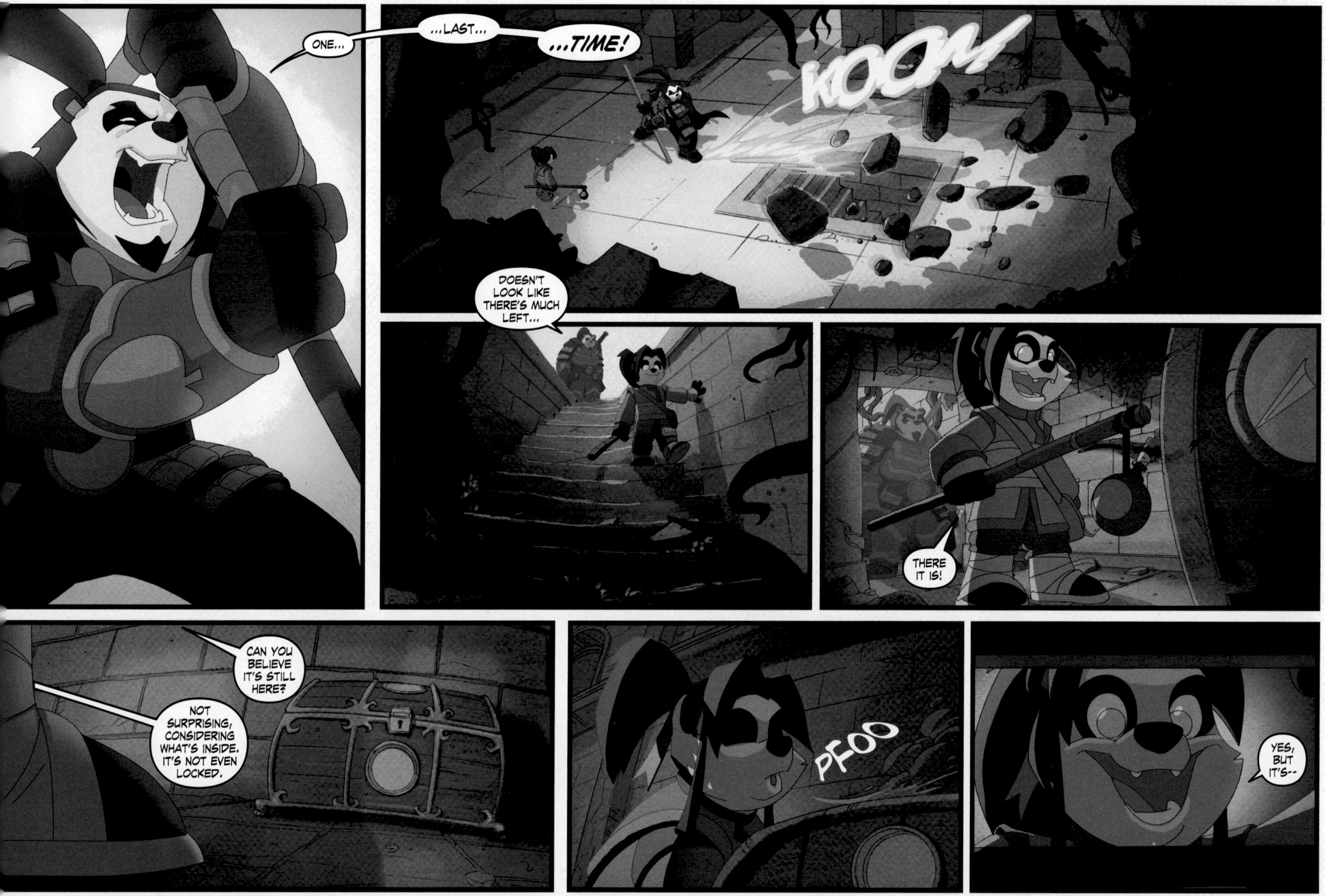
ONE...
...LAST...
...TIME!
KOOM!
DOESN'T LOOK LIKE THERE'S MUCH LEFT...
THERE IT IS!
CAN YOU BELIEVE IT'S STILL HERE?
NOT SURPRISING, CONSIDERING WHAT'S INSIDE. IT'S NOT EVEN LOCKED.
PFOO
YES, BUT IT'S--

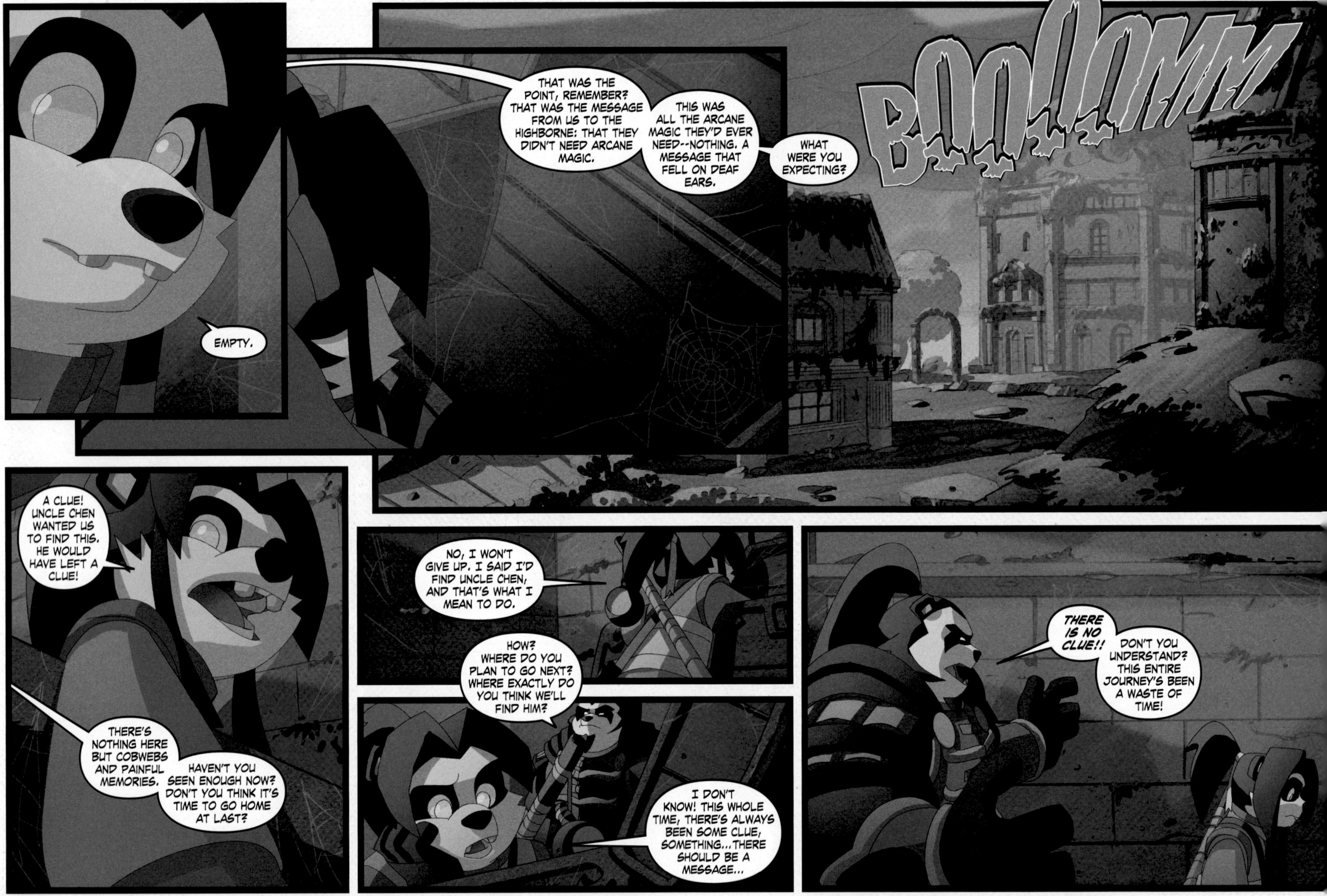
EMPTY.
THAT WAS THE POINT, REMEMBER? THAT WAS THE MESSAGE FROM US TO THE HIGHBORNE: THAT THEY DIDN'T NEED ARCANE MAGIC.
THIS WAS ALL THE ARCANE MAGIC THEY'D EVER NEED--NOTHING. A MESSAGE THAT FELL ON DEAF EARS.
WHAT WERE YOU EXPECTING?
BOOOOOMM
A CLUE! UNCLE CHEN WANTED US TO FIND THIS. HE WOULD HAVE LEFT A CLUE!
THERE'S NOTHING HERE BUT COBWEBS AND PAINFUL MEMORIES.
HAVEN'T YOU SEEN ENOUGH NOW? DON'T YOU THINK IT'S TIME TO GO HOME AT LAST?
NO, I WON'T GIVE UP. I SAID I'D FIND UNCLE CHEN, AND THAT'S WHAT I MEAN TO DO.
HOW? WHERE DO YOU PLAN TO GO NEXT? WHERE EXACTLY DO YOU THINK WE'LL FIND HIM?
I DON'T KNOW! THIS WHOLE TIME, THERE'S ALWAYS BEEN SOME CLUE, SOMETHING...THERE SHOULD BE A MESSAGE...
THERE IS NO CLUE!!
DON'T YOU UNDERSTAND? THIS ENTIRE JOURNEY'S BEEN A WASTE OF TIME!

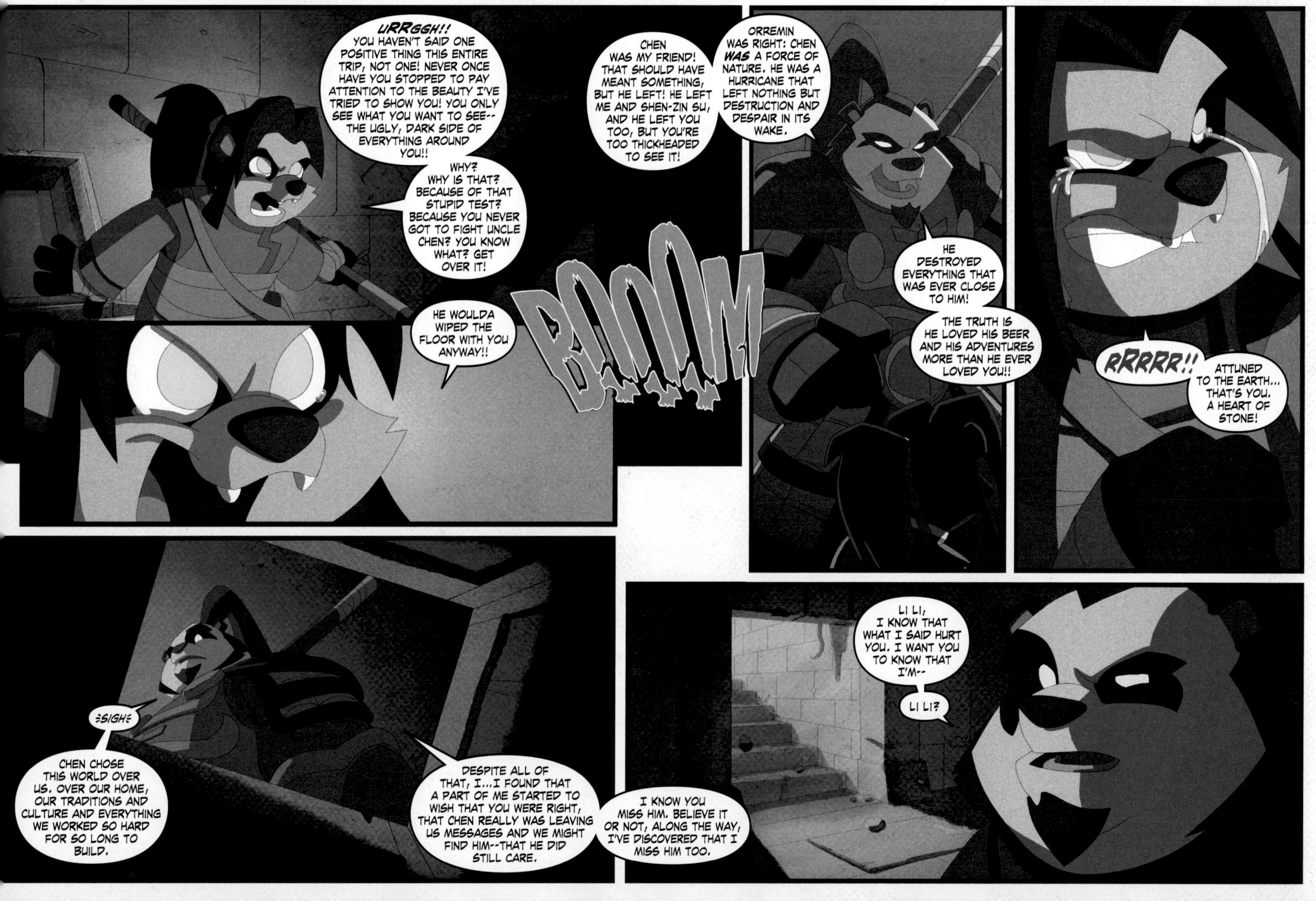
uRRggh!! YOU HAVEN'T SAID ONE POSITIVE THING THIS ENTIRE TRIP, NOT ONE! NEVER ONCE HAVE YOU STOPPED TO PAY ATTENTION TO THE BEAUTY I'VE TRIED TO SHOW YOU! YOU ONLY SEE WHAT YOU WANT TO SEE-- THE UGLY, DARK SIDE OF EVERYTHING AROUND YOU!!
WHY? WHY IS THAT? BECAUSE OF THAT STUPID TEST? BECAUSE YOU NEVER GOT TO FIGHT UNCLE CHEN? YOU KNOW WHAT? GET OVER IT!
HE WOULDA WIPED THE FLOOR WITH YOU ANYWAY!!
BOOOM
CHEN WAS MY FRIEND! THAT SHOULD HAVE MEANT SOMETHING, BUT HE LEFT! HE LEFT ME AND SHEN-ZIN SU, AND HE LEFT YOU TOO, BUT YOU'RE TOO THICKHEADED TO SEE IT!
ORREMIN WAS RIGHT: CHEN WAS A FORCE OF NATURE. HE WAS A HURRICANE THAT LEFT NOTHING BUT DESTRUCTION AND DESPAIR IN ITS WAKE.
HE DESTROYED EVERYTHING THAT WAS EVER CLOSE TO HIM!
THE TRUTH IS HE LOVED HIS BEER AND HIS ADVENTURES MORE THAN HE EVER LOVED YOU!!
RRRRR!!
ATTUNED TO THE EARTH... THAT'S YOU. A HEART OF STONE!
SIGH
CHEN CHOSE THIS WORLD OVER US. OVER OUR HOME, OUR TRADITIONS AND CULTURE AND EVERYTHING WE WORKED SO HARD FOR SO LONG TO BUILD.
DESPITE ALL OF THAT, I...I FOUND THAT A PART OF ME STARTED TO WISH THAT YOU WERE RIGHT, THAT CHEN REALLY WAS LEAVING US MESSAGES AND WE MIGHT FIND HIM--THAT HE DID STILL CARE.
I KNOW YOU MISS HIM. BELIEVE IT OR NOT, ALONG THE WAY, I'VE DISCOVERED THAT I MISS HIM TOO.
LI LI, I KNOW THAT WHAT I SAID HURT YOU. I WANT YOU TO KNOW THAT I'M--
LI LI?

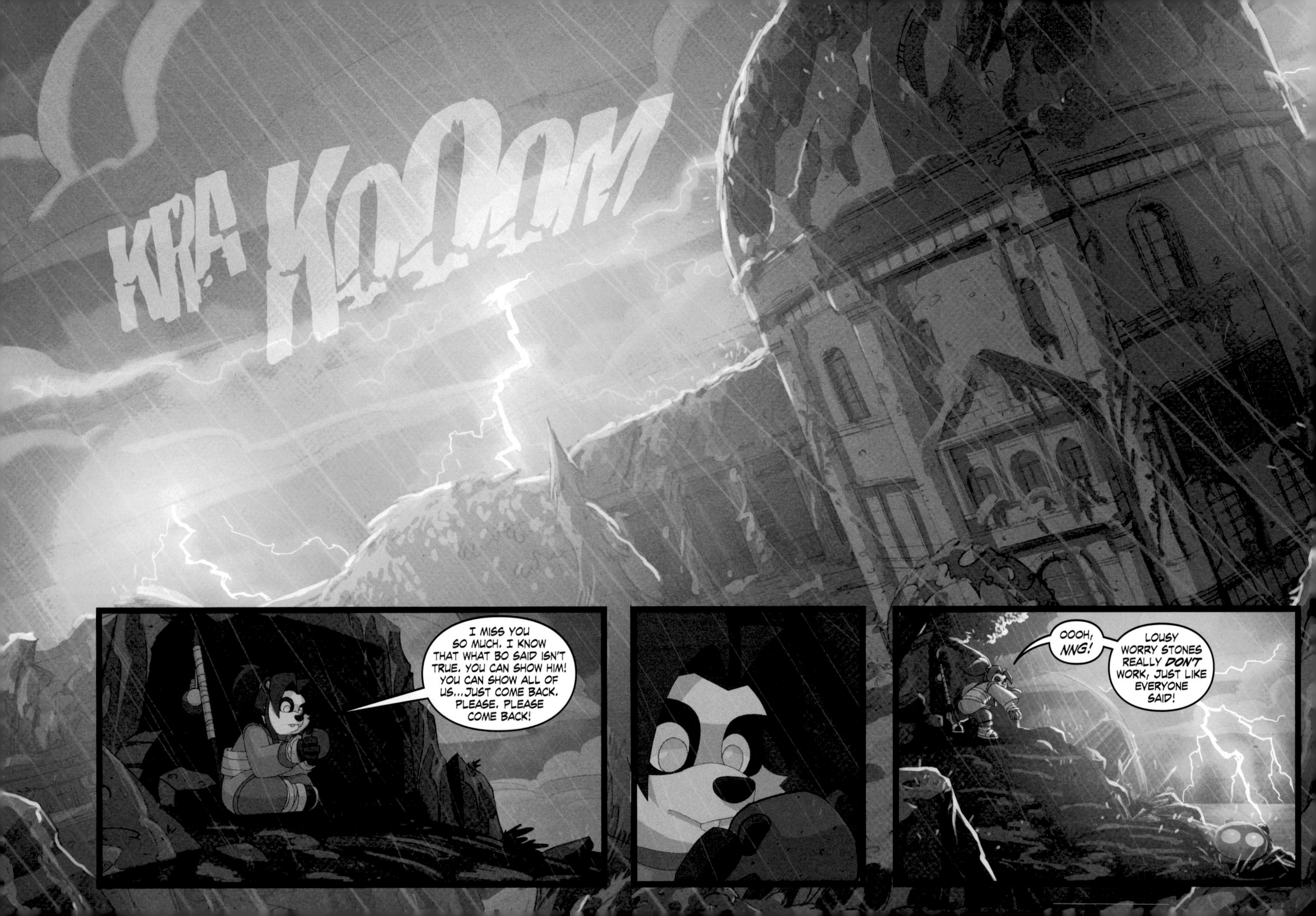
KRA KOOOOM
I MISS YOU SO MUCH. I KNOW THAT WHAT BO SAID ISN'T TRUE. YOU CAN SHOW HIM! YOU CAN SHOW ALL OF US...JUST COME BACK. PLEASE. PLEASE COME BACK!
OOOH, NNG!
LOUSY WORRY STONES REALLY DON'T WORK, JUST LIKE EVERYONE SAID!

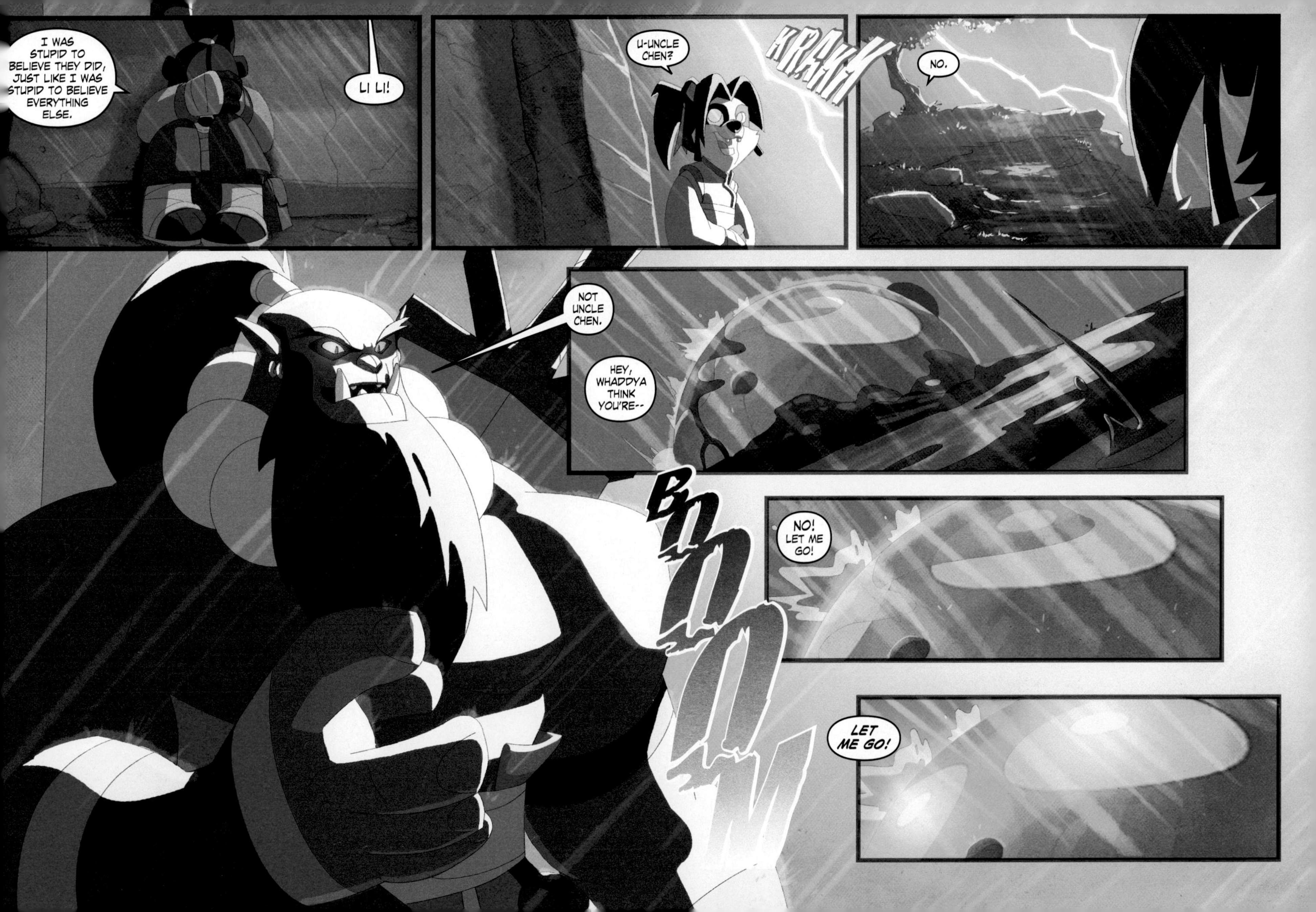
I WAS STUPID TO BELIEVE THEY DID, JUST LIKE I WAS STUPID TO BELIEVE EVERYTHING ELSE.
LI LI!
U-UNCLE CHEN?
KRAKK
NO.
NOT UNCLE CHEN.
HEY, WHADDYA THINK YOU'RE--
BOOOM
NO! LET ME GO!
LET ME GO!

CHAPTER FIVE

Journey's End

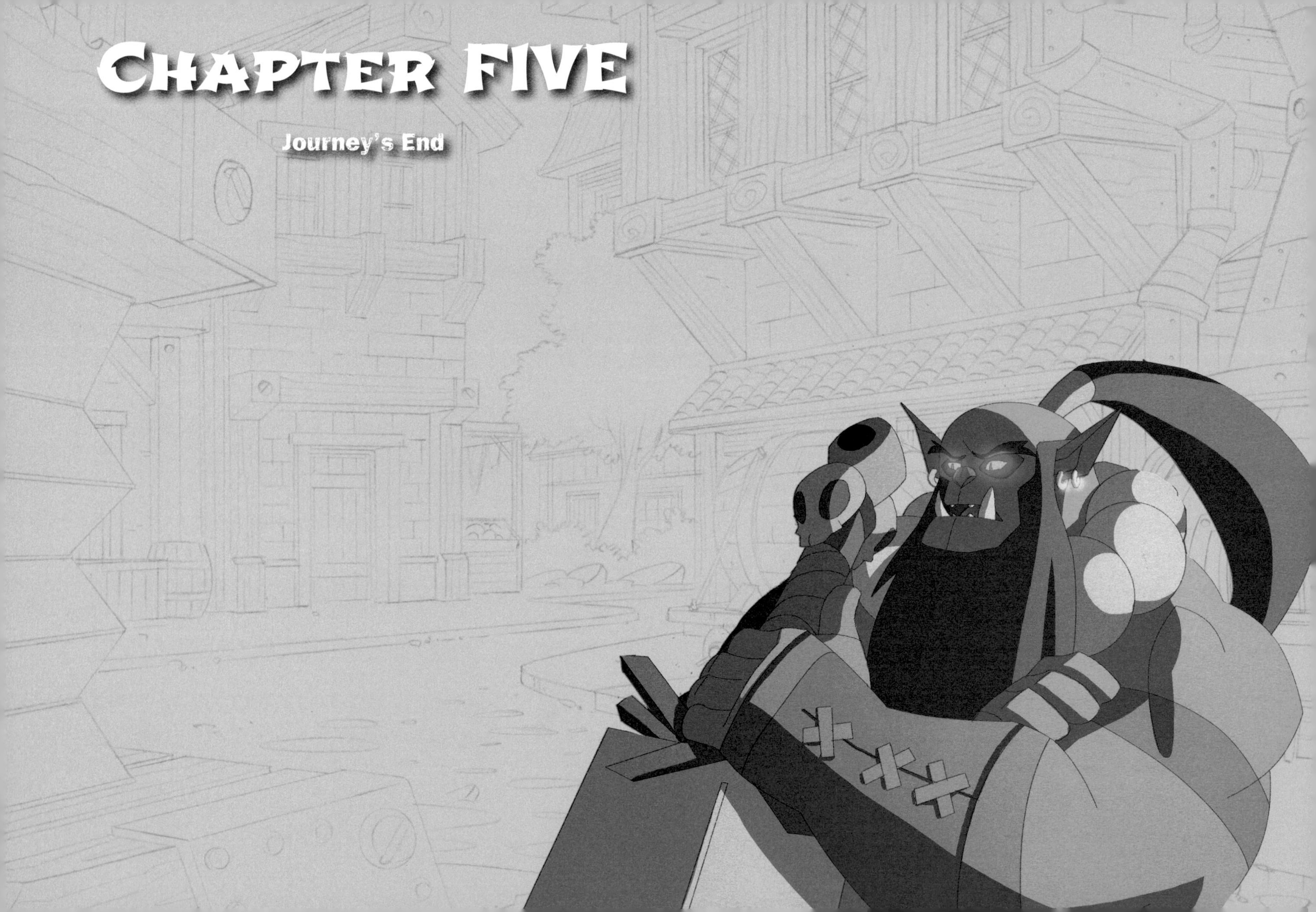

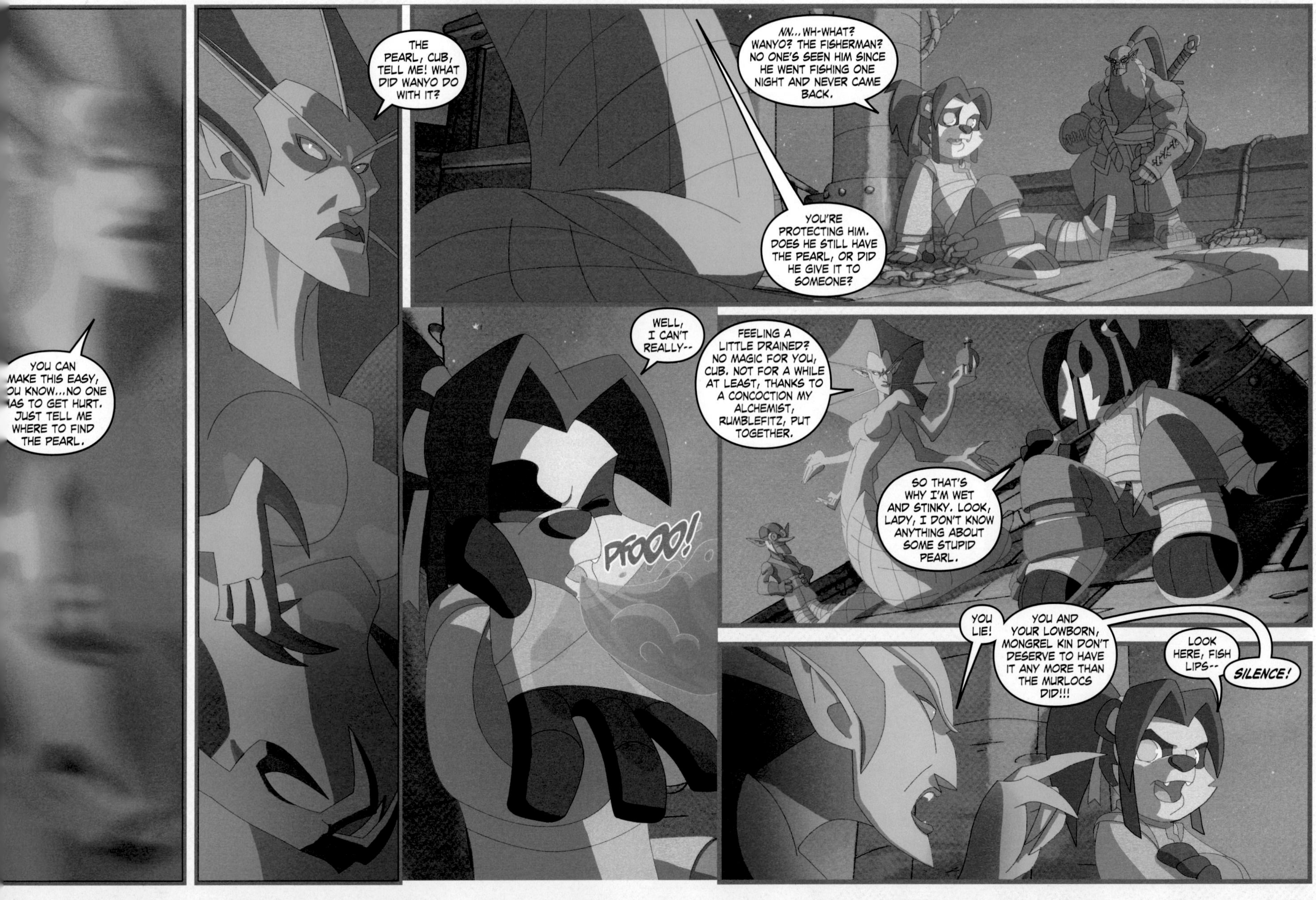
YOU CAN MAKE THIS EASY, OU KNOW...NO ONE HAS TO GET HURT. JUST TELL ME WHERE TO FIND THE PEARL.
THE PEARL, CUB, TELL ME! WHAT DID WANYO DO WITH IT?
NN...WH-WHAT? WANYO? THE FISHERMAN? NO ONE'S SEEN HIM SINCE HE WENT FISHING ONE NIGHT AND NEVER CAME BACK.
YOU'RE PROTECTING HIM. DOES HE STILL HAVE THE PEARL, OR DID HE GIVE IT TO SOMEONE?
WELL, I CAN'T REALLY--
PFOOO!
FEELING A LITTLE DRAINED? NO MAGIC FOR YOU, CUB. NOT FOR A WHILE AT LEAST, THANKS TO A CONCOCTION MY ALCHEMIST, RUMBLEFITZ, PUT TOGETHER.
SO THAT'S WHY I'M WET AND STINKY. LOOK, LADY, I DON'T KNOW ANYTHING ABOUT SOME STUPID PEARL.
YOU LIE!
YOU AND YOUR LOWBORN, MONGREL KIN DON'T DESERVE TO HAVE IT ANY MORE THAN THE MURLOCS DID!!!
LOOK HERE, FISH LIPS--
SILENCE!

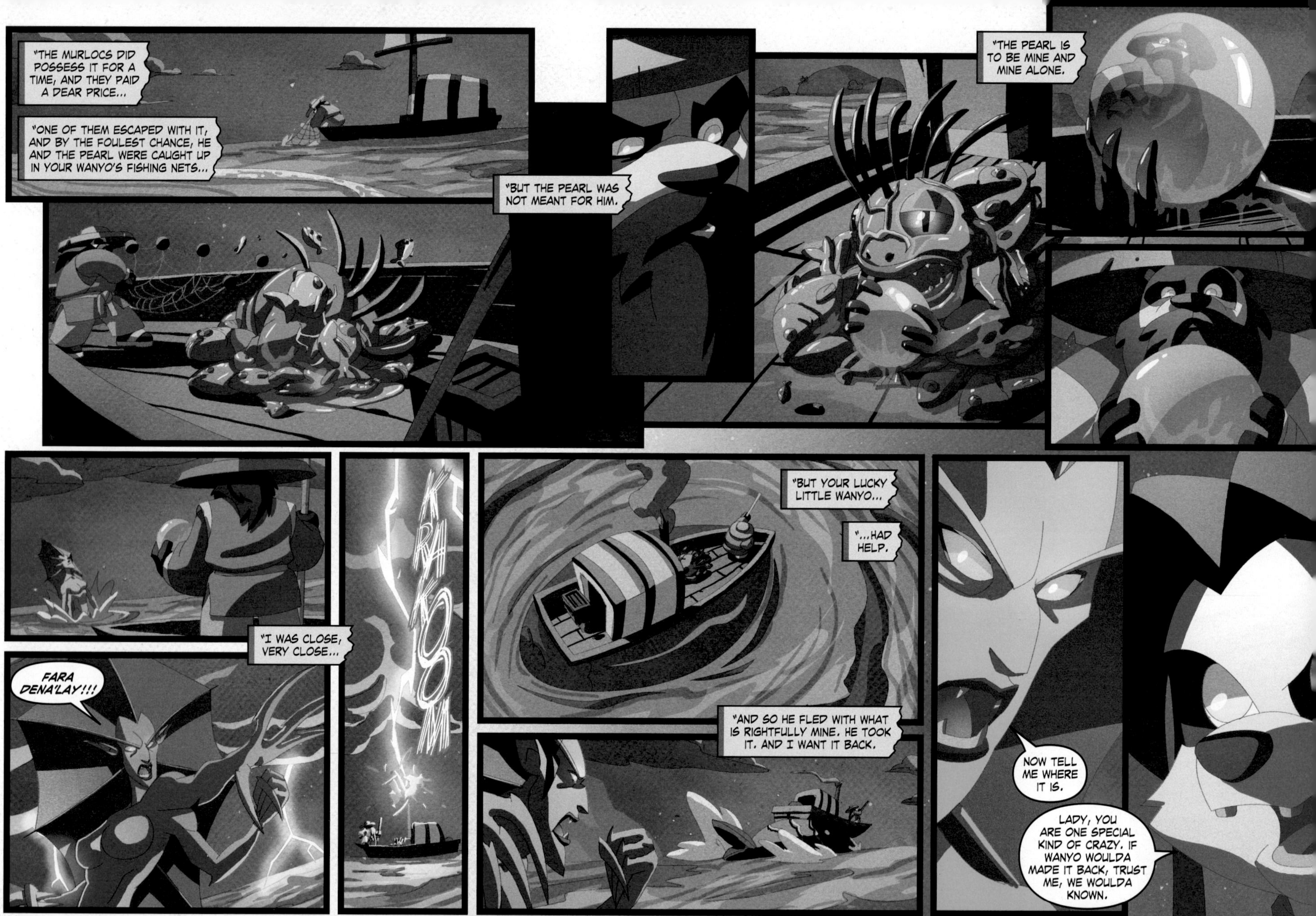
"THE MURLOCS DID POSSESS IT FOR A TIME, AND THEY PAID A DEAR PRICE...
"ONE OF THEM ESCAPED WITH IT, AND BY THE FOULEST CHANCE, HE AND THE PEARL WERE CAUGHT UP IN YOUR WANYO'S FISHING NETS...
"BUT THE PEARL WAS NOT MEANT FOR HIM.
"THE PEARL IS TO BE MINE AND MINE ALONE.
"I WAS CLOSE, VERY CLOSE...
FARA DENA'LAY!!!
KRAKOOM
"BUT YOUR LUCKY LITTLE WANYO...
"...HAD HELP.
"AND SO HE FLED WITH WHAT IS RIGHTFULLY MINE. HE TOOK IT. AND I WANT IT BACK.
NOW TELL ME WHERE IT IS.
LADY, YOU ARE ONE SPECIAL KIND OF CRAZY. IF WANYO WOULDA MADE IT BACK, TRUST ME, WE WOULDA KNOWN.

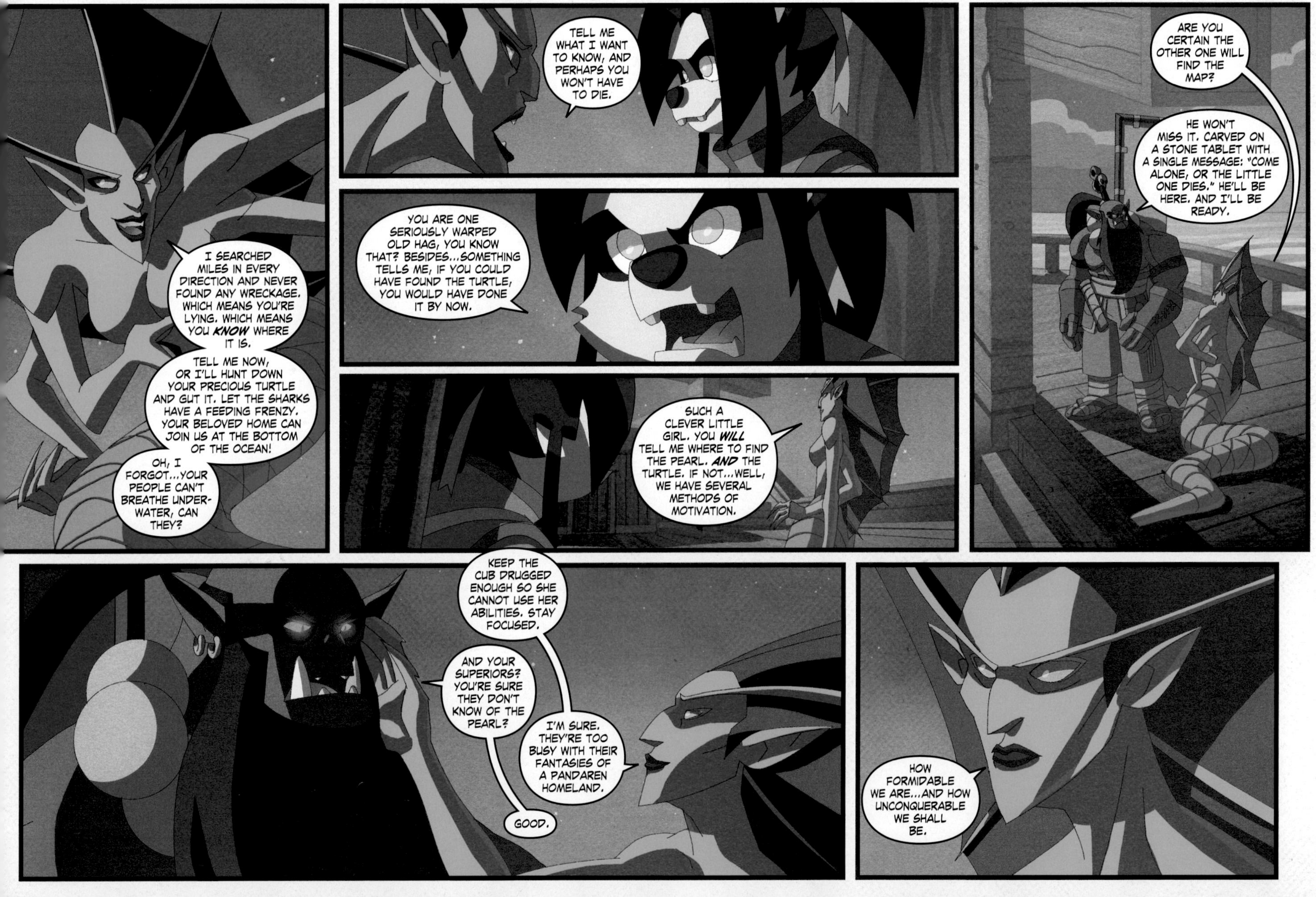
I SEARCHED MILES IN EVERY DIRECTION AND NEVER FOUND ANY WRECKAGE. WHICH MEANS YOU'RE LYING. WHICH MEANS YOU ***KNOW*** WHERE IT IS.
TELL ME NOW, OR I'LL HUNT DOWN YOUR PRECIOUS TURTLE AND GUT IT. LET THE SHARKS HAVE A FEEDING FRENZY. YOUR BELOVED HOME CAN JOIN US AT THE BOTTOM OF THE OCEAN!
OH, I FORGOT...YOUR PEOPLE CAN'T BREATHE UNDER-WATER, CAN THEY?
TELL ME WHAT I WANT TO KNOW, AND PERHAPS YOU WON'T HAVE TO DIE.
YOU ARE ONE SERIOUSLY WARPED OLD HAG, YOU KNOW THAT? BESIDES...SOMETHING TELLS ME, IF YOU COULD HAVE FOUND THE TURTLE, YOU WOULD HAVE DONE IT BY NOW.
SUCH A CLEVER LITTLE GIRL. YOU ***WILL*** TELL ME WHERE TO FIND THE PEARL. ***AND*** THE TURTLE. IF NOT...WELL, WE HAVE SEVERAL METHODS OF MOTIVATION.
ARE YOU CERTAIN THE OTHER ONE WILL FIND THE MAP?
HE WON'T MISS IT. CARVED ON A STONE TABLET WITH A SINGLE MESSAGE: "COME ALONE, OR THE LITTLE ONE DIES." HE'LL BE HERE. AND I'LL BE READY.
KEEP THE CUB DRUGGED ENOUGH SO SHE CANNOT USE HER ABILITIES. STAY FOCUSED.
AND YOUR SUPERIORS? YOU'RE SURE THEY DON'T KNOW OF THE PEARL?
I'M SURE. THEY'RE TOO BUSY WITH THEIR FANTASIES OF A PANDAREN HOMELAND.
GOOD.
HOW FORMIDABLE WE ARE...AND HOW UNCONQUERABLE WE SHALL BE.

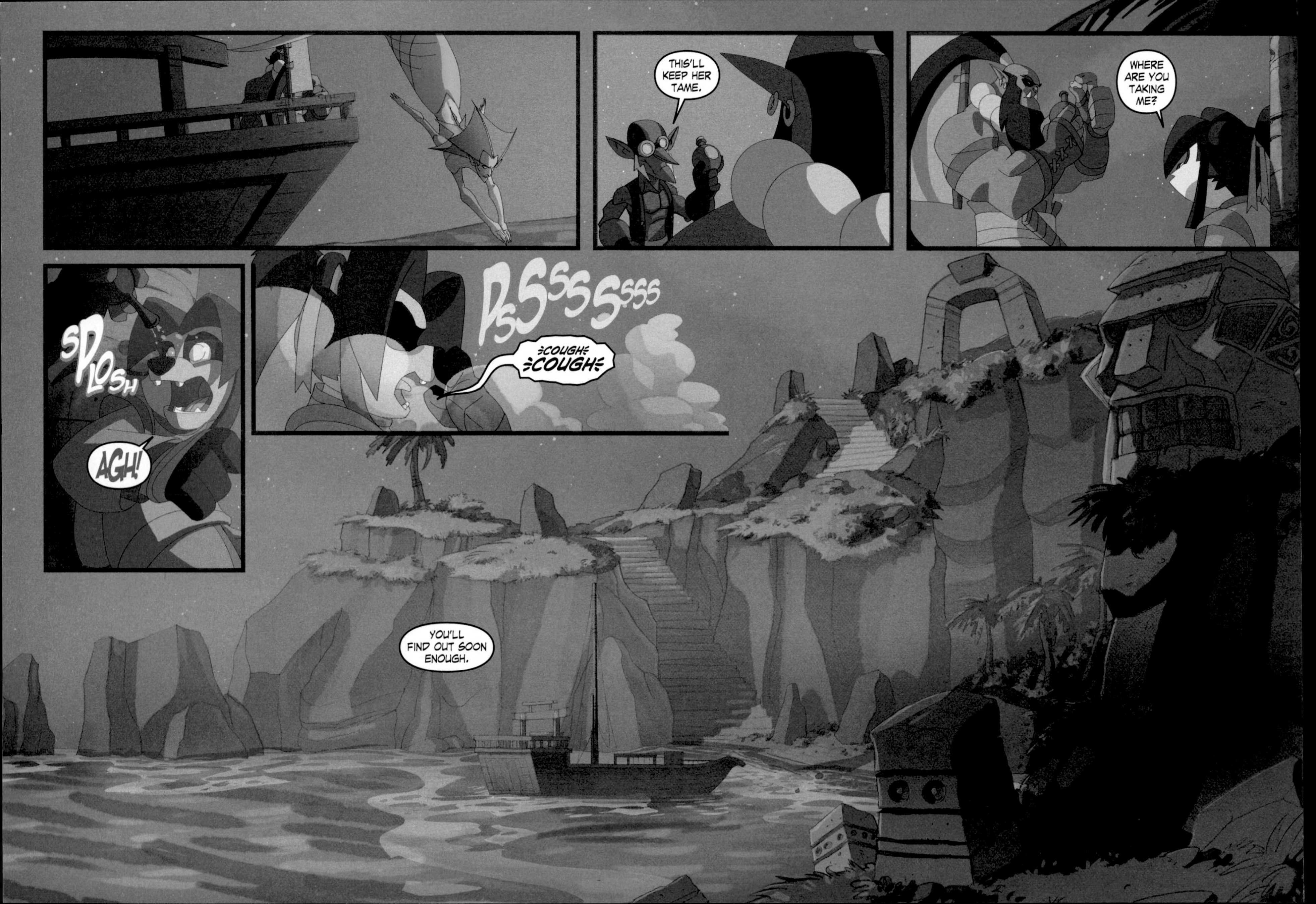
THIS'LL KEEP HER TAME.
WHERE ARE YOU TAKING ME?
SPLOSH
AGH!
PSSSSSSSS
COUGH COUGH
YOU'LL FIND OUT SOON ENOUGH.

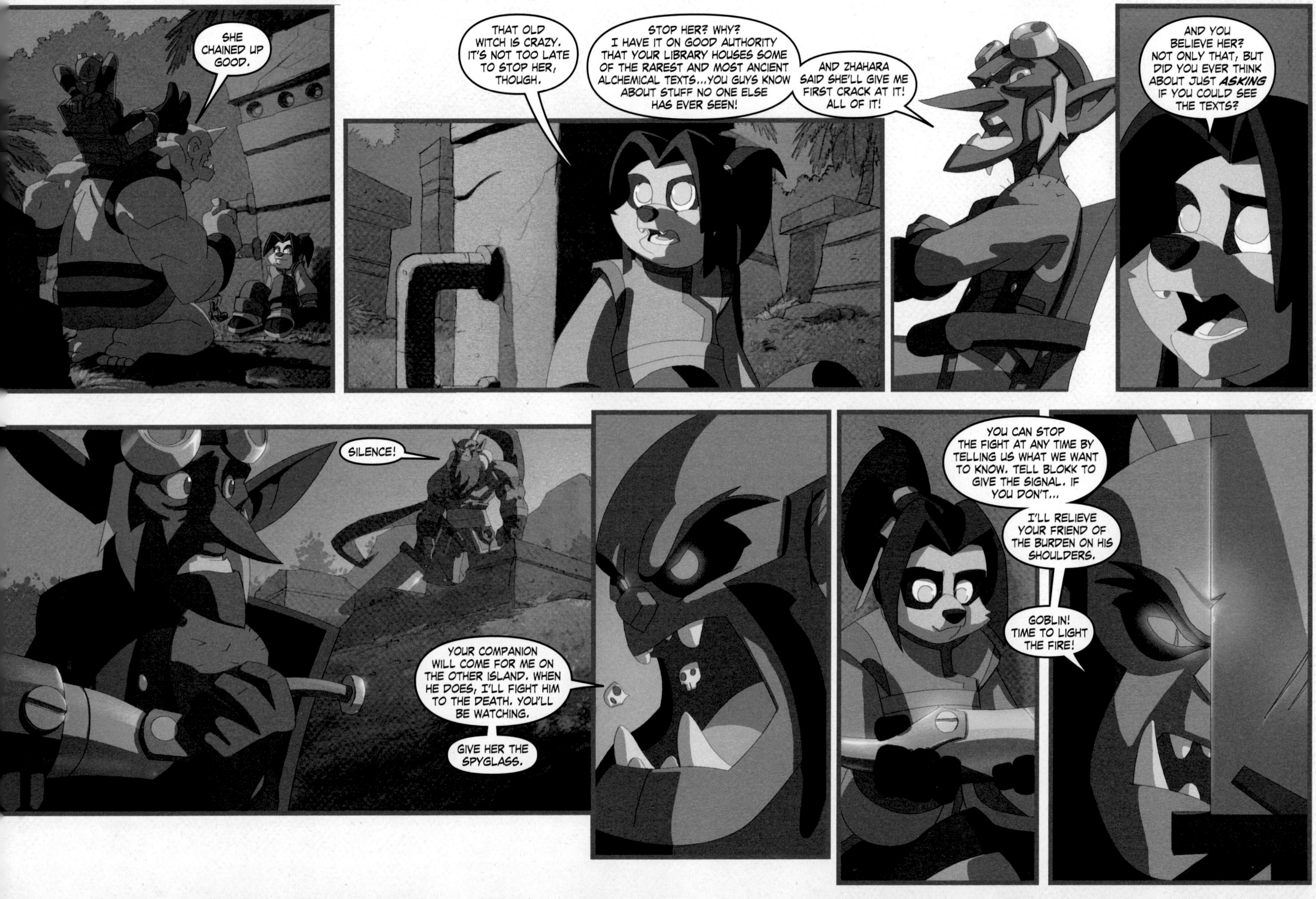
SHE CHAINED UP GOOD.
THAT OLD WITCH IS CRAZY. IT'S NOT TOO LATE TO STOP HER, THOUGH.
STOP HER? WHY? I HAVE IT ON GOOD AUTHORITY THAT YOUR LIBRARY HOUSES SOME OF THE RAREST AND MOST ANCIENT ALCHEMICAL TEXTS...YOU GUYS KNOW ABOUT STUFF NO ONE ELSE HAS EVER SEEN!
AND ZHAHARA SAID SHE'LL GIVE ME FIRST CRACK AT IT! ALL OF IT!
AND YOU BELIEVE HER? NOT ONLY THAT, BUT DID YOU EVER THINK ABOUT JUST ASKING IF YOU COULD SEE THE TEXTS?
SILENCE!
YOUR COMPANION WILL COME FOR ME ON THE OTHER ISLAND. WHEN HE DOES, I'LL FIGHT HIM TO THE DEATH. YOU'LL BE WATCHING.
GIVE HER THE SPYGLASS.
YOU CAN STOP THE FIGHT AT ANY TIME BY TELLING US WHAT WE WANT TO KNOW. TELL BLOKK TO GIVE THE SIGNAL. IF YOU DON'T...
I'LL RELIEVE YOUR FRIEND OF THE BURDEN ON HIS SHOULDERS.
GOBLIN! TIME TO LIGHT THE FIRE!

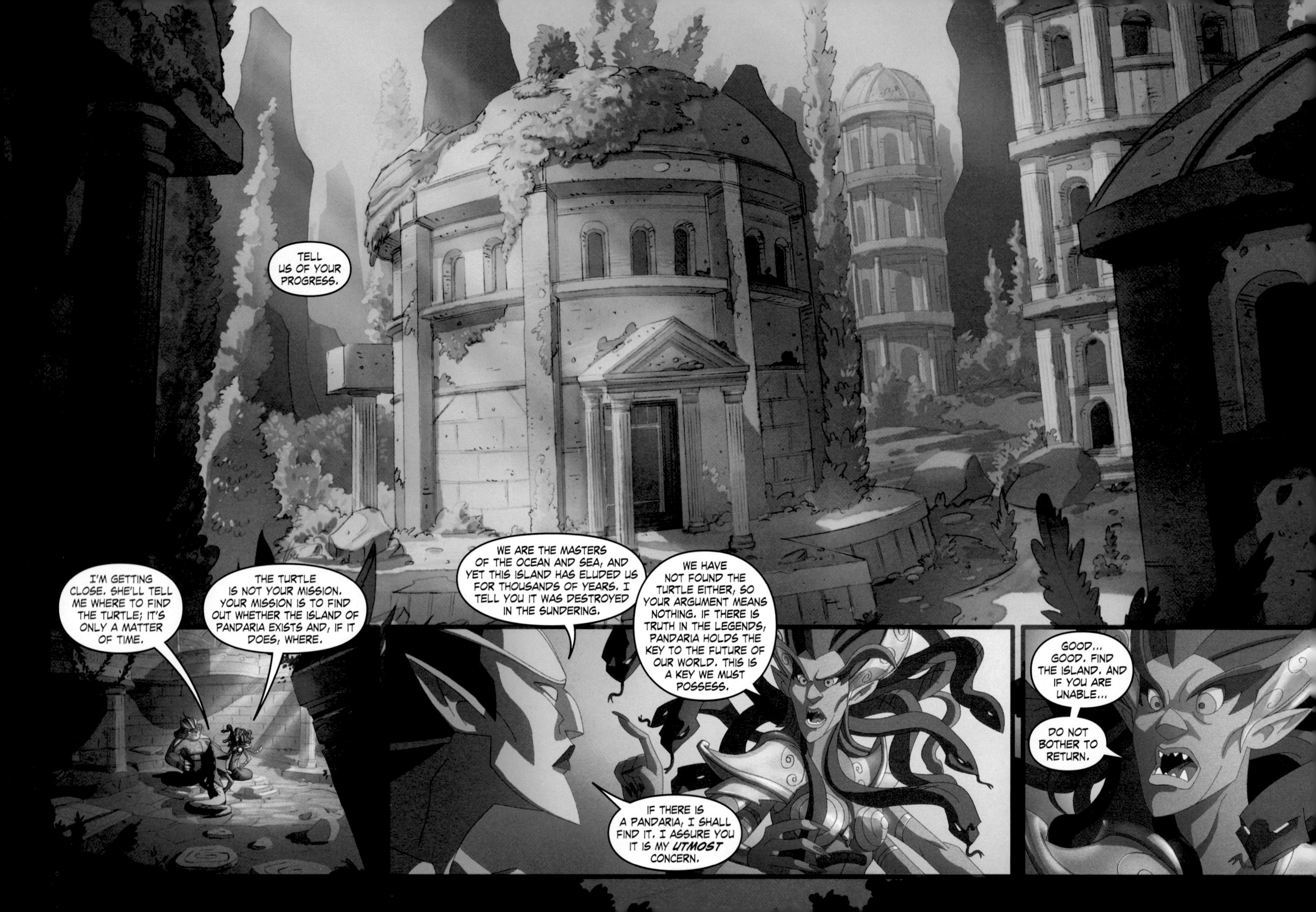
TELL US OF YOUR PROGRESS.
I'M GETTING CLOSE. SHE'LL TELL ME WHERE TO FIND THE TURTLE; IT'S ONLY A MATTER OF TIME.
THE TURTLE IS NOT YOUR MISSION. YOUR MISSION IS TO FIND OUT WHETHER THE ISLAND OF PANDARIA EXISTS AND, IF IT DOES, WHERE.
WE ARE THE MASTERS OF THE OCEAN AND SEA, AND YET THIS ISLAND HAS ELUDED US FOR THOUSANDS OF YEARS. I TELL YOU IT WAS DESTROYED IN THE SUNDERING.
WE HAVE NOT FOUND THE TURTLE EITHER, SO YOUR ARGUMENT MEANS NOTHING. IF THERE IS TRUTH IN THE LEGENDS, PANDARIA HOLDS THE KEY TO THE FUTURE OF OUR WORLD. THIS IS A KEY WE MUST POSSESS.
IF THERE IS A PANDARIA, I SHALL FIND IT. I ASSURE YOU IT IS MY *UTMOST* CONCERN.
GOOD... GOOD. FIND THE ISLAND. AND IF YOU ARE UNABLE...
DO NOT BOTHER TO RETURN.

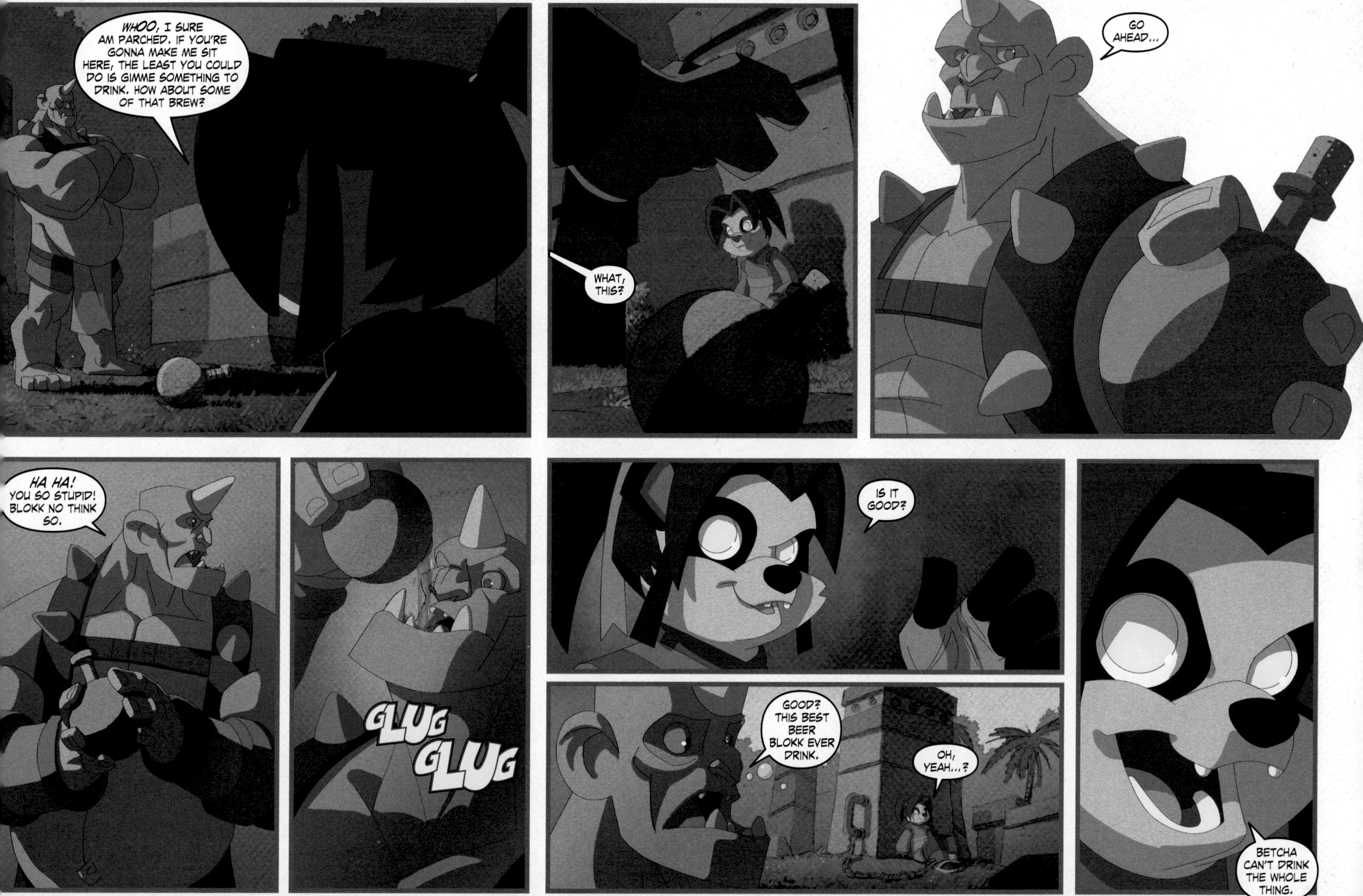
WHOO, I SURE AM PARCHED. IF YOU'RE GONNA MAKE ME SIT HERE, THE LEAST YOU COULD DO IS GIMME SOMETHING TO DRINK. HOW ABOUT SOME OF THAT BREW?
WHAT, THIS?
GO AHEAD...
HA HA! YOU SO STUPID! BLOKK NO THINK SO.
GLUG GLUG
IS IT GOOD?
GOOD? THIS BEST BEER BLOKK EVER DRINK.
OH, YEAH...?
BETCHA CAN'T DRINK THE WHOLE THING.

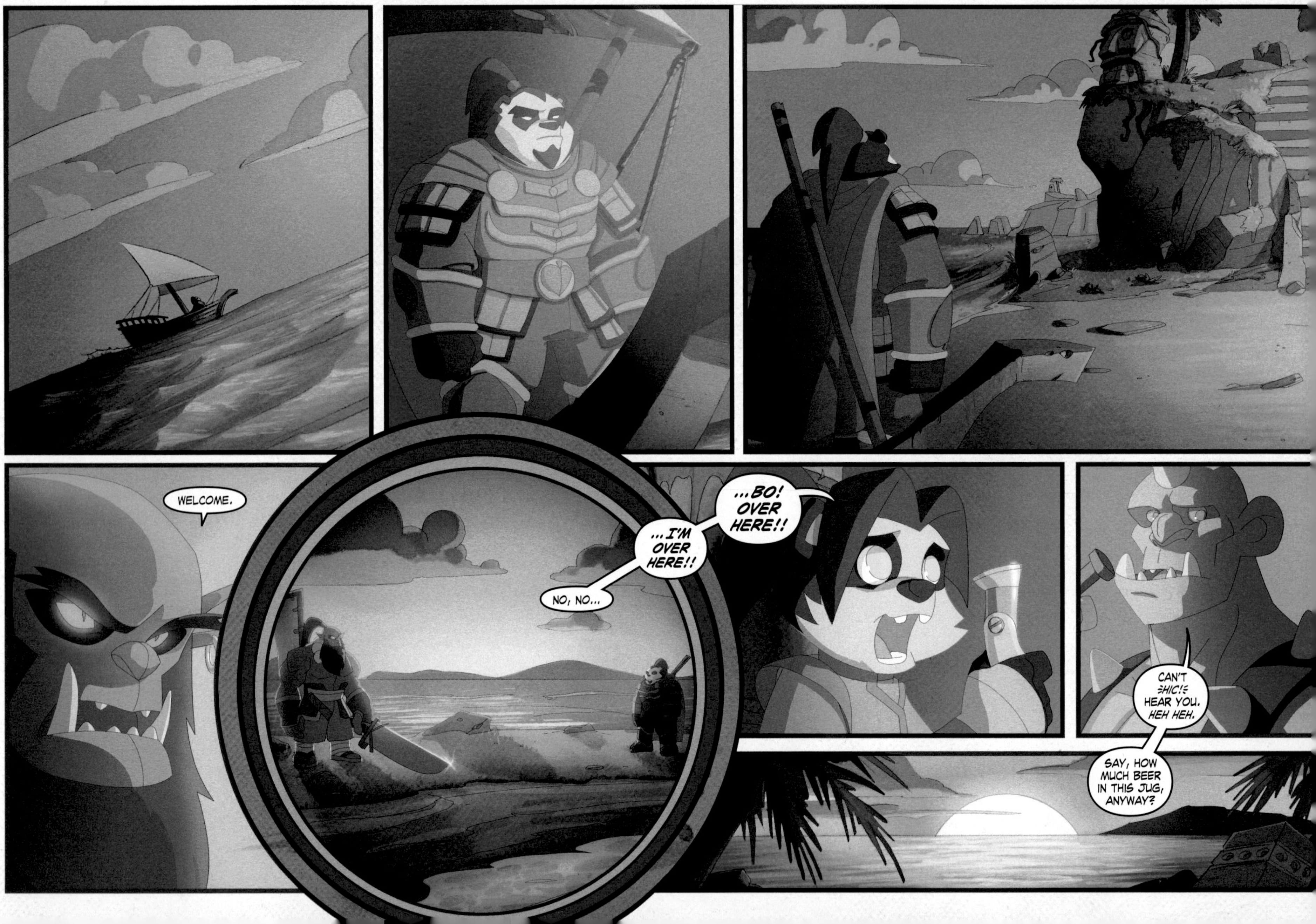
WELCOME.
NO, NO...
...I'M OVER HERE!!
...BO! OVER HERE!!
CAN'T *HIC!* HEAR YOU. HEH HEH.
SAY, HOW MUCH BEER IN THIS JUG, ANYWAY?

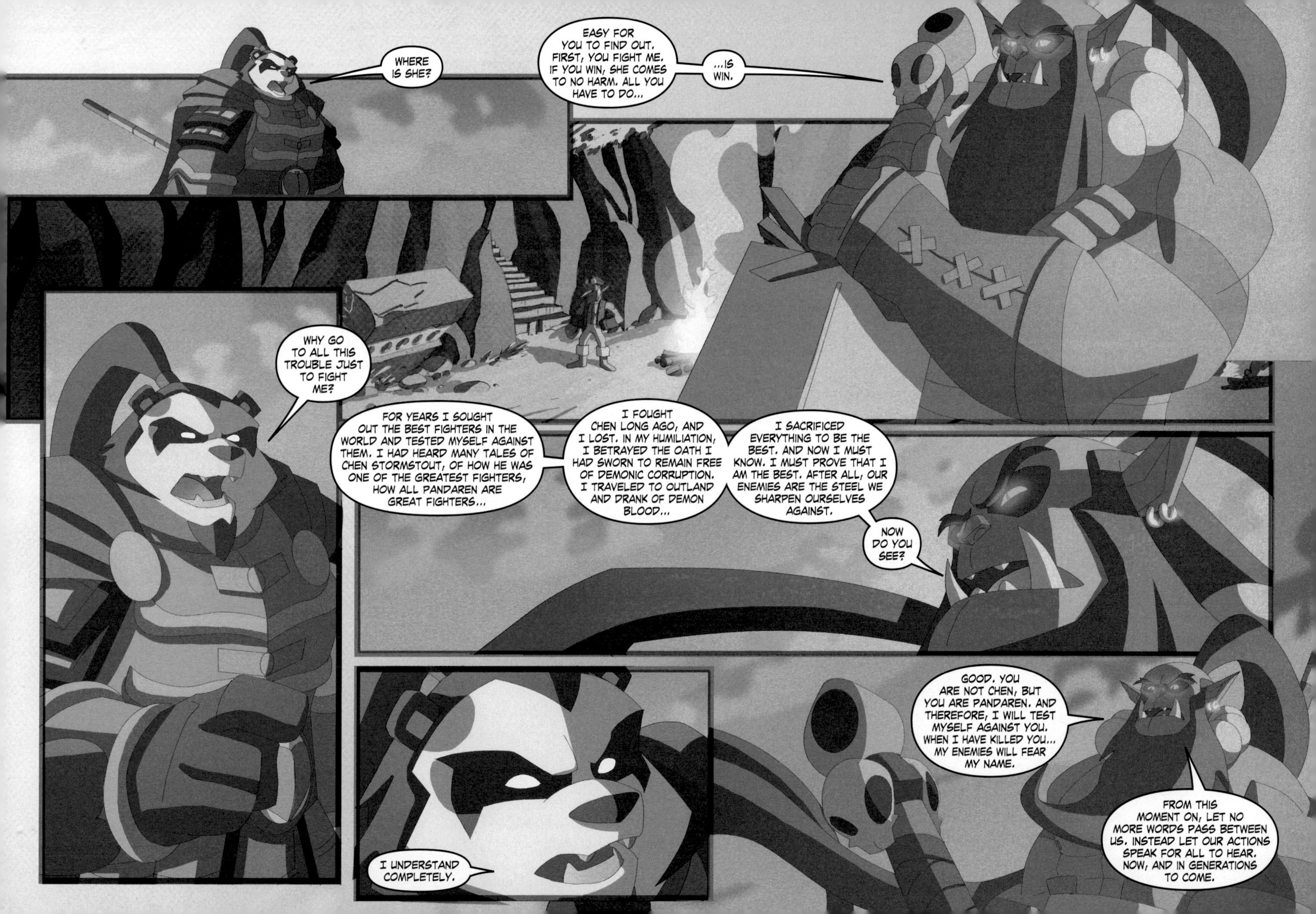
WHERE IS SHE?
EASY FOR YOU TO FIND OUT. FIRST, YOU FIGHT ME. IF YOU WIN, SHE COMES TO NO HARM. ALL YOU HAVE TO DO...
...IS WIN.
WHY GO TO ALL THIS TROUBLE JUST TO FIGHT ME?
FOR YEARS I SOUGHT OUT THE BEST FIGHTERS IN THE WORLD AND TESTED MYSELF AGAINST THEM. I HAD HEARD MANY TALES OF CHEN STORMSTOUT, OF HOW HE WAS ONE OF THE GREATEST FIGHTERS, HOW ALL PANDAREN ARE GREAT FIGHTERS...
I FOUGHT CHEN LONG AGO, AND I LOST. IN MY HUMILIATION, I BETRAYED THE OATH I HAD SWORN TO REMAIN FREE OF DEMONIC CORRUPTION. I TRAVELED TO OUTLAND AND DRANK OF DEMON BLOOD...
I SACRIFICED EVERYTHING TO BE THE BEST. AND NOW I MUST KNOW. I MUST PROVE THAT I AM THE BEST. AFTER ALL, OUR ENEMIES ARE THE STEEL WE SHARPEN OURSELVES AGAINST.
NOW DO YOU SEE?
I UNDERSTAND COMPLETELY.
GOOD. YOU ARE NOT CHEN, BUT YOU ARE PANDAREN. AND THEREFORE, I WILL TEST MYSELF AGAINST YOU. WHEN I HAVE KILLED YOU... MY ENEMIES WILL FEAR MY NAME.
FROM THIS MOMENT ON, LET NO MORE WORDS PASS BETWEEN US. INSTEAD LET OUR ACTIONS SPEAK FOR ALL TO HEAR. NOW, AND IN GENERATIONS TO COME.

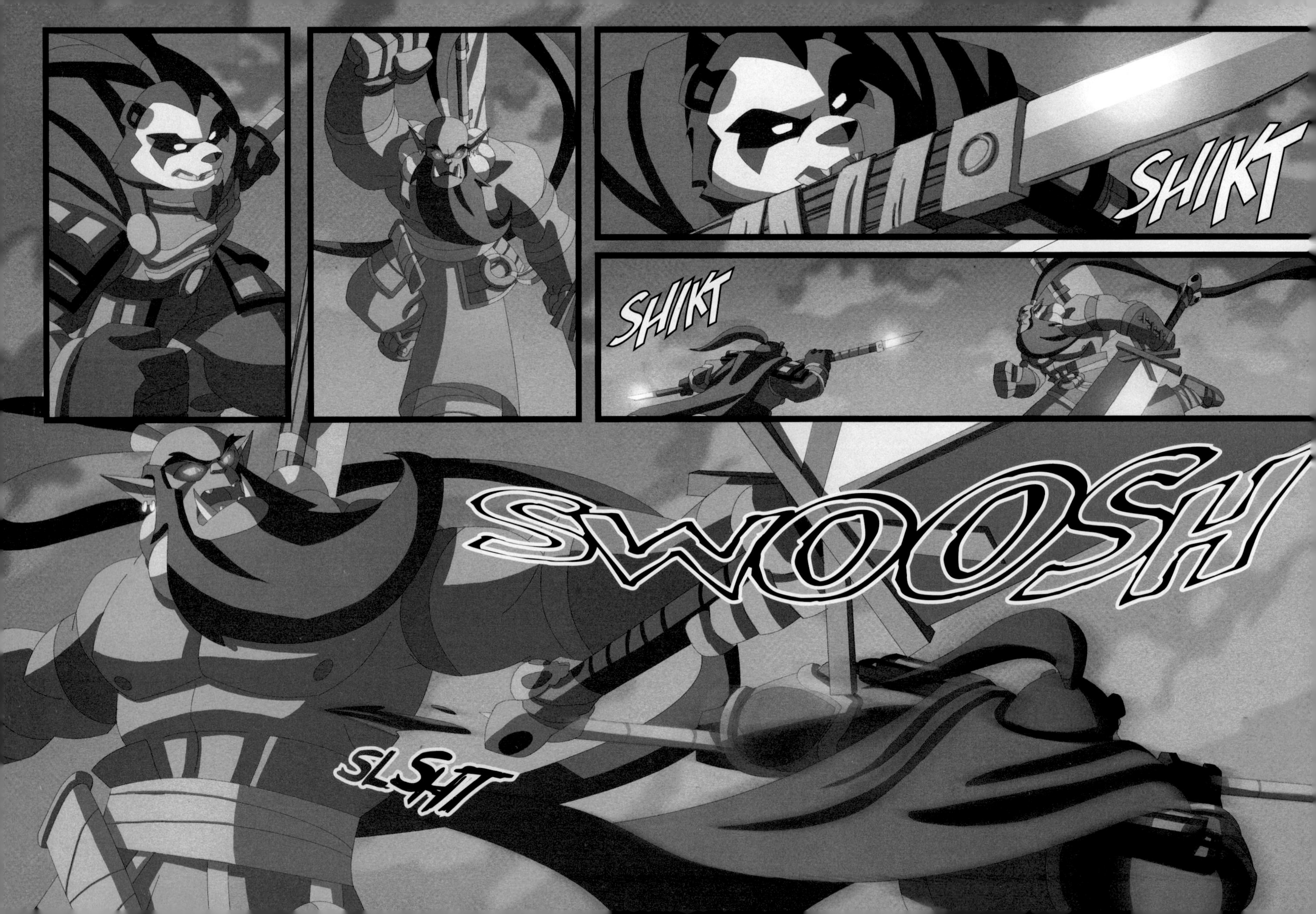
SHIKT
SHIKT
SWOOSH
SLSHT

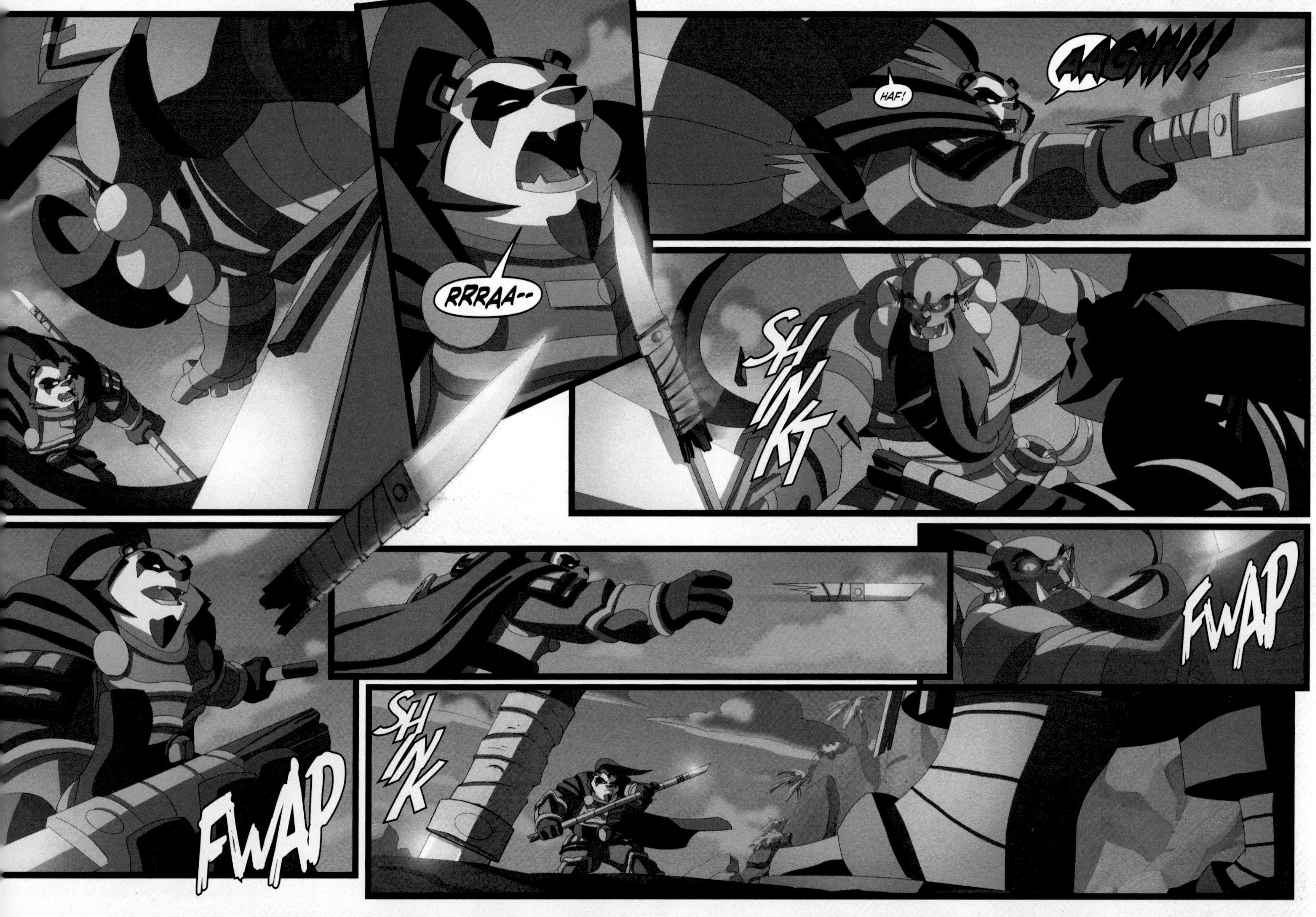
RRRAA--
HAF!
AAGHH!!
SHINKT
FWAP
FWAP
SHINK

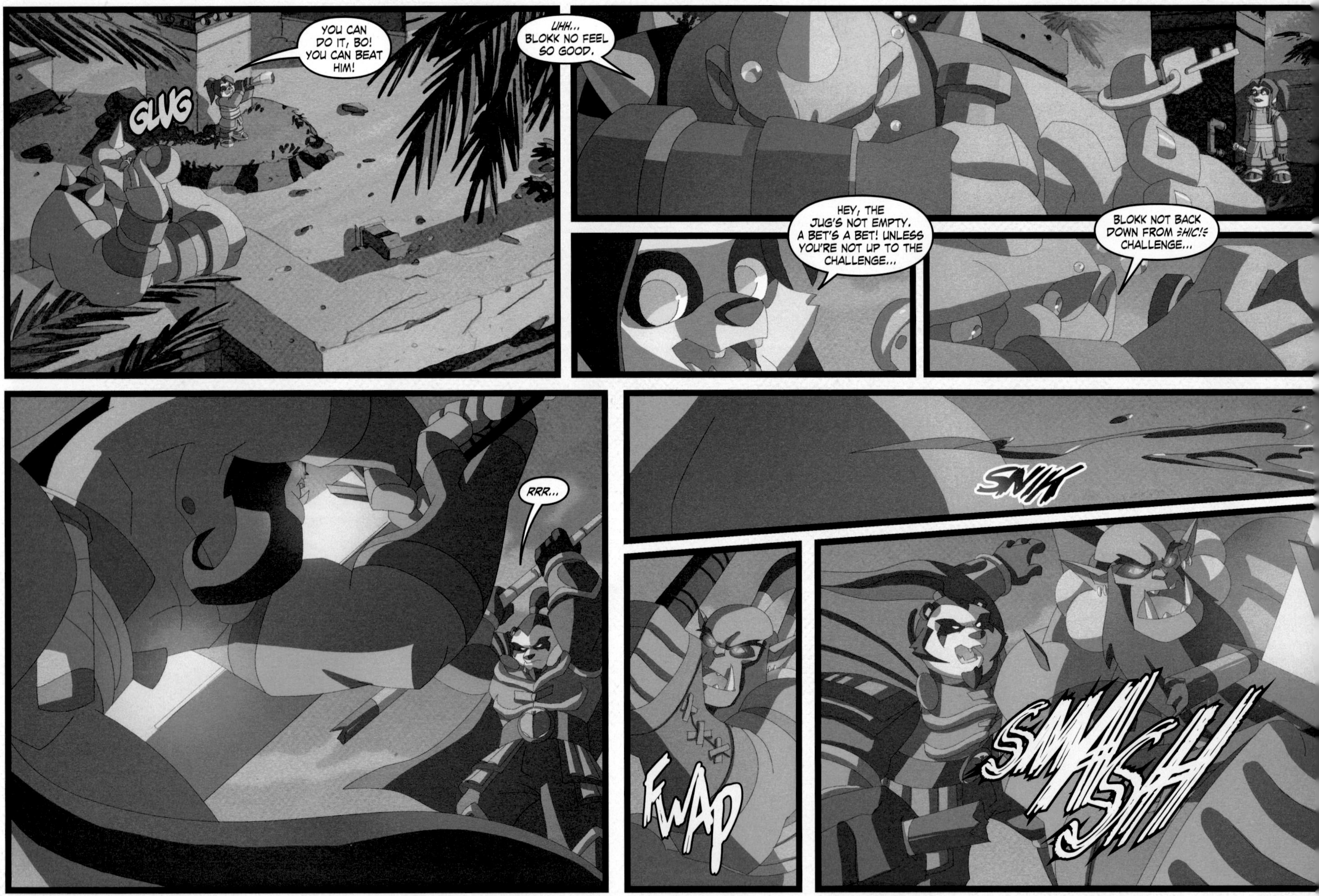
YOU CAN DO IT, BO! YOU CAN BEAT HIM!
GLUG
UHH... BLOKK NO FEEL SO GOOD.
HEY, THE JUG'S NOT EMPTY. A BET'S A BET! UNLESS YOU'RE NOT UP TO THE CHALLENGE...
BLOKK NOT BACK DOWN FROM *HIC!* CHALLENGE...
RRR...
SNIK
FWAP
SMASH

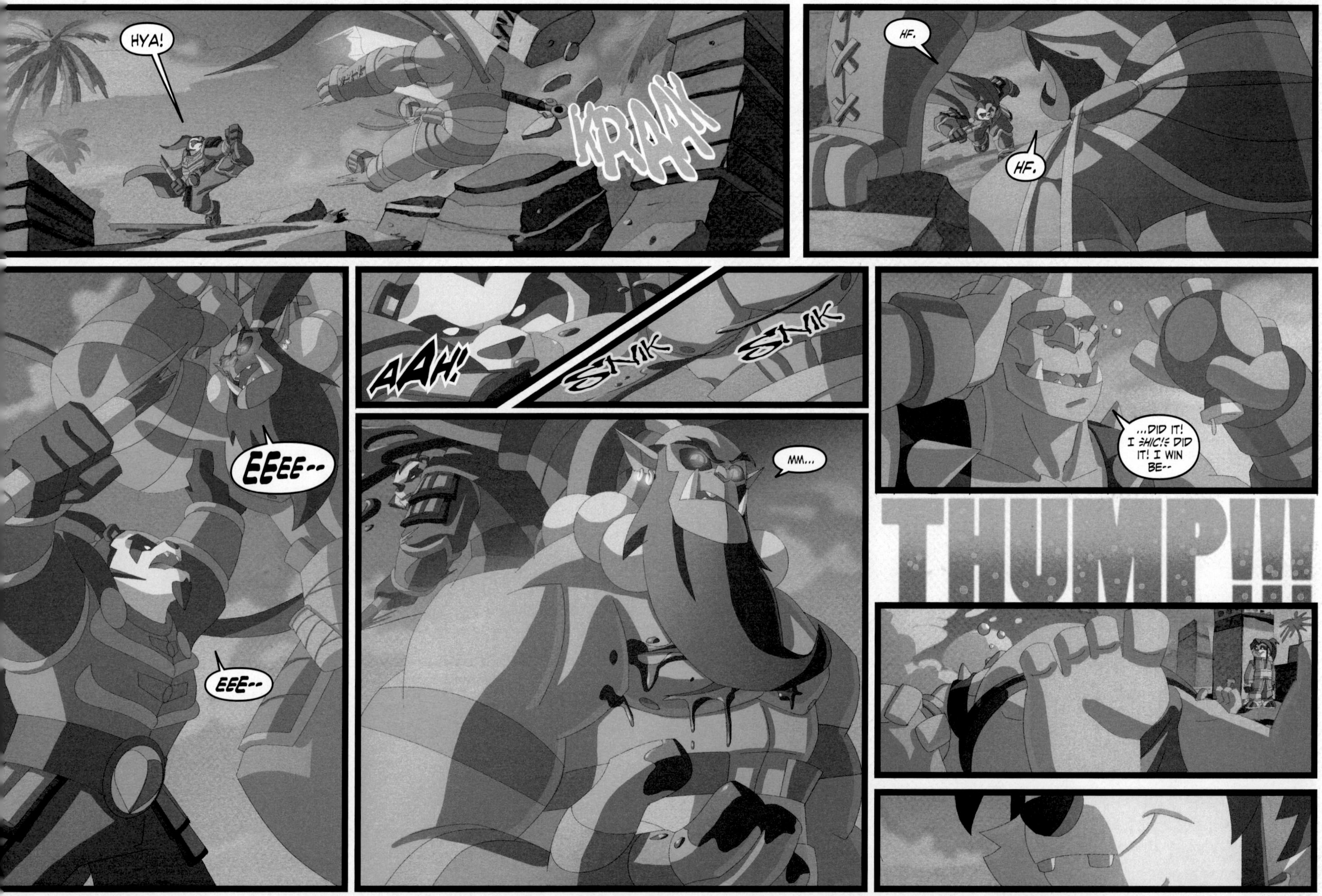
HYA!
KRAAK
HF.
HF.
EEEE--
EEE--
AAH!
SNIK
SNIK
MM...
...DID IT! I HIC! DID IT! I WIN BE--
THUMP!!!!

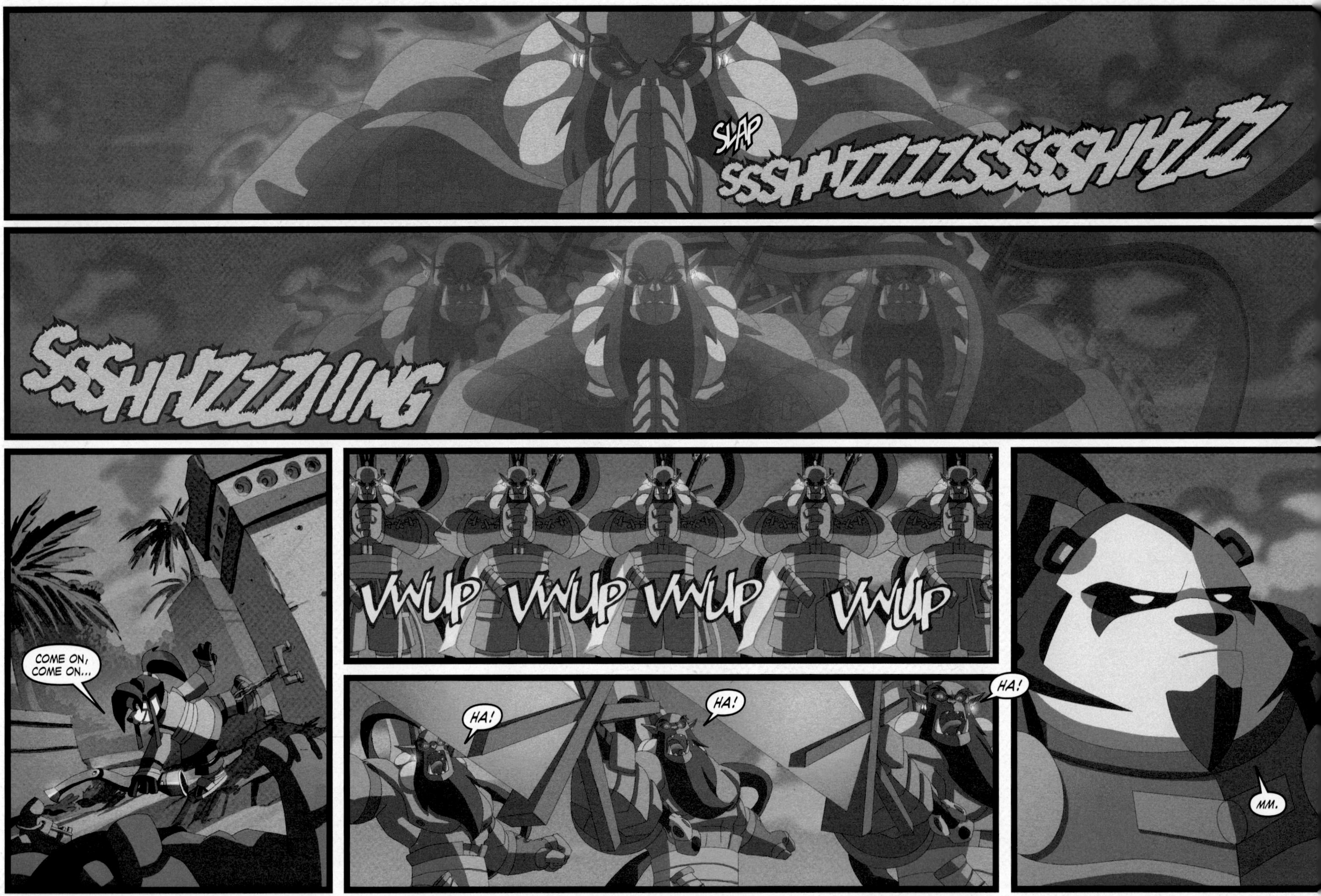
SLAP
SSSHHZZZZZZSSSSSHHZZZ
SSSHHZZZZIING
COME ON, COME ON...
VWUP
VWUP
VWUP
VWUP
HA!
HA!
HA!
MM.

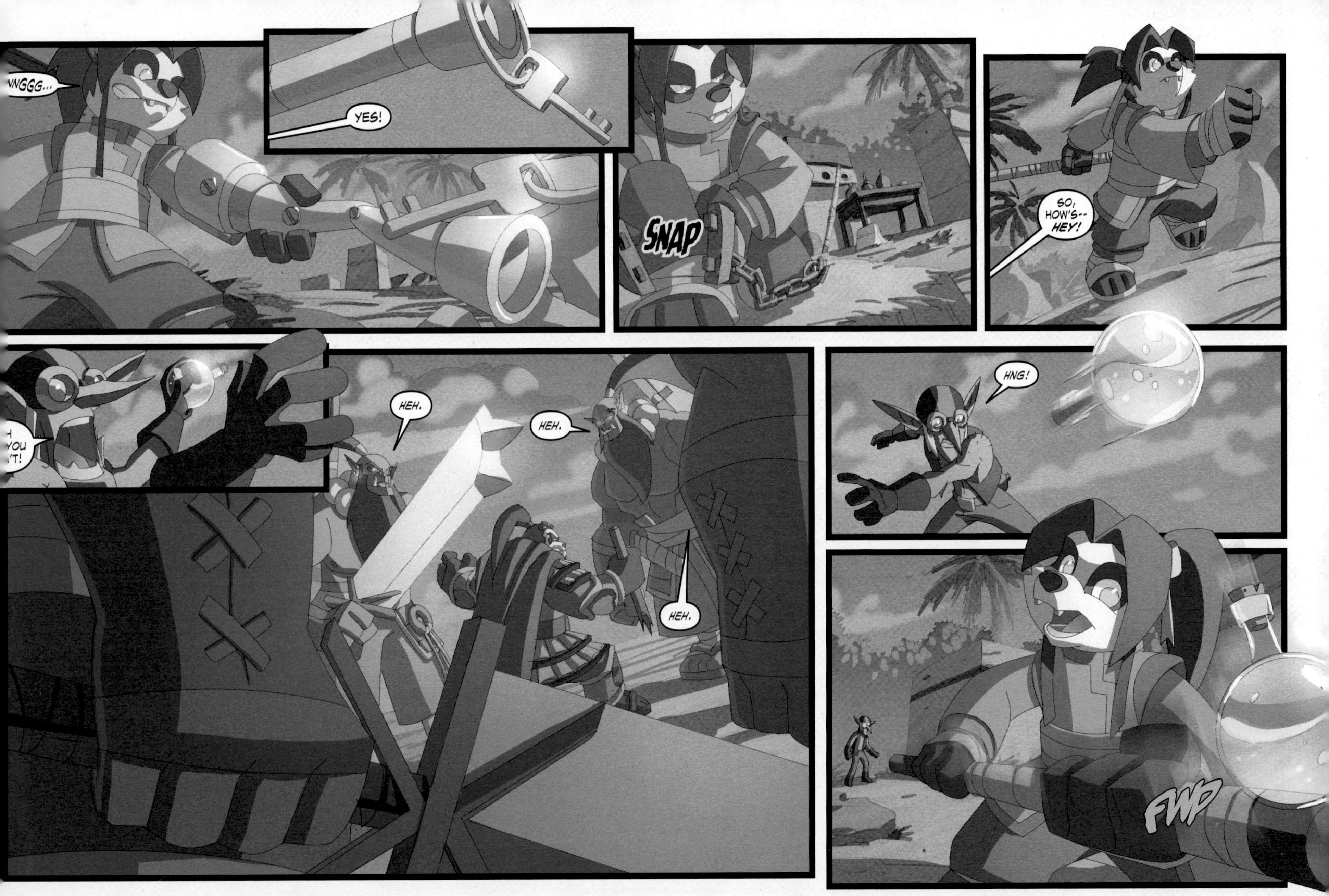
NNGGG...
YES!
SNAP
SO, HOW'S-- HEY!
HEH.
HEH.
HEH.
HNG!
FWP

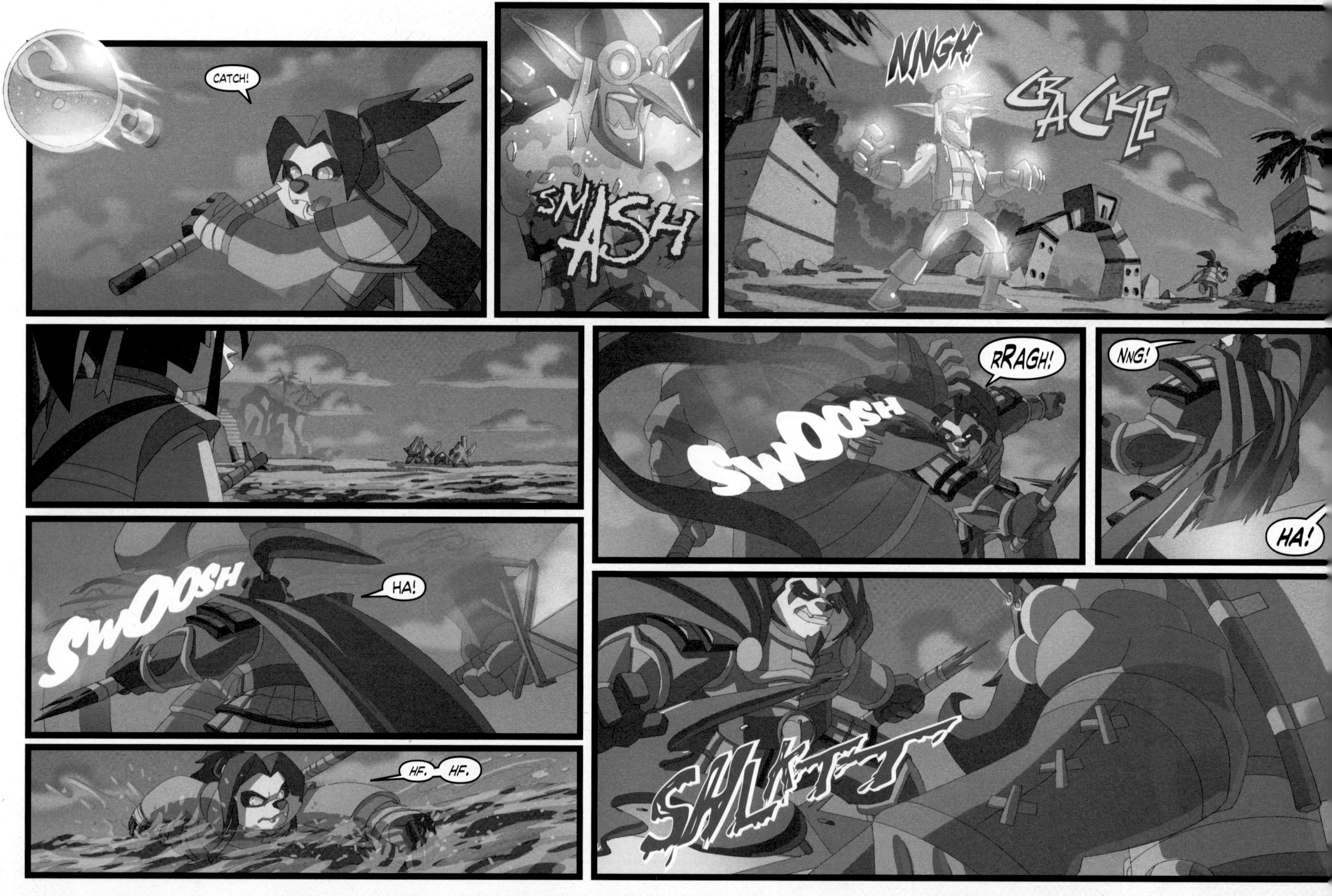
CATCH!
SMASH
NNGH!
CRACKLE
RRAGH!
SWOOSH
NNG!
HA!
SWOOSH
HA!
HF. HF.
SHKTT

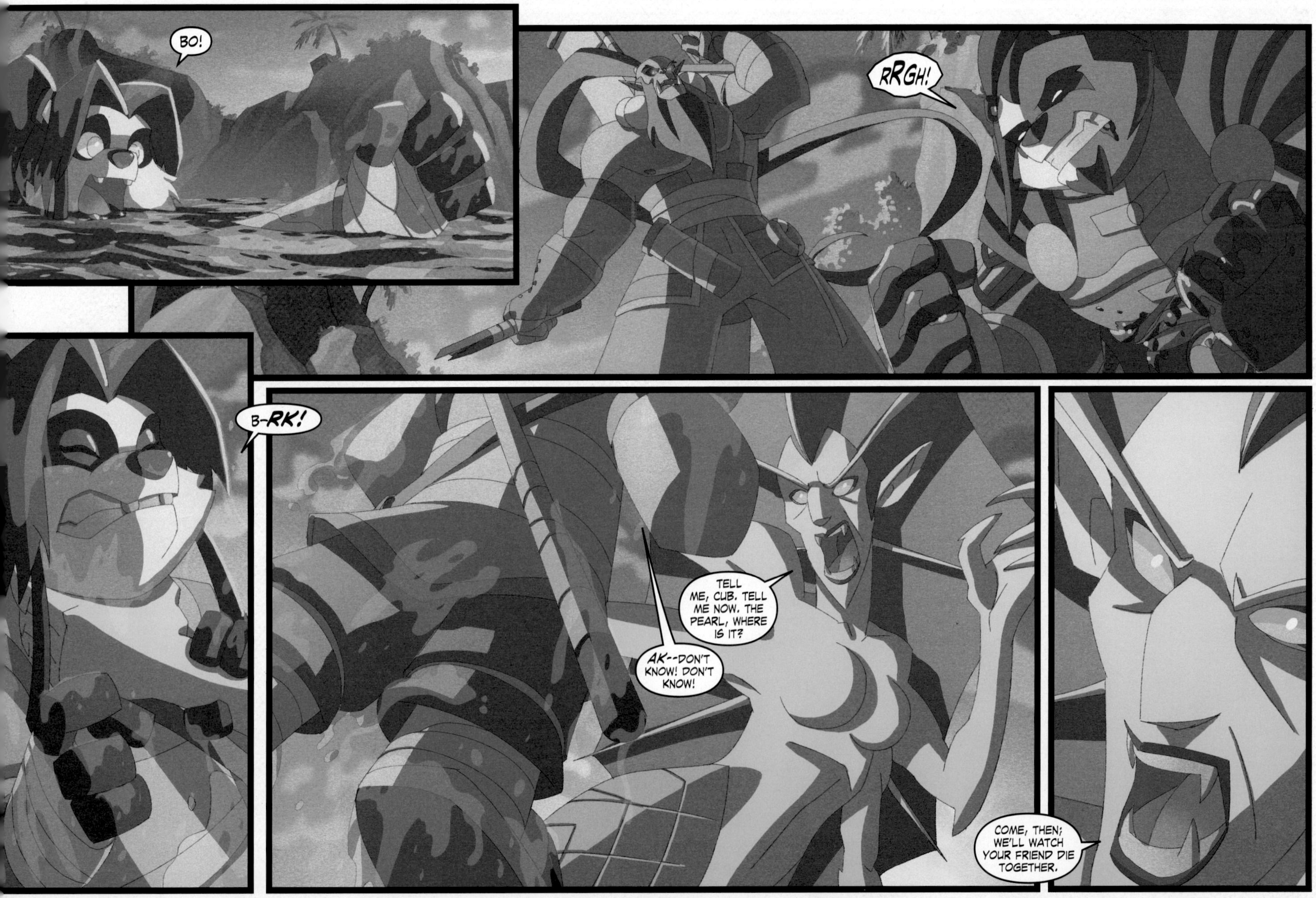

BO!
RRGH!
B-RK!
TELL ME, CUB. TELL ME NOW. THE PEARL, WHERE IS IT?
AK--DON'T KNOW! DON'T KNOW!
COME, THEN; WE'LL WATCH YOUR FRIEND DIE TOGETHER.

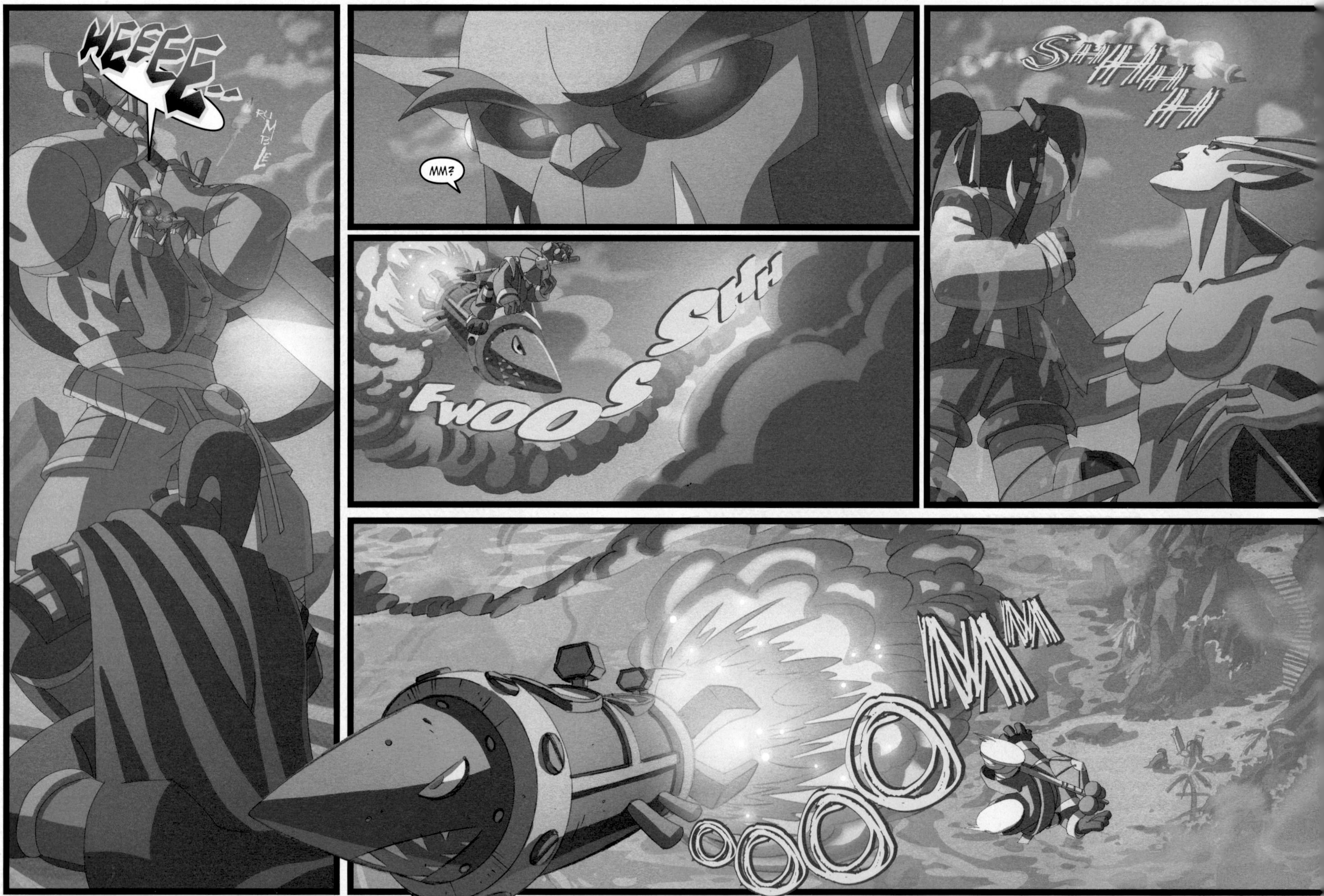

HEEEE...
RUMBLE
MM?
FWOOSSHH
SHHHHHH

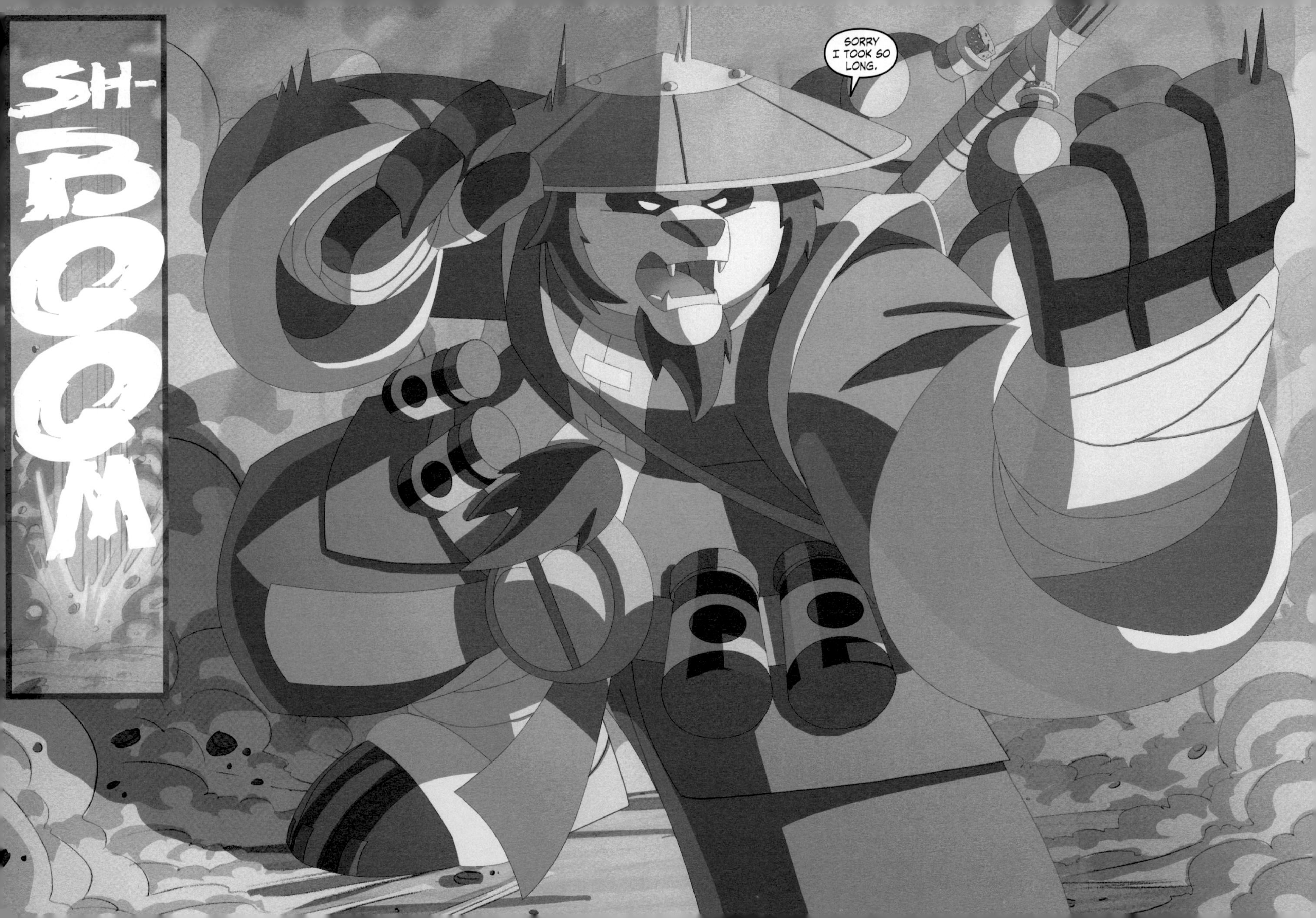
SH-BOOM
SORRY I TOOK SO LONG.

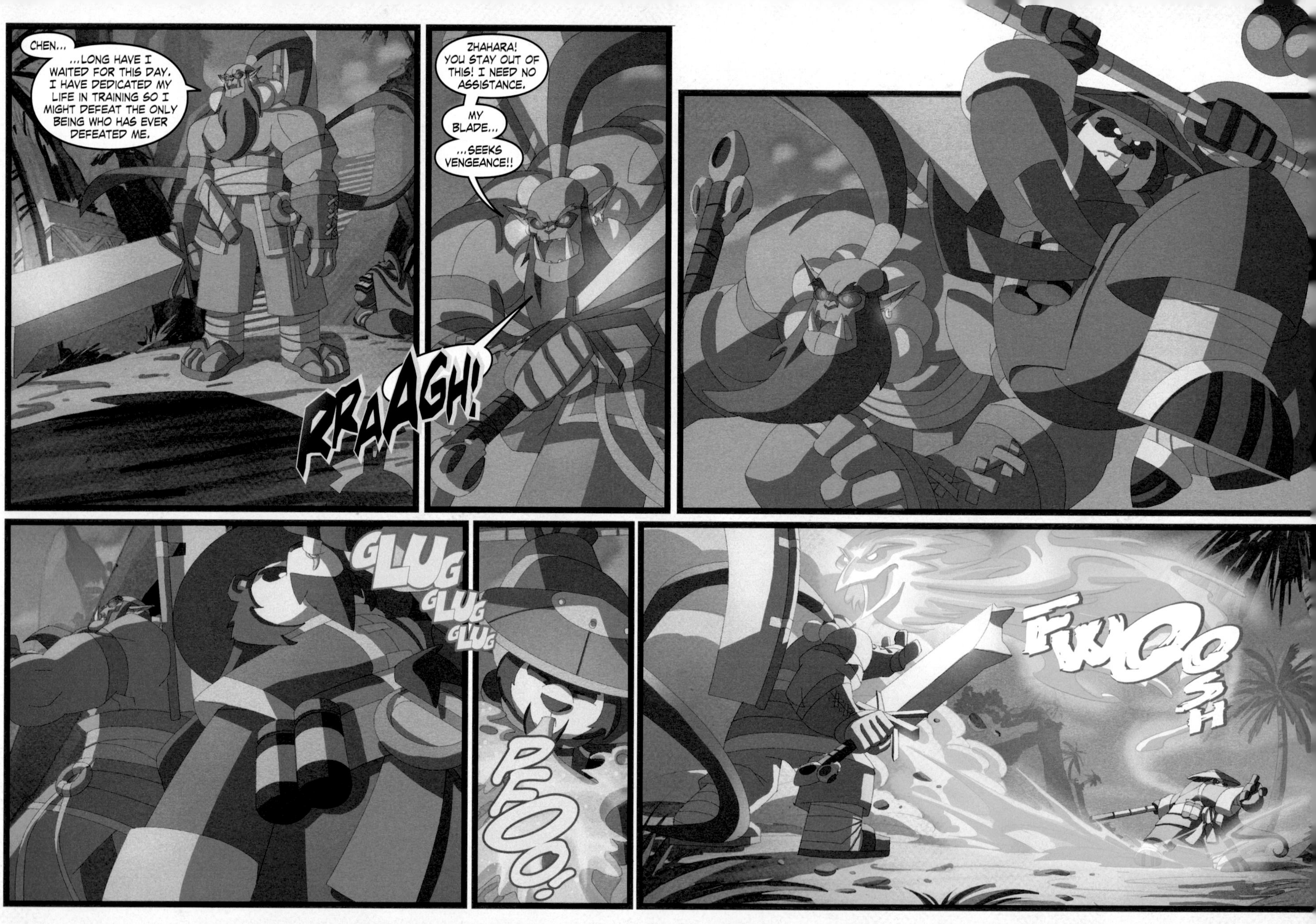
CHEN...
...LONG HAVE I WAITED FOR THIS DAY. I HAVE DEDICATED MY LIFE IN TRAINING SO I MIGHT DEFEAT THE ONLY BEING WHO HAS EVER DEFEATED ME.
RRAAGH!
ZHAHARA! YOU STAY OUT OF THIS! I NEED NO ASSISTANCE.
MY BLADE...
...SEEKS VENGEANCE!!
GLUG
GLUG
GLUG
PFOOO!
FWOOOSH

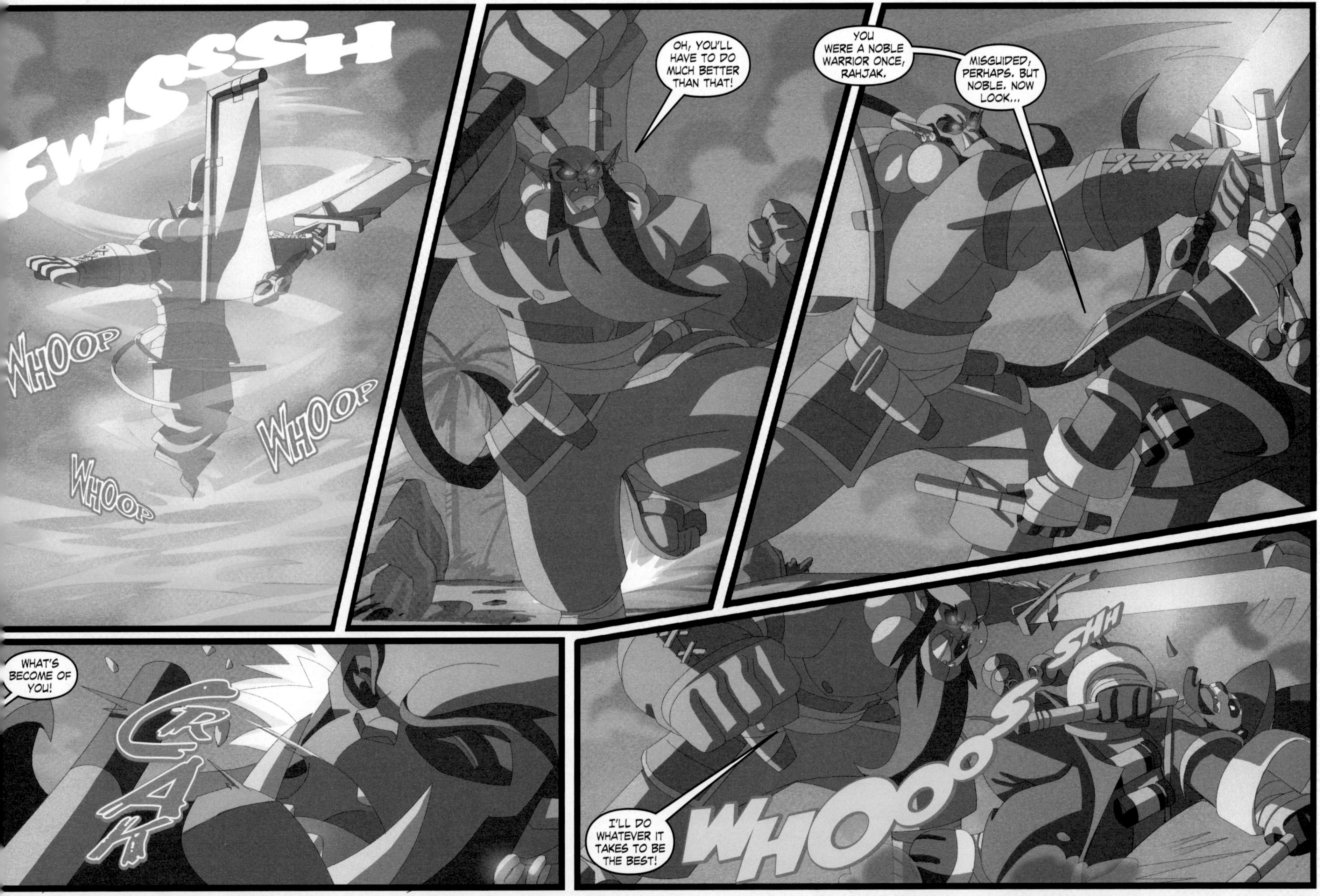
FWISSSH
WHOOP
WHOOP
WHOOP
OH, YOU'LL HAVE TO DO MUCH BETTER THAN THAT!
YOU WERE A NOBLE WARRIOR ONCE, RAHJAK.
MISGUIDED, PERHAPS. BUT NOBLE. NOW LOOK...
WHAT'S BECOME OF YOU!
CRAK
SHH
I'LL DO WHATEVER IT TAKES TO BE THE BEST!
WHOOOOOS

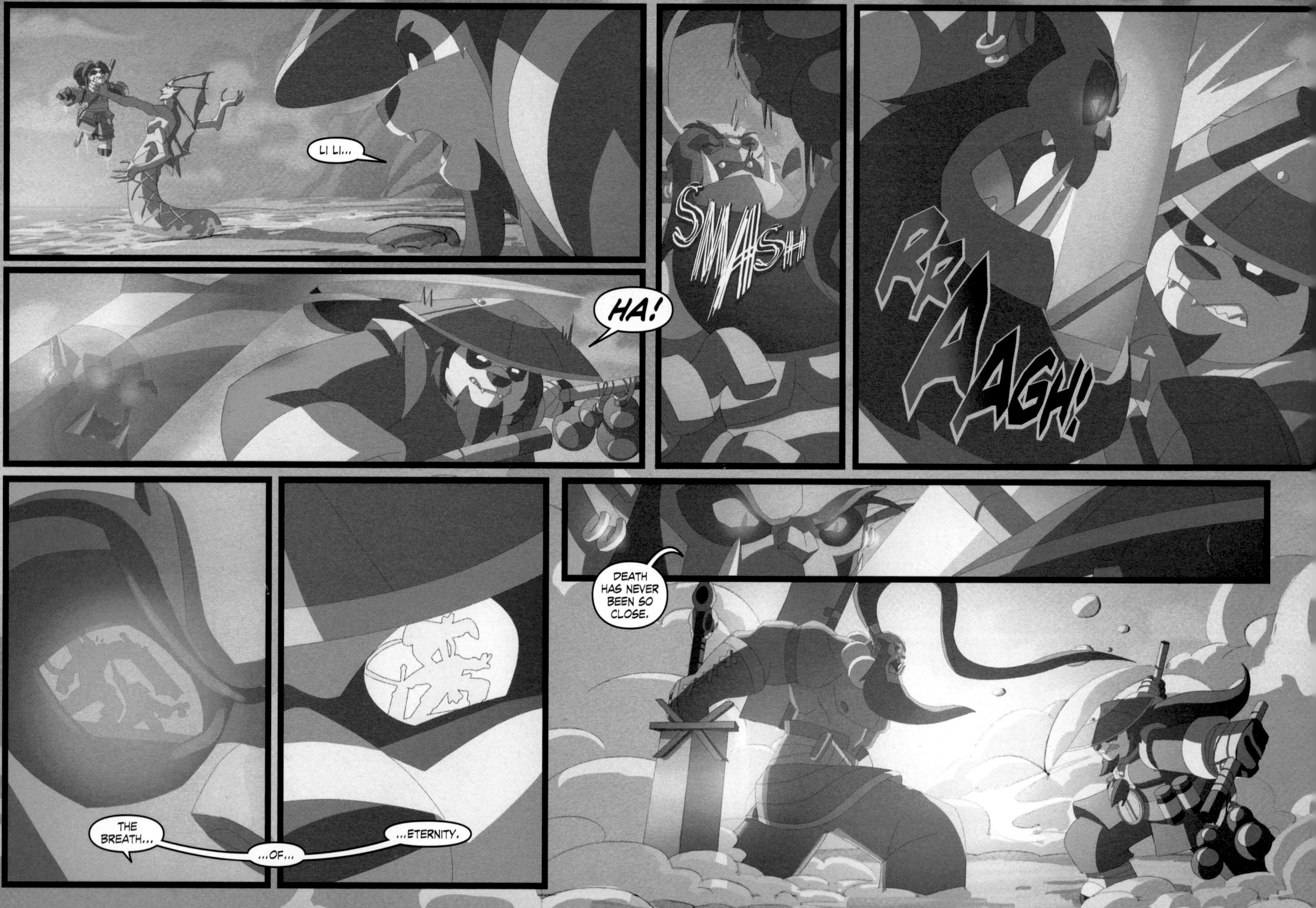

LI LI...
HA!
SMASH
RRAAGH!
DEATH HAS NEVER BEEN SO CLOSE.
THE BREATH...
...OF...
...ETERNITY.

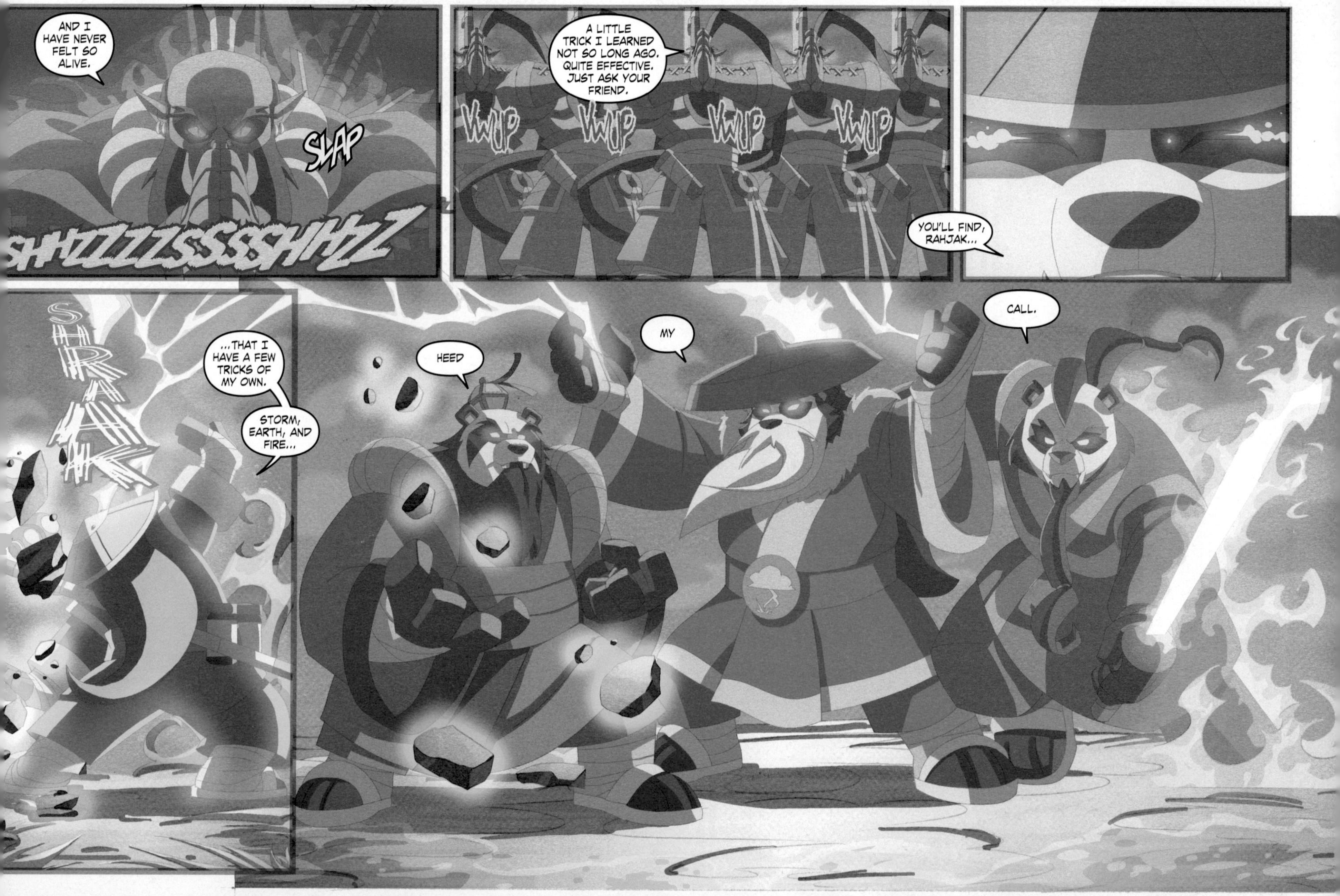
AND I HAVE NEVER FELT SO ALIVE.
SLAP
SHZZZZSSSSHHZZ
A LITTLE TRICK I LEARNED NOT SO LONG AGO. QUITE EFFECTIVE. JUST ASK YOUR FRIEND.
VWUP
VWUP
VWUP
VWUP
YOU'LL FIND, RAHJAK...
SHRAAK
...THAT I HAVE A FEW TRICKS OF MY OWN.
STORM, EARTH, AND FIRE...
HEED
MY
CALL.

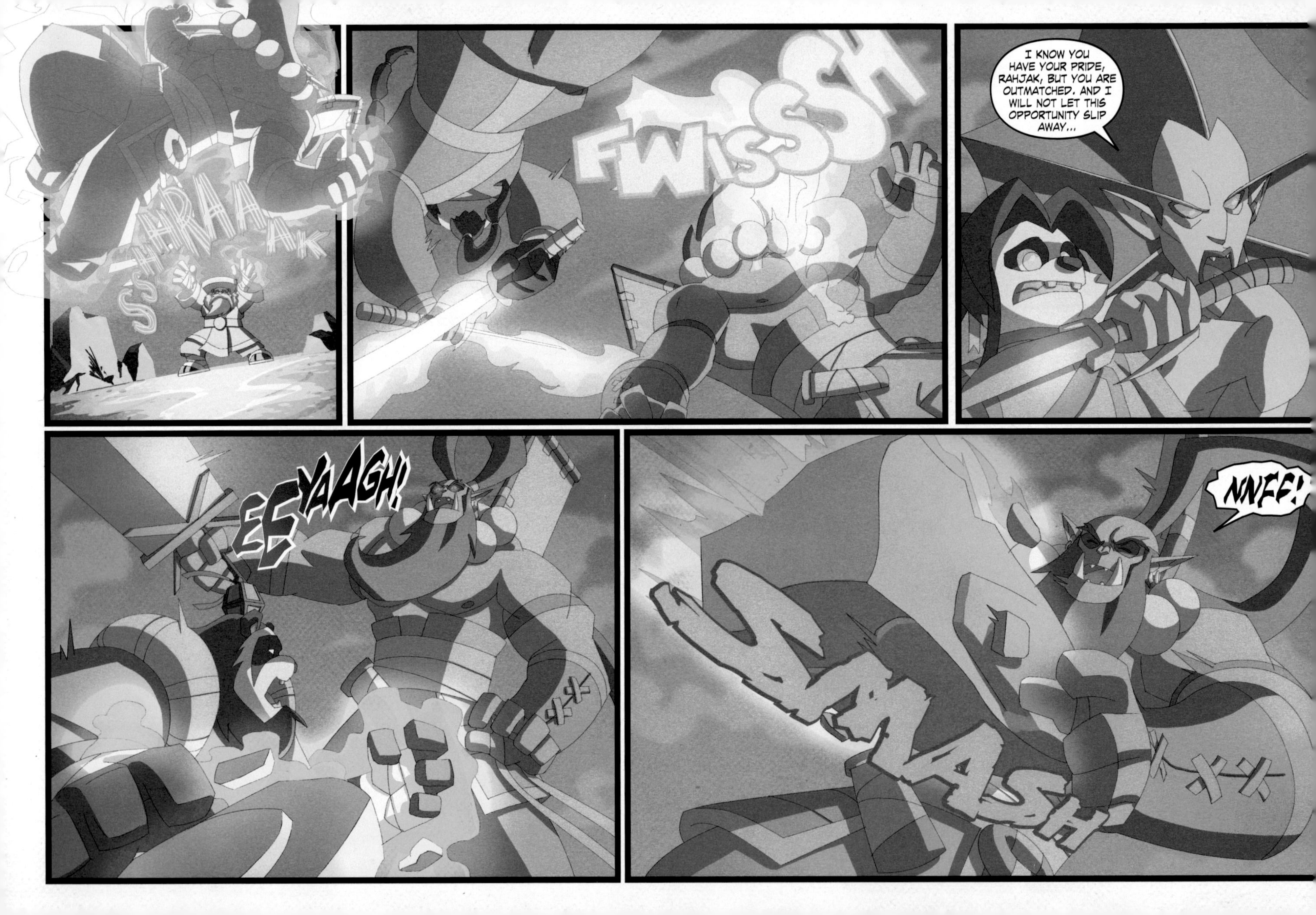
SHRAAAK
FWISSSH
I KNOW YOU HAVE YOUR PRIDE, RAHJAK, BUT YOU ARE OUTMATCHED. AND I WILL NOT LET THIS OPPORTUNITY SLIP AWAY...
EEYAAGH!
NNFF!
SMASH

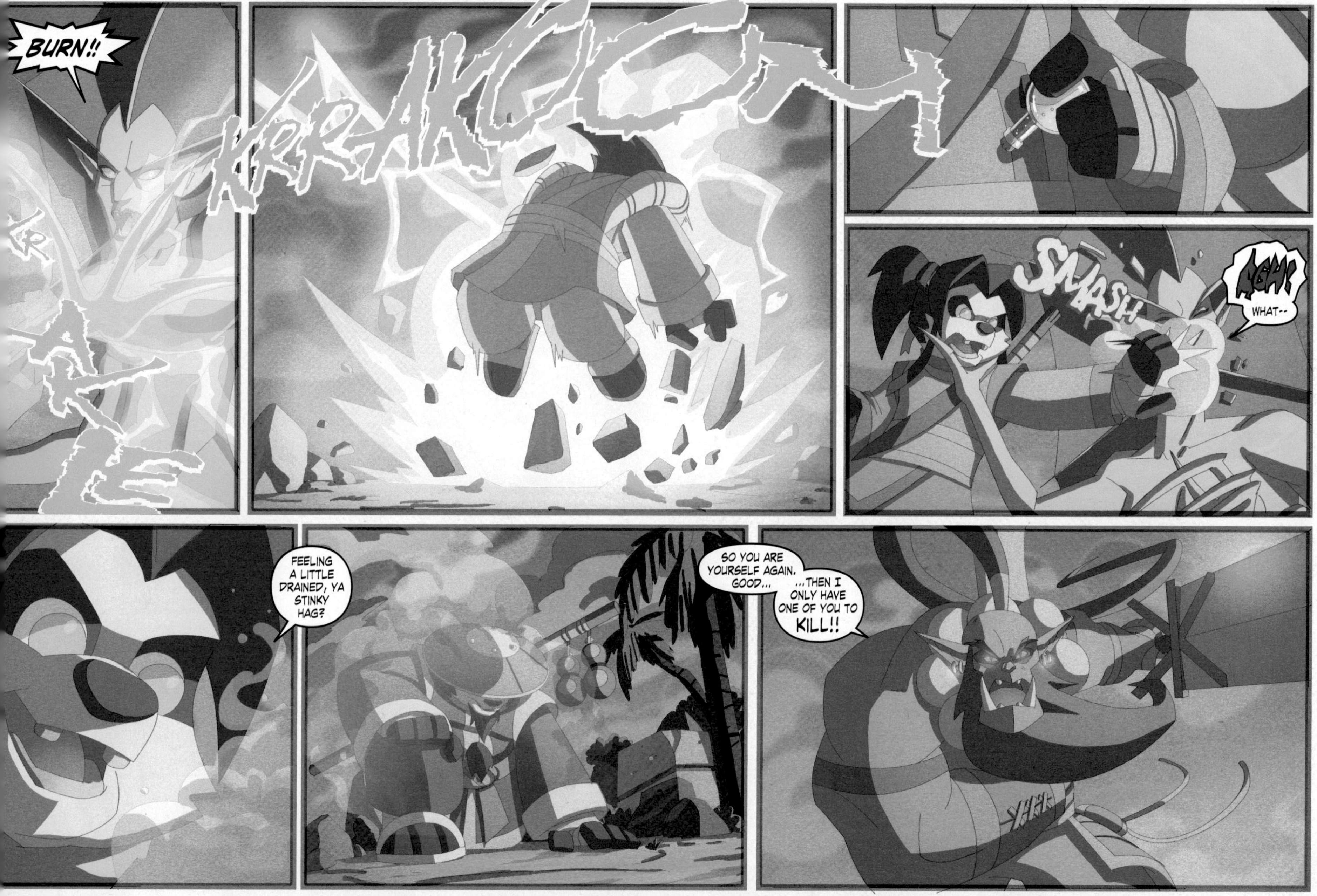

BURN!!
KRRAKOOM
SMASH
AGH!
WHAT--
FEELING A LITTLE DRAINED, YA STINKY HAG?
SO YOU ARE YOURSELF AGAIN. GOOD...
...THEN I ONLY HAVE ONE OF YOU TO KILL!!

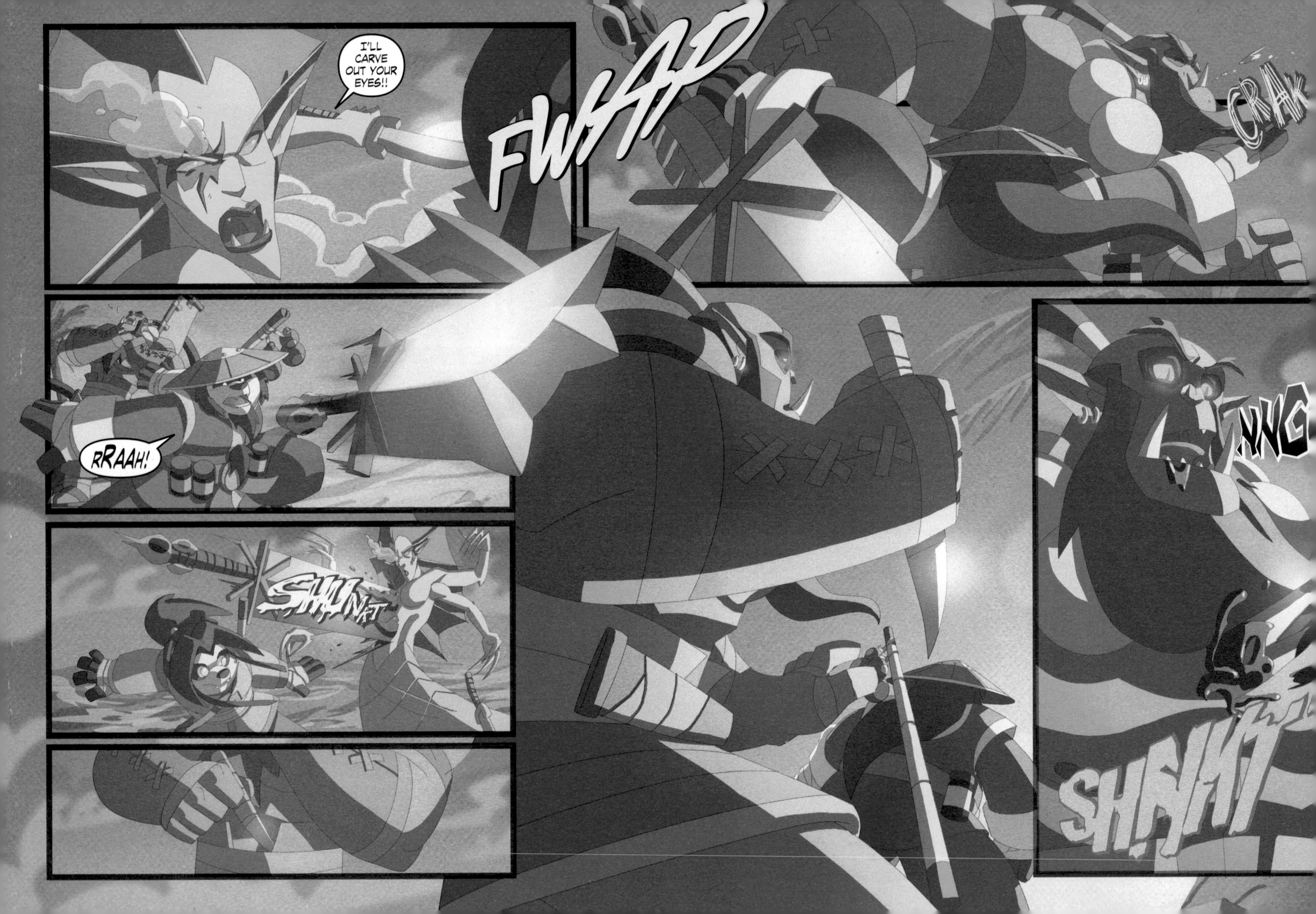
I'LL CARVE OUT YOUR EYES!!
FWAP
CRAK
RRAAH!
SHUNKT
NNG
SHNNT

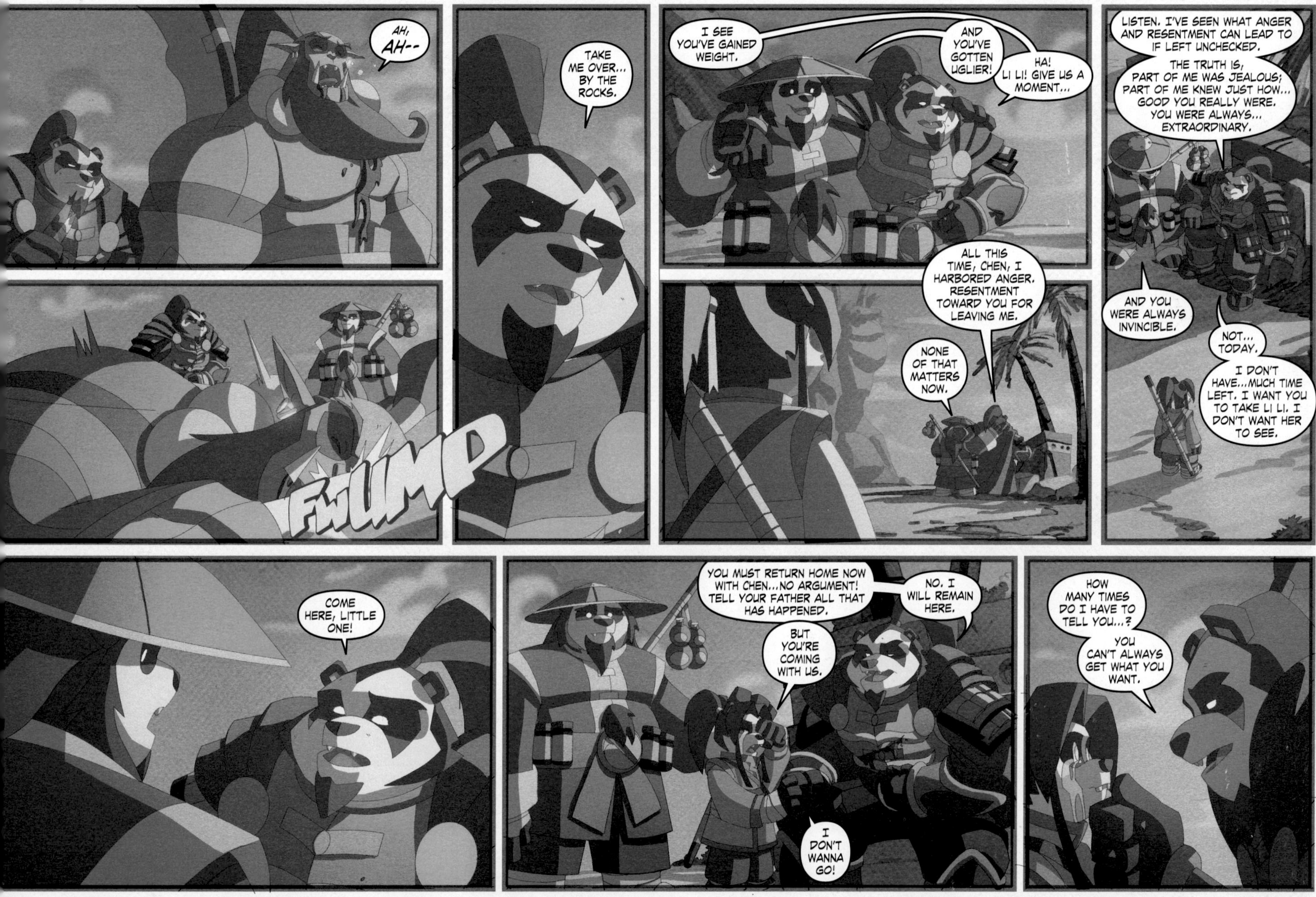
AH, AH--
TAKE ME OVER... BY THE ROCKS.
FWUMP
I SEE YOU'VE GAINED WEIGHT.
AND YOU'VE GOTTEN UGLIER!
HA! LI LI! GIVE US A MOMENT...
ALL THIS TIME, CHEN, I HARBORED ANGER. RESENTMENT TOWARD YOU FOR LEAVING ME.
NONE OF THAT MATTERS NOW.
LISTEN. I'VE SEEN WHAT ANGER AND RESENTMENT CAN LEAD TO IF LEFT UNCHECKED.
THE TRUTH IS, PART OF ME WAS JEALOUS; PART OF ME KNEW JUST HOW... GOOD YOU REALLY WERE. YOU WERE ALWAYS... EXTRAORDINARY.
AND YOU WERE ALWAYS INVINCIBLE.
NOT... TODAY.
I DON'T HAVE...MUCH TIME LEFT. I WANT YOU TO TAKE LI LI. I DON'T WANT HER TO SEE.
COME HERE, LITTLE ONE!
YOU MUST RETURN HOME NOW WITH CHEN...NO ARGUMENT! TELL YOUR FATHER ALL THAT HAS HAPPENED.
NO. I WILL REMAIN HERE.
BUT YOU'RE COMING WITH US.
I DON'T WANNA GO!
HOW MANY TIMES DO I HAVE TO TELL YOU...?
YOU CAN'T ALWAYS GET WHAT YOU WANT.

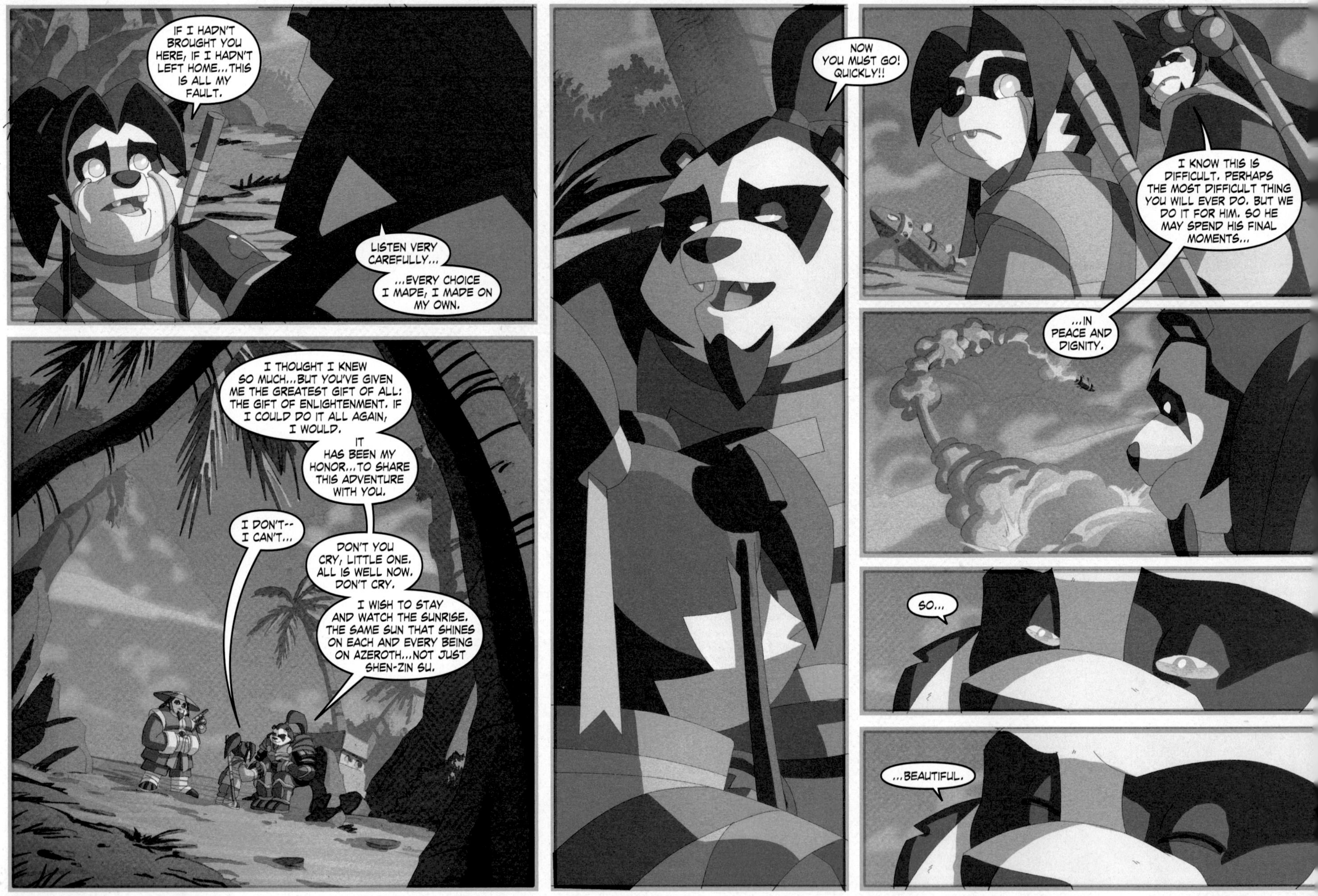
IF I HADN'T BROUGHT YOU HERE, IF I HADN'T LEFT HOME...THIS IS ALL MY FAULT.
LISTEN VERY CAREFULLY...
...EVERY CHOICE I MADE, I MADE ON MY OWN.
I THOUGHT I KNEW SO MUCH...BUT YOU'VE GIVEN ME THE GREATEST GIFT OF ALL: THE GIFT OF ENLIGHTENMENT. IF I COULD DO IT ALL AGAIN, I WOULD.
IT HAS BEEN MY HONOR...TO SHARE THIS ADVENTURE WITH YOU.
I DON'T-- I CAN'T...
DON'T YOU CRY, LITTLE ONE. ALL IS WELL NOW. DON'T CRY.
I WISH TO STAY AND WATCH THE SUNRISE. THE SAME SUN THAT SHINES ON EACH AND EVERY BEING ON AZEROTH...NOT JUST SHEN-ZIN SU.
NOW YOU MUST GO! QUICKLY!!
I KNOW THIS IS DIFFICULT. PERHAPS THE MOST DIFFICULT THING YOU WILL EVER DO. BUT WE DO IT FOR HIM. SO HE MAY SPEND HIS FINAL MOMENTS...
...IN PEACE AND DIGNITY.
SO...
...BEAUTIFUL.

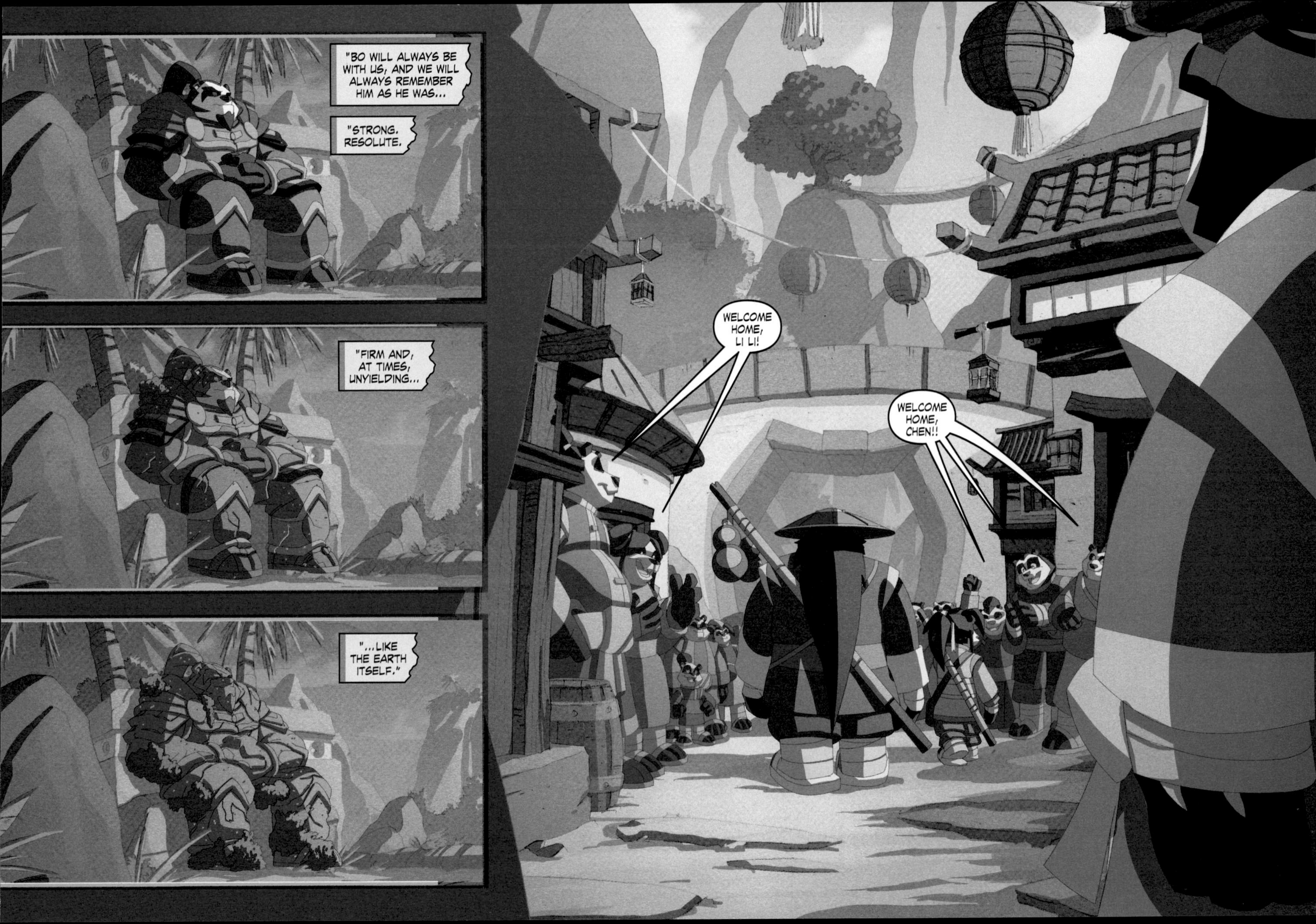
"BO WILL ALWAYS BE WITH US, AND WE WILL ALWAYS REMEMBER HIM AS HE WAS...
"STRONG. RESOLUTE.
"FIRM AND, AT TIMES, UNYIELDING...
"...LIKE THE EARTH ITSELF."
WELCOME HOME, LI LI!
WELCOME HOME, CHEN!!

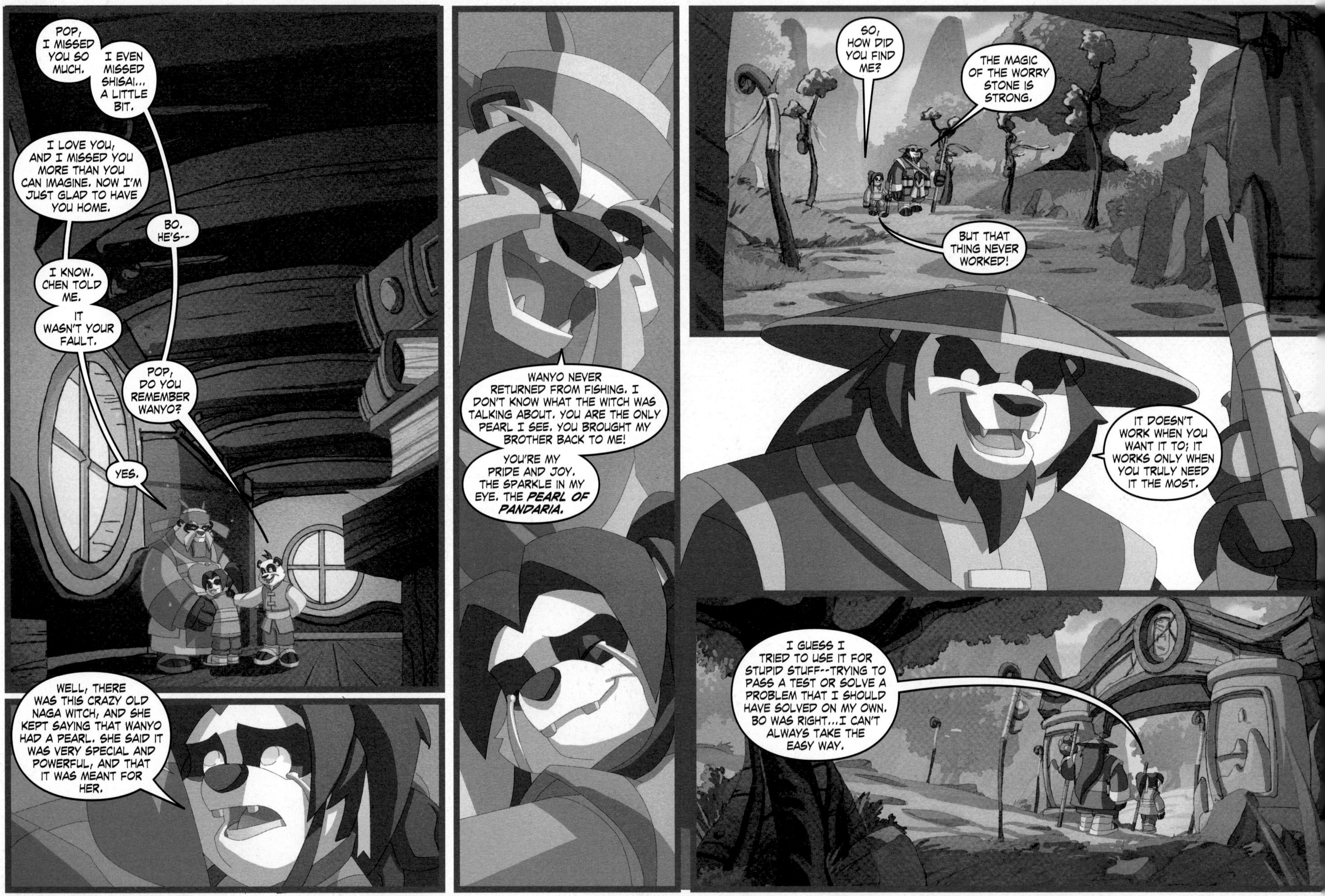
POP, I MISSED YOU SO MUCH.
I EVEN MISSED SHISAI... A LITTLE BIT.
I LOVE YOU, AND I MISSED YOU MORE THAN YOU CAN IMAGINE. NOW I'M JUST GLAD TO HAVE YOU HOME.
BO. HE'S--
I KNOW. CHEN TOLD ME.
IT WASN'T YOUR FAULT.
POP, DO YOU REMEMBER WANYO?
YES.
WELL, THERE WAS THIS CRAZY OLD NAGA WITCH, AND SHE KEPT SAYING THAT WANYO HAD A PEARL. SHE SAID IT WAS VERY SPECIAL AND POWERFUL, AND THAT IT WAS MEANT FOR HER.
WANYO NEVER RETURNED FROM FISHING. I DON'T KNOW WHAT THE WITCH WAS TALKING ABOUT. YOU ARE THE ONLY PEARL I SEE. YOU BROUGHT MY BROTHER BACK TO ME!
YOU'RE MY PRIDE AND JOY. THE SPARKLE IN MY EYE. THE ***PEARL OF PANDARIA.***
SO, HOW DID YOU FIND ME?
THE MAGIC OF THE WORRY STONE IS STRONG.
BUT THAT THING NEVER WORKED!
IT DOESN'T WORK WHEN YOU WANT IT TO; IT WORKS ONLY WHEN YOU TRULY NEED IT THE MOST.
I GUESS I TRIED TO USE IT FOR STUPID STUFF--TRYING TO PASS A TEST OR SOLVE A PROBLEM THAT I SHOULD HAVE SOLVED ON MY OWN. BO WAS RIGHT...I CAN'T ALWAYS TAKE THE EASY WAY.

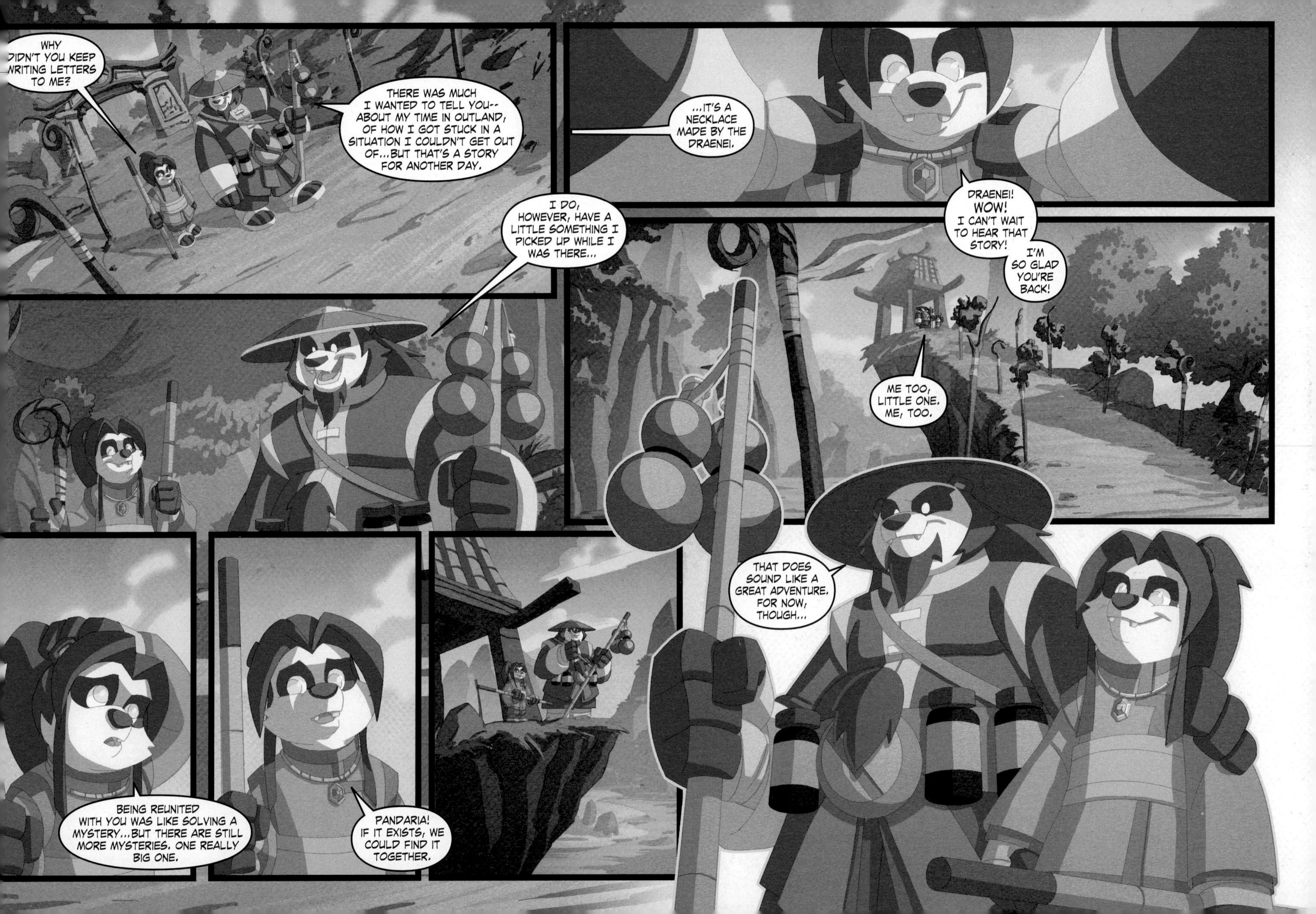

WHY DIDN'T YOU KEEP WRITING LETTERS TO ME?
THERE WAS MUCH I WANTED TO TELL YOU-- ABOUT MY TIME IN OUTLAND, OF HOW I GOT STUCK IN A SITUATION I COULDN'T GET OUT OF...BUT THAT'S A STORY FOR ANOTHER DAY.
I DO, HOWEVER, HAVE A LITTLE SOMETHING I PICKED UP WHILE I WAS THERE...
...IT'S A NECKLACE MADE BY THE DRAENEI.
DRAENEI! WOW! I CAN'T WAIT TO HEAR THAT STORY!
I'M SO GLAD YOU'RE BACK!
ME TOO, LITTLE ONE. ME, TOO.
BEING REUNITED WITH YOU WAS LIKE SOLVING A MYSTERY...BUT THERE ARE STILL MORE MYSTERIES. ONE REALLY BIG ONE.
PANDARIA! IF IT EXISTS, WE COULD FIND IT TOGETHER.
THAT DOES SOUND LIKE A GREAT ADVENTURE. FOR NOW, THOUGH...

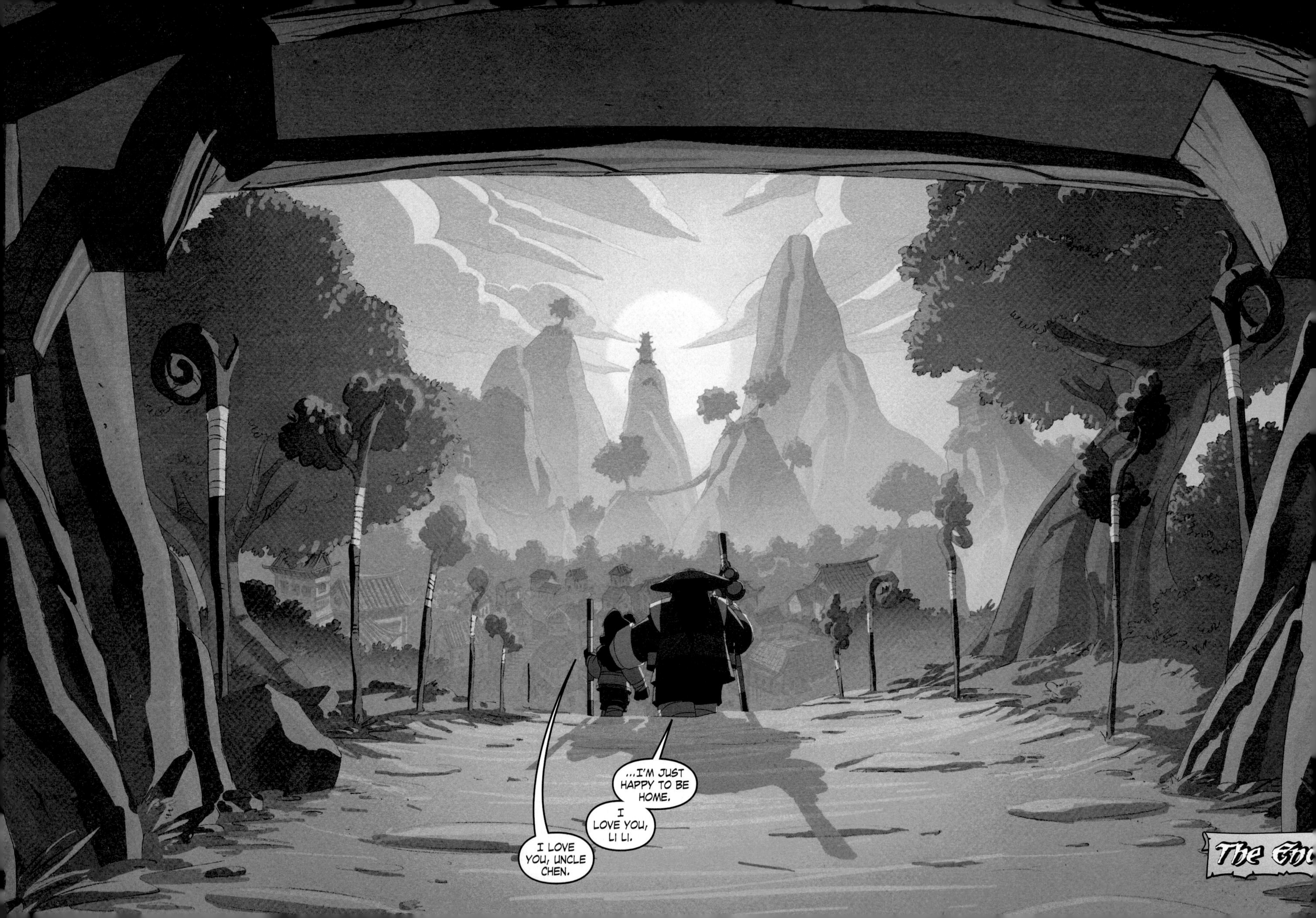
...I'M JUST HAPPY TO BE HOME.
I LOVE YOU, LI LI.
I LOVE YOU, UNCLE CHEN.
The

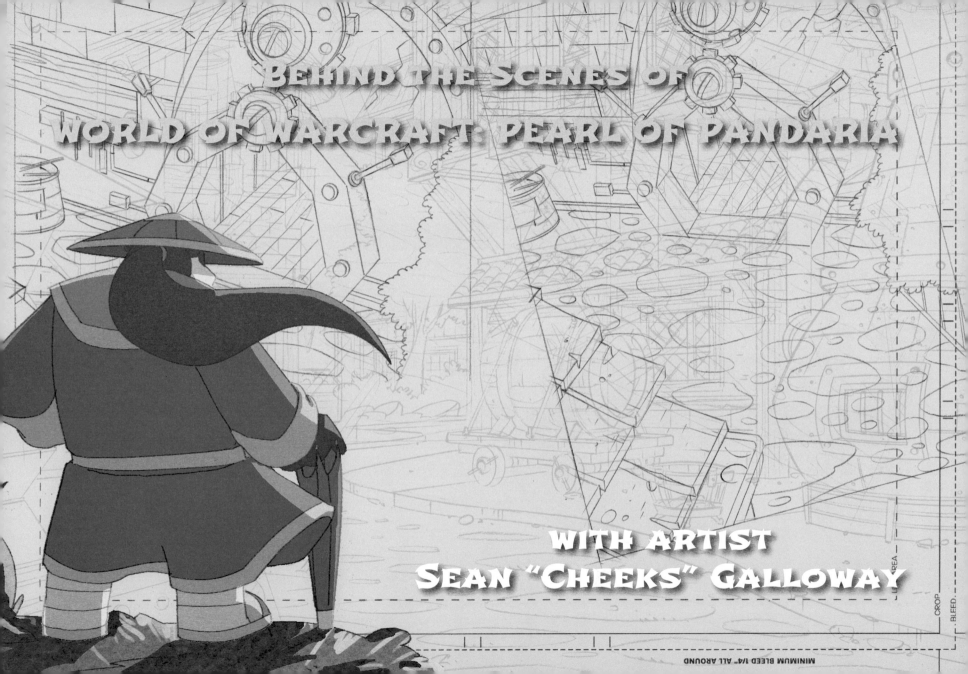

Behind the Scenes of
World of Warcraft: Pearl of Pandaria

with Artist
Sean "Cheeks" Galloway

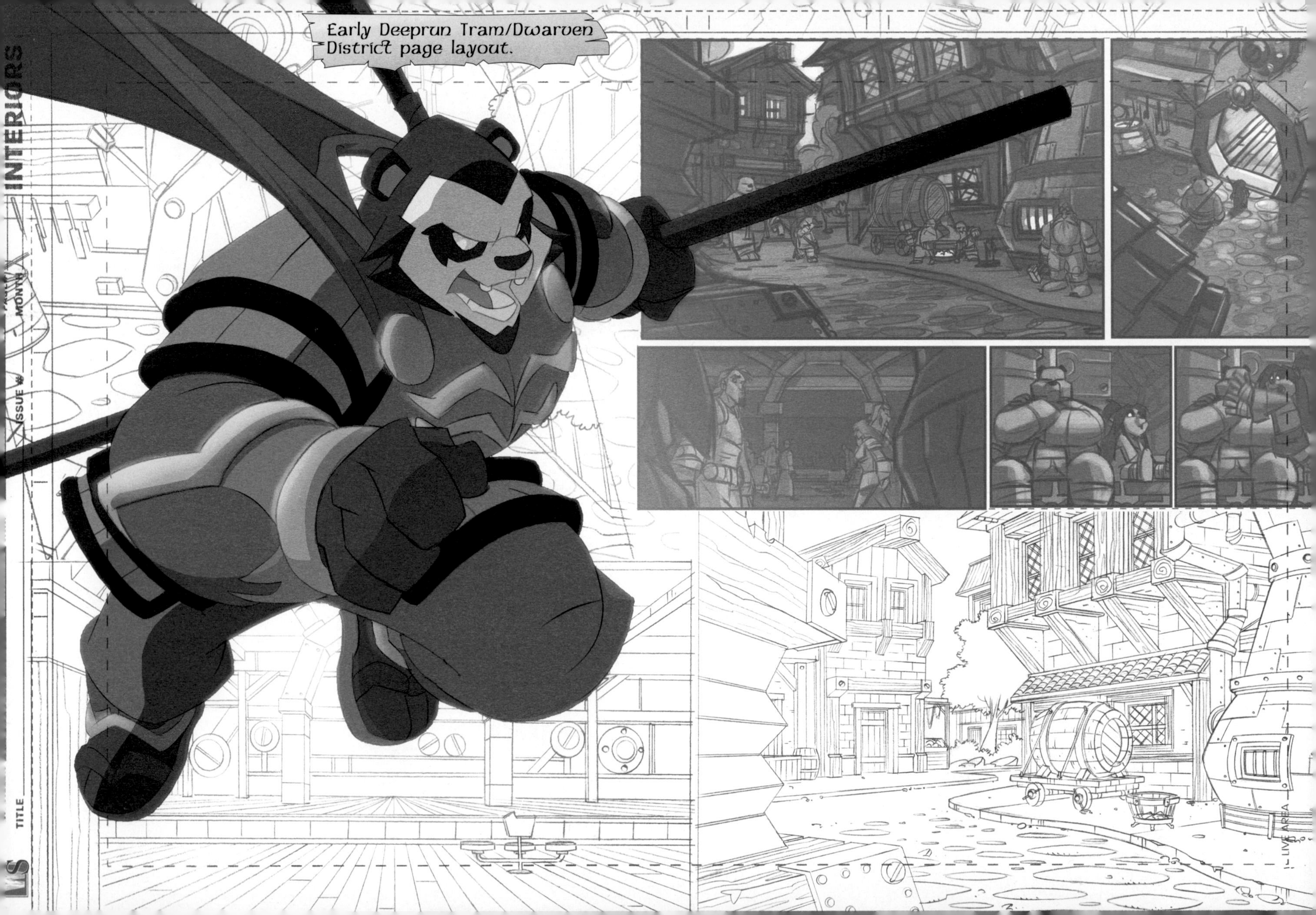
INTERIORS
MONTH
ISSUE #
TITLE
LIVE AREA
Early Deeprun Tram/Dwarven District page layout.

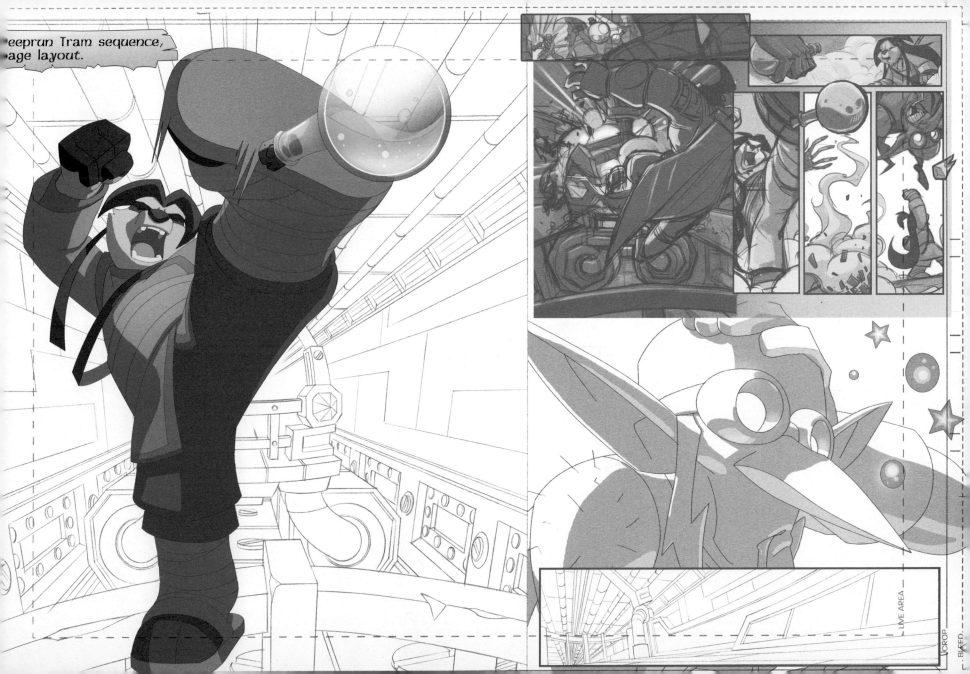

eeprun Tram sequence,
age layout.

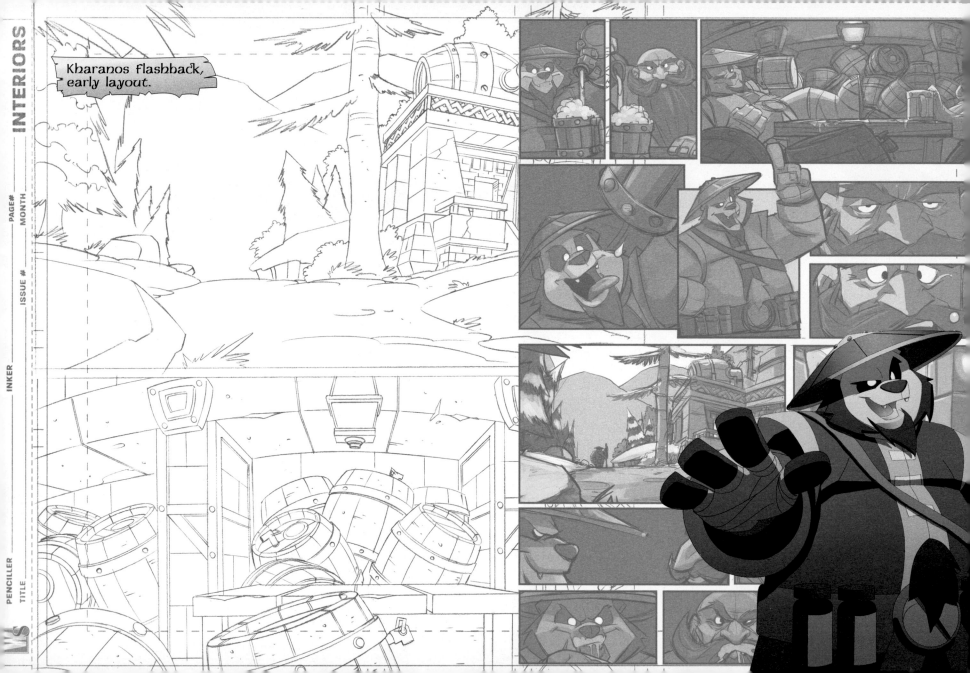

Kharanos flashback, early layout.

PENCILLER
INKER
TITLE
ISSUE #
PAGE#
MONTH

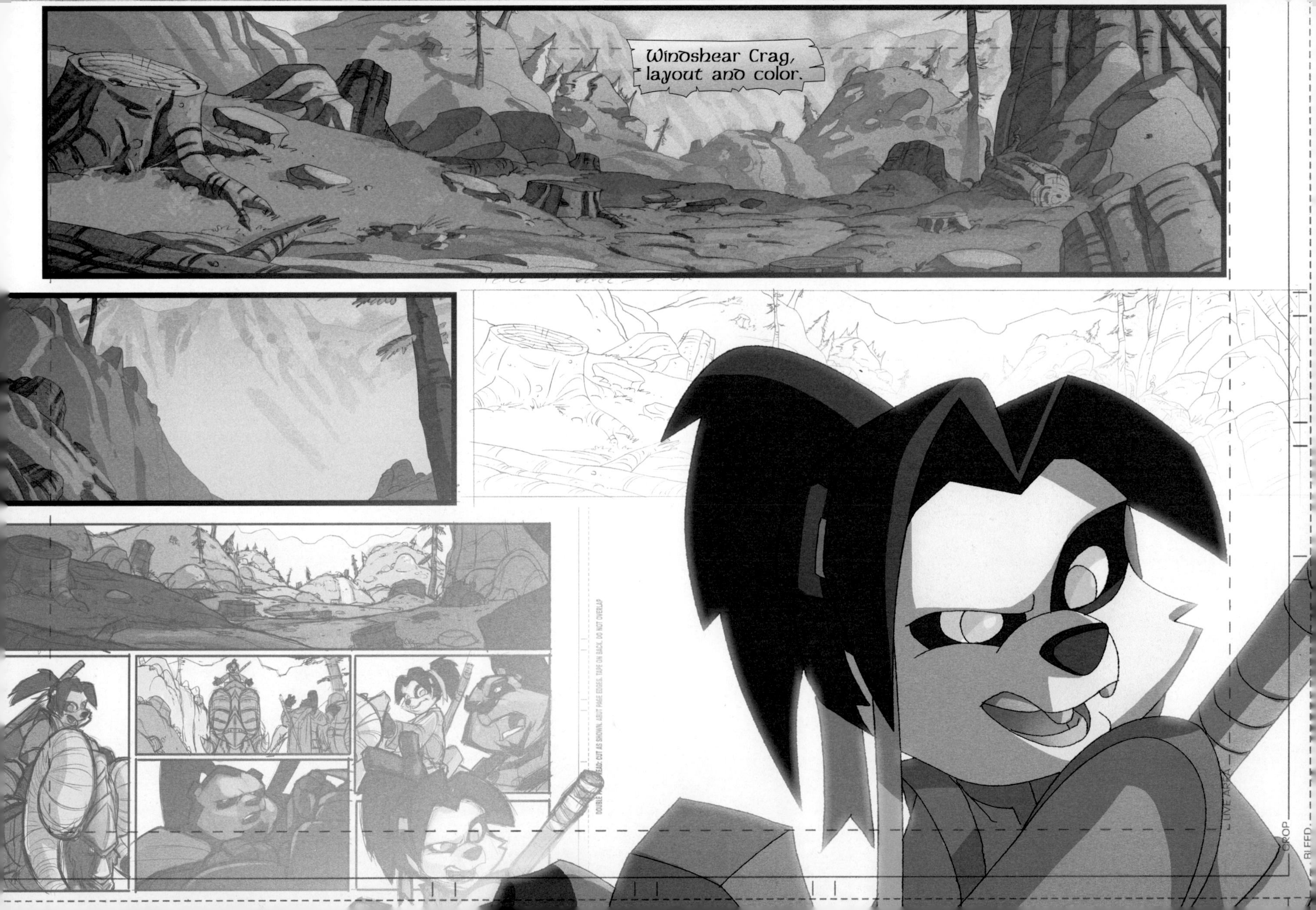
Windshear Crag,
layout and color.

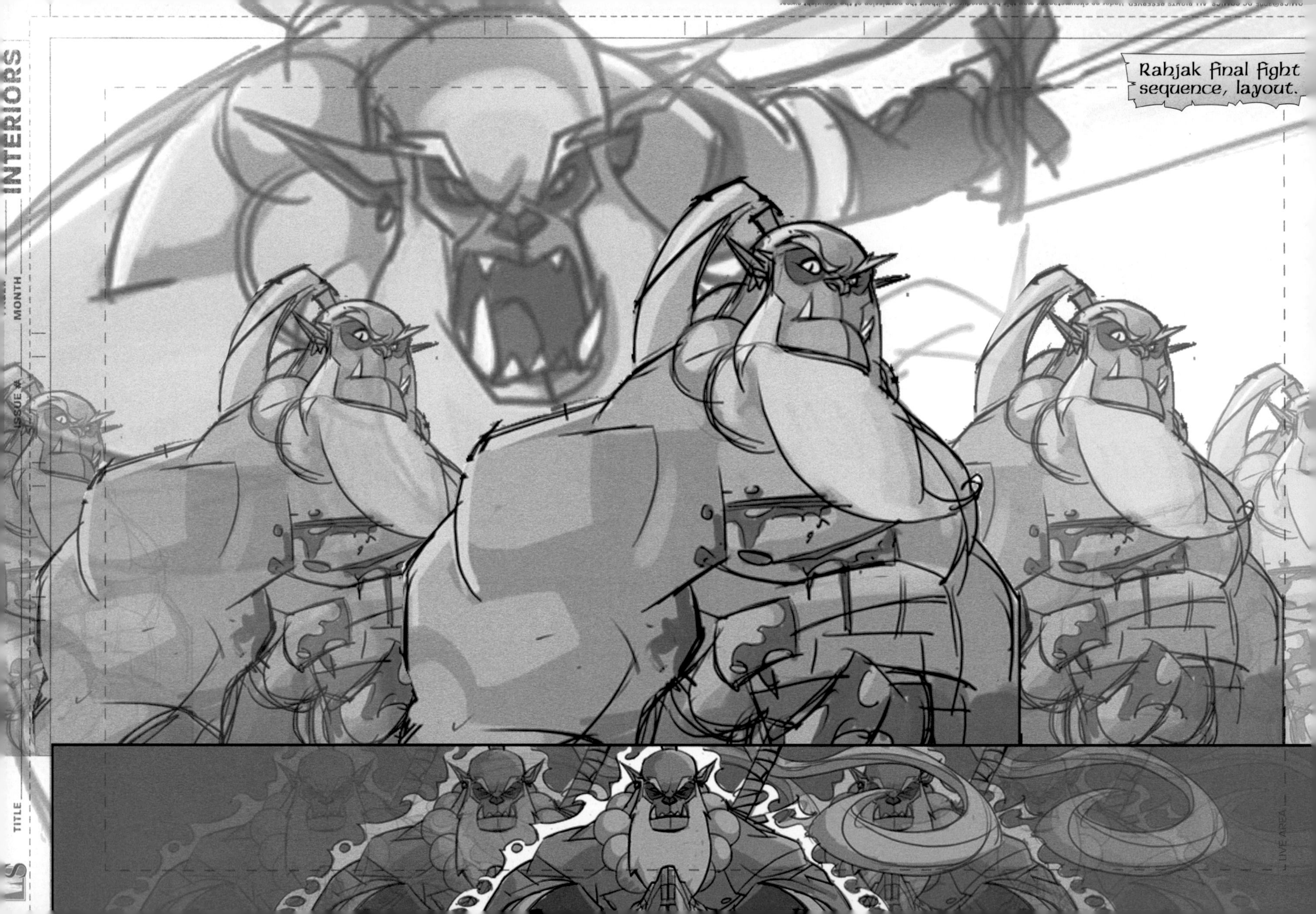
INTERIORS
MONTH
ISSUE #
TITLE
LIVE AREA

Rahjak final fight sequence, layout.

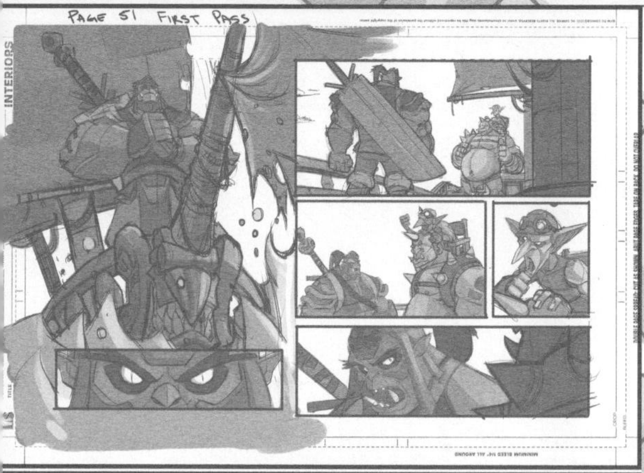
PAGE 51 FIRST PASS
INTERIORS

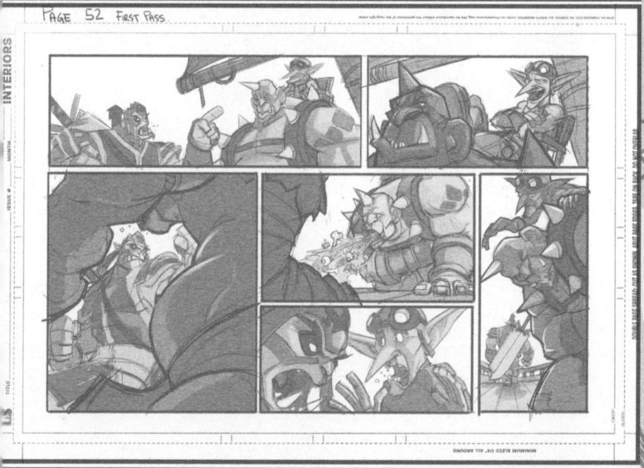
PAGE 52 FIRST PASS
INTERIORS

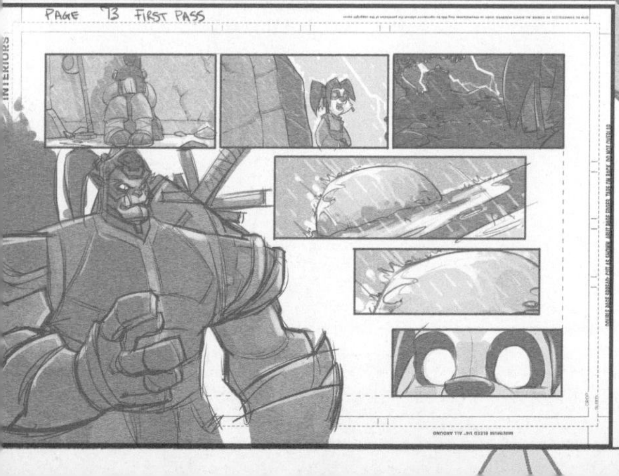
PAGE 73 FIRST PASS
INTERIORS

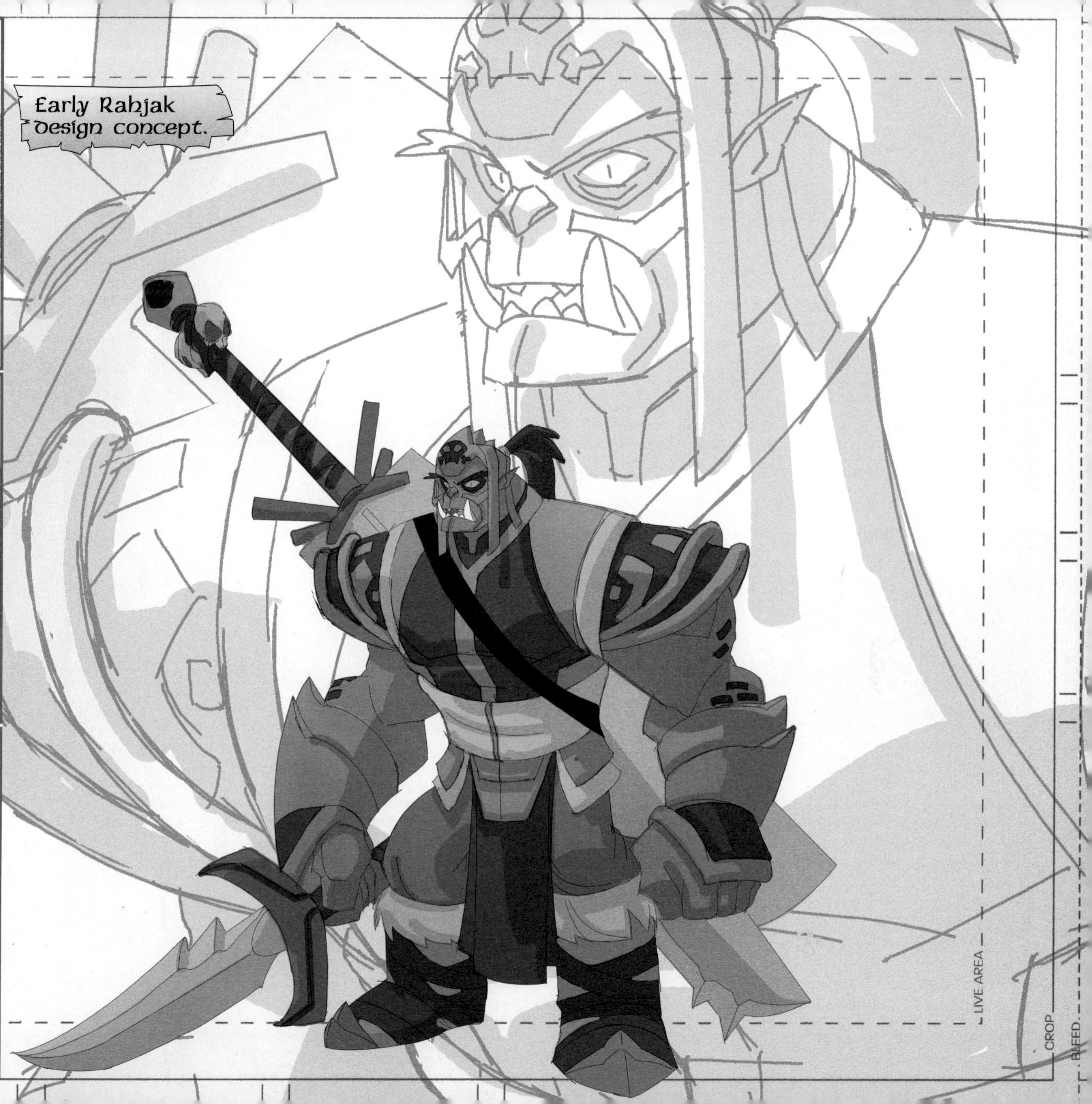
LIVE AREA
CROP
BLEED

Early Rahjak design concept.

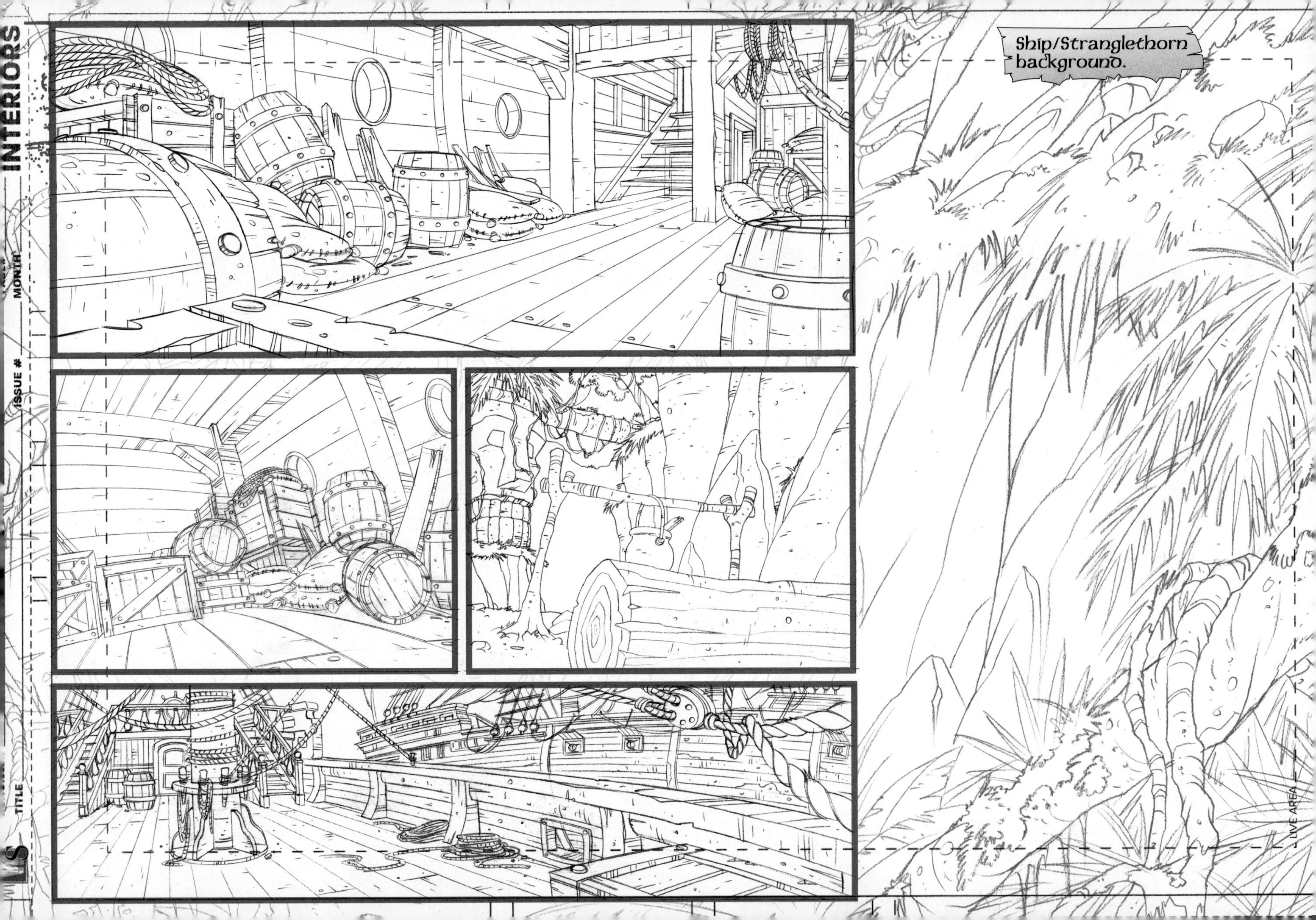
Ship/Stranglethorn background.
INTERIORS
MONTH
ISSUE #
TITLE
LIVE AREA

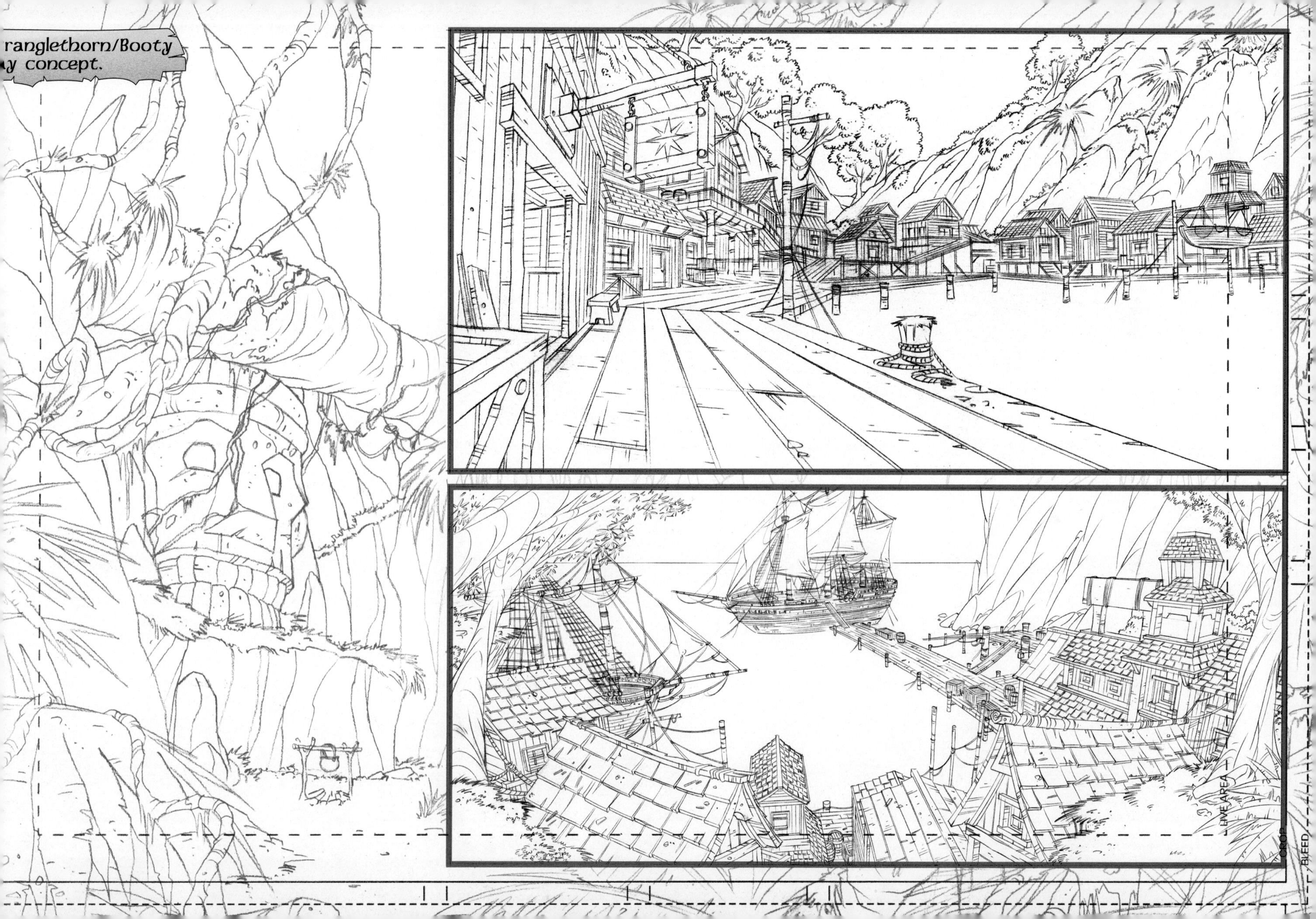
LIVE AREA
CROP
BLEED

rangletorn/Booty
y concept.

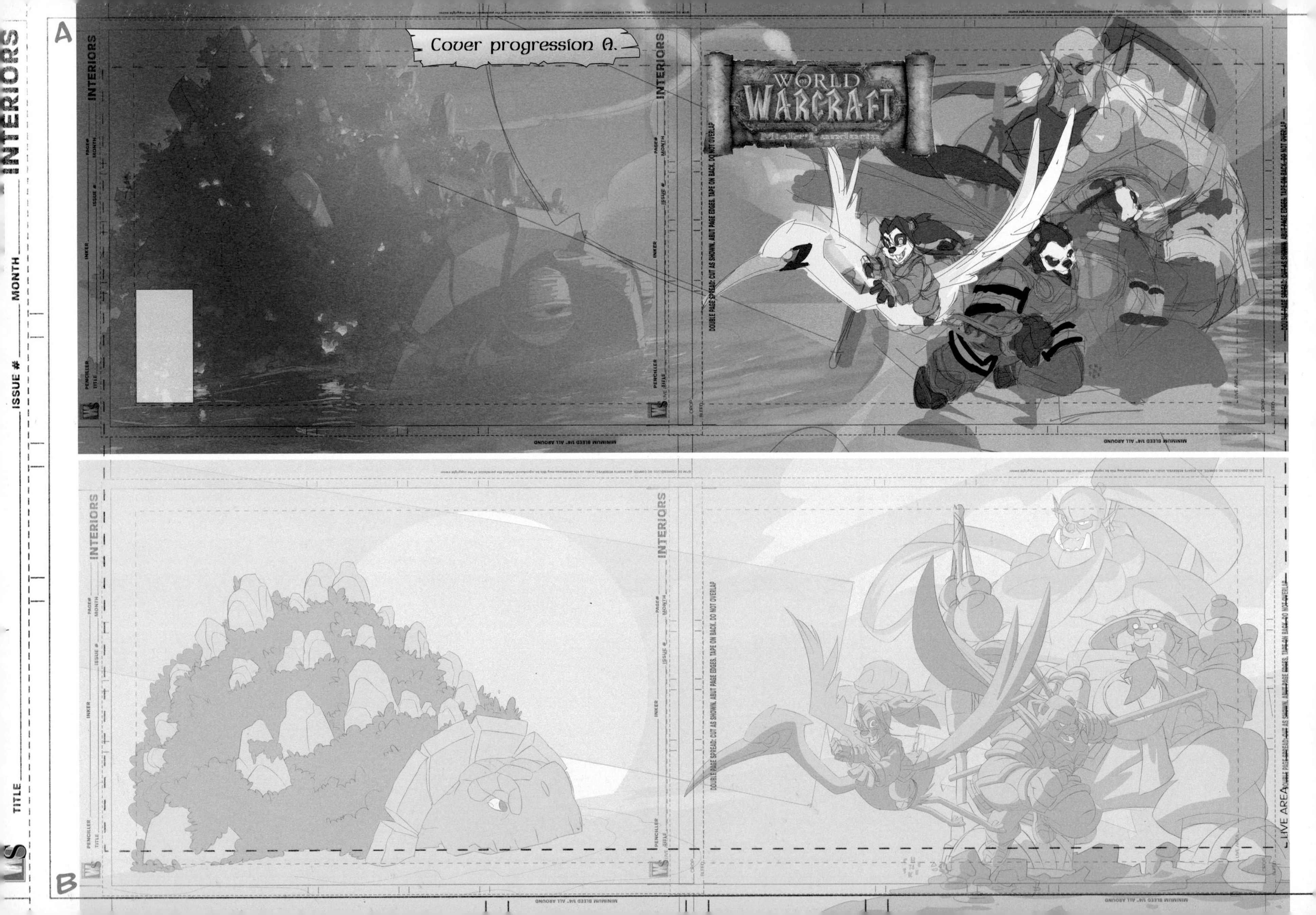
A
Cover progression A.
WORLD OF WARCRAFT
B
INTERIORS
TITLE
ISSUE #
MONTH

Cover progression B.

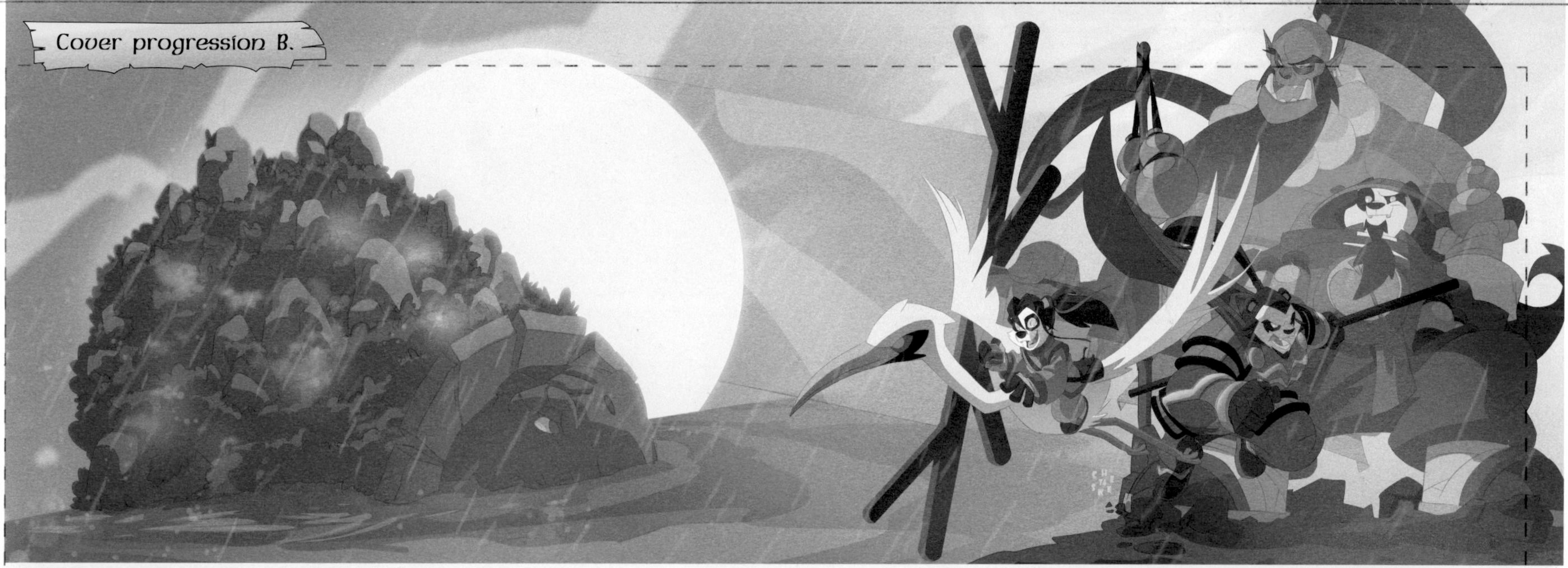

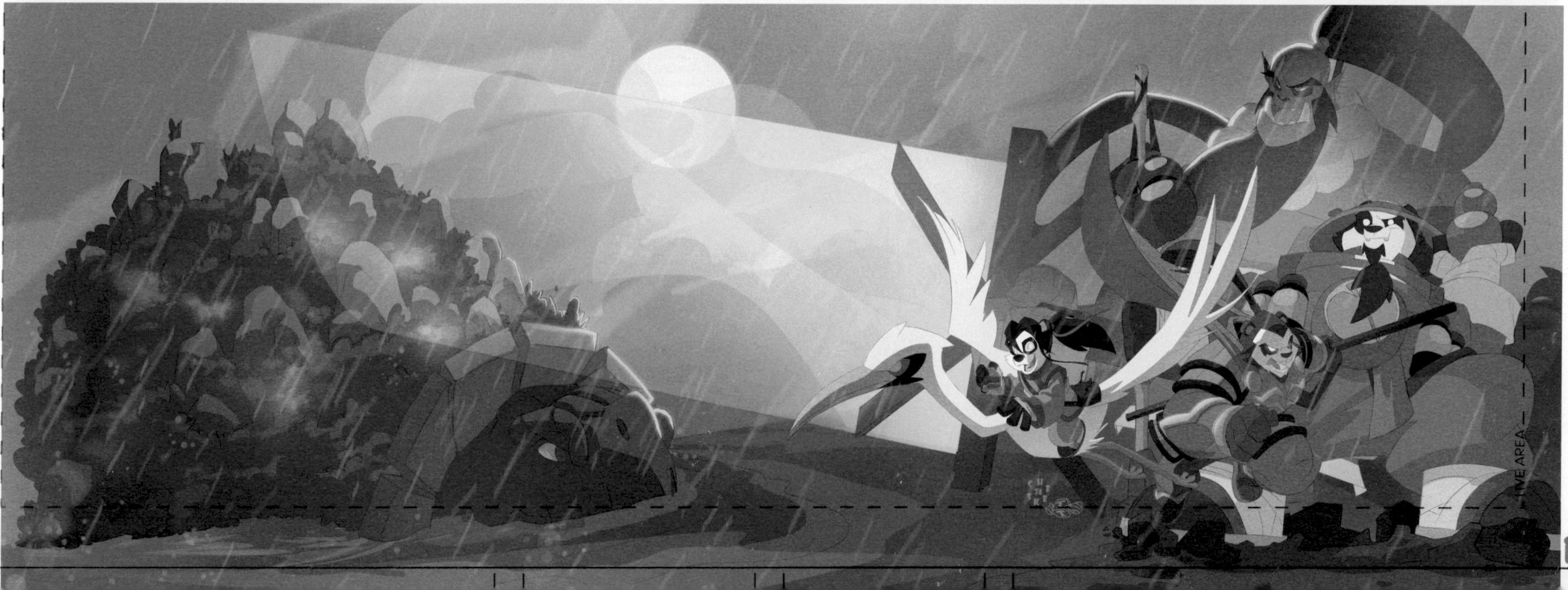

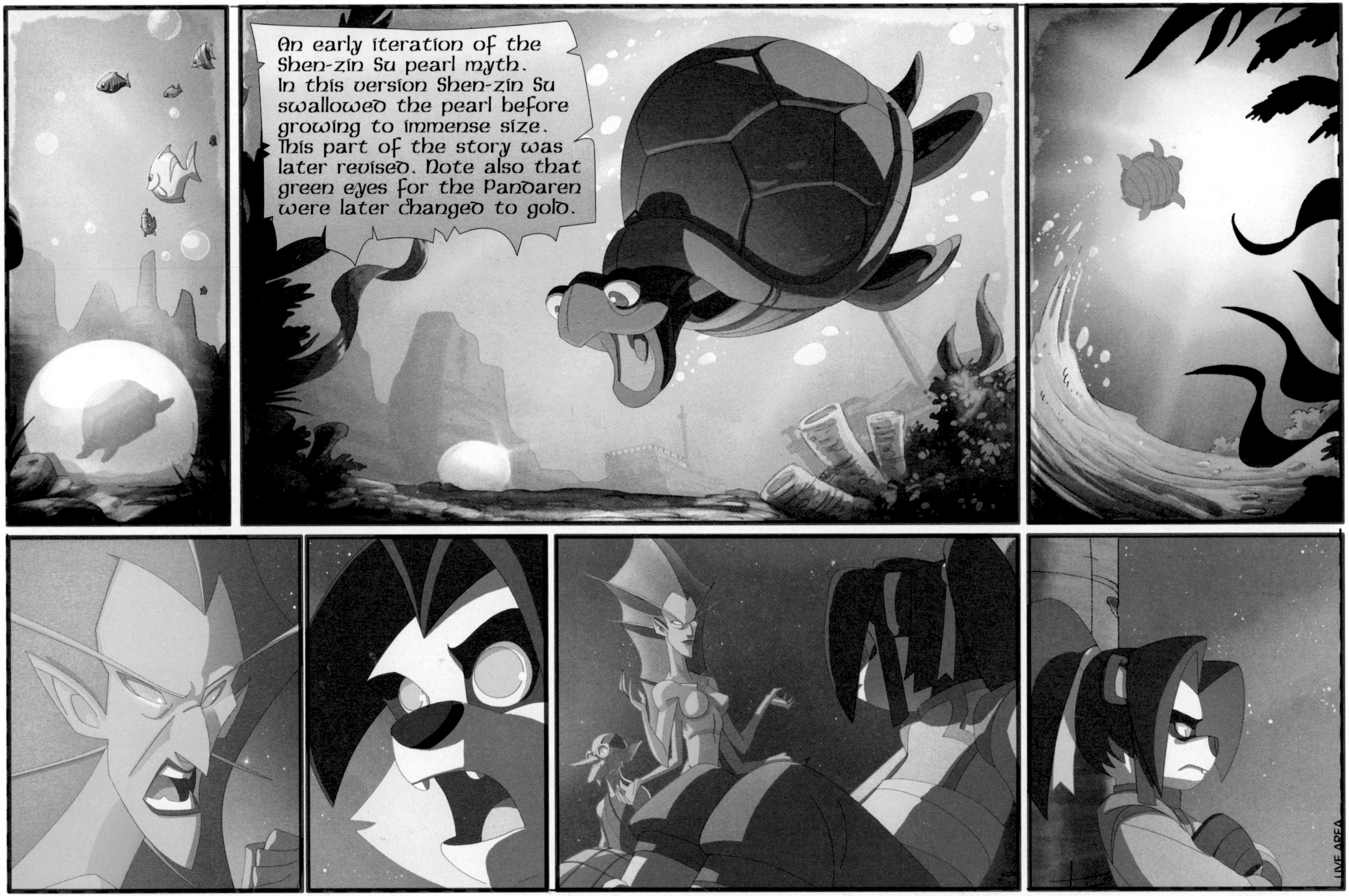
An early iteration of the Shen-zin Su pearl myth. In this version Shen-zin Su swallowed the pearl before growing to immense size. This part of the story was later revised. Note also that green eyes for the Pandaren were later changed to gold.
LIVE AREA

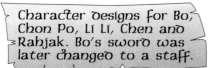

Character designs for Bo, Chon Po, Li Li, Chen and Rahjak. Bo's sword was later changed to a staff.

Chen and Li Li's adventures will continue in the free online novella Quest for Pandaria. Look for it soon at: www.worldofwarcraft.com!